The Chattahoochee Chiefdo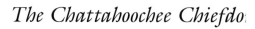

A Dan Josselyn Memorial Publication

The Chattahoochee Chiefdoms

JOHN H. BLITZ and
KARL G. LORENZ

THE UNIVERSITY OF ALABAMA PRESS
Tuscaloosa

Copyright © 2006
The University of Alabama Press
Tuscaloosa, Alabama 35487-0380
All rights reserved
Manufactured in the United States of America

Typeface is Galliard

∞
The paper on which this book is printed meets the minimum requirements of
American National Standard for Information Sciences-Permanence of Paper for
Printed Library Materials, ANSI Z39.48–1984.

Library of Congress Cataloging-in-Publication Data

Blitz, John Howard.
    The Chattahoochee chiefdoms / John H. Blitz and Karl G. Lorenz.
        p. cm.
    Includes bibliographical references and index.
    ISBN-13: 978-0-8173-1494-1 (cloth : alk. paper)
    ISBN-10: 0-8173-1494-6 (cloth : alk. paper)
    ISBN-13: 978-0-8173-5277-6 (pbk. : alk. paper)
    ISBN-10: 0-8173-5277-5 (pbk. : alk. paper)
    1. Mississippian culture—Chattahoochee River Valley. 2. Indians of North
America—Chattahoochee River Valley—Kings and rulers. 3. Indians of North
America—Chattahoochee River Valley—Politics and government. 4. Chiefdoms—
Chattahoochee River Valley. 5. Excavations (Archaeology)—Chattahoochee River
Valley. 6. Chattahoochee River Valley—Antiquities. I. Lorenz, Karl G. (Karl
Gregory), 1961– . II. Title.
    E99.M6815B56 2006
    975.8′01—dc22

2005022266

Contents

Illustrations

Acknowledgments

We take this opportunity to thank those individuals and institutions that aided us in this research. In particular, Frank T. Schnell shared his knowledge, encouraged us to pursue this project, and provided access to many of the materials that made it possible. Thanks, Frank.

The research reported here was supported by the University of Oklahoma and Shippensburg University. We thank these institutions for granting access to research materials: Alabama Archaeological Society, Columbus Museum, Florida Anthropological Society, National Anthropological Archives, Museum of the American Indian, Smithsonian Museum Support Center, Society for American Archaeology, and the Southeastern Archaeological Conference. Additional thanks are due to the Anthropology Sampling Committee, National Museum of Natural History, Smithsonian Institution, for permission to submit samples for radiocarbon assays.

Many thanks to those individuals who assisted the project in various ways: Donald Gordy, Deborah Hull-Walski, Ned J. Jenkins, Adam King, Vernon J. Knight Jr., James Krakker, Robert W. Neuman, Thomas Pluck-hahn, Margaret C. Russell, John F. Scarry, Gail S. Schnell, Vyrtis Thomas, and Nancy M. White.

Our deepest appreciation goes to Lisa J. LeCount and Kathleen M. Cain Lorenz for their unending show of love, understanding, and support through a long and demanding project.

The Chattahoochee Chiefdoms

1   Political and Social Integration in Rank Societies

A Mississippian Case Study

Along the banks of the lower Chattahoochee River, the remains of ancient settlements are abundant. Some of these archaeological sites, produced by American Indians between 900 and 350 years ago, are noticeable by the presence of large earthen mounds. Like similar monuments elsewhere in the southeastern United States, the lower Chattahoochee River mounds have long attracted the attention of travelers, antiquarians, and archaeologists. The eighteenth-century naturalist William Bartram described in his *Travels* how he passed through the region and encountered "one instance of the tetragon terraces which was in the Apalachucla old town, on the west banks of that river; here were yet remaining conspicuous monuments, as vast four square terraces, chunk yards, etc. almost equalling [*sic*] those eminent ones at the Oakmulge fields" (Bartram 1958:331–332, emphasis added).

Over the next 150 years, objects from the mounds were unearthed, occasionally illustrated, and discussed in print (Brandon 1909; Moore 1907). Attention was focused on the aesthetic qualities of the artifacts, speculation about the origins of the remains, and possible relationships to the Creek Indians. Beginning in the twentieth century, new concerns emerged as the developing science of archaeology was introduced to the region. Trained archaeologists from the University of Alabama, the University of Georgia, the Columbus Museum (Georgia), and the Smithsonian Institution initiated extensive excavations of the mounds as many of the sites were threatened or destroyed by reservoir construction. Although classification of artifacts and sites into a chronological progression of cultures was the thrust of this effort, a second concern, sometimes more latent than manifest, was the reconstruction of a past way of life. Archaeologists hoped to achieve a better understanding of the sociopolitical organization of the peoples who built the mounds, and how those organizations changed through time.

Contemporary archaeologists, while in agreement on many aspects of the ancient cultures, debate the causes, forms, and degrees of sociopolitical complexity in the ancient Southeast. Written accounts from the time of early contact with Europeans in the sixteenth century provide one source of information (Clayton et al. 1993). Spanish conquistadors encountered native southeastern peoples with powerful leaders who lived on flat-topped earthen mounds in fortified communities. Narrators portrayed these societies in terms derived from their own feudal order: as warring provinces of lords and vassals giving and taking tribute over extensive territories. By Bartram's day, the Lower Creeks of the Chattahoochee region, like other native southeastern peoples, no longer constructed mounds, nor did their societies conform to the earlier Spanish accounts (Smith 1987). Some archaeologists argue for a high degree of centralized authority in the late precolumbian societies, not unlike the Spanish descriptions, whereby communities were integrated into political organizations that encompassed whole regions (DePratter 1991; Hudson et al. 1985). Others depict these societies with social structures and political forms no more complex or centralized than the historic Creeks when Bartram sojourned among them (Muller 1997).

Do the mounds mark the capitals of political territories? If so, what was the scale and scope of these ancient "provinces"? What manner of society constructed the mound settlements? What was the sociopolitical organization of these long-dead populations? How can archaeologists answer such queries with the mute and sometimes ordinary materials with which they work: pottery, stone tools, organic residues, and the strata of remnant settlements, buildings, and mounds?

Prehistoric Politics

This book presents the results of our efforts to find answers to these questions. In this study we address the development of complex society in the ancient American Southeast by generating models of sociopolitical organization that can be evaluated through archaeology. It is a case study based on archaeological excavations. Our research is designed to measure and assess the form and scale of political and social integration in the lower Chattahoochee River valley of Alabama and Georgia (Figure 1.1). Our use of the term integration refers to the cultural practices that linked people together into communities that interacted on a regular and sustained basis. Aided by settlement distributions and pottery style analysis, we document the locations, sizes, and occupation histories of mound centers, a form of archaeological site that functioned as a civic-ceremonial capital of an ancient political territory.

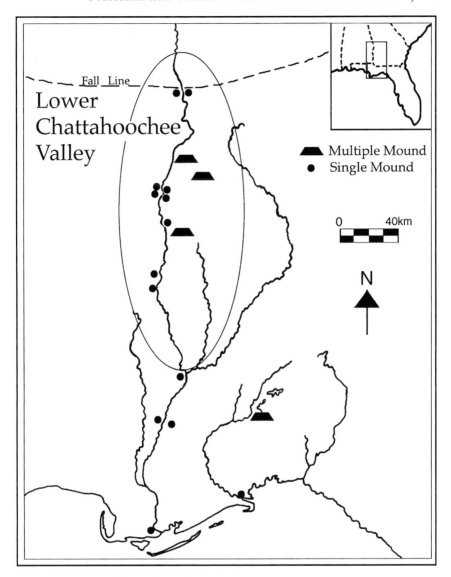

1.1. Distribution of mound centers in the lower Chattahoochee River region A.D. 1100–1650.

The precolumbian peoples who built the mound centers, known as Mississippian, lived in societies with ranked kin groups and strong leaders. The term Mississippian refers to an American Indian cultural development beginning just over 1,000 years ago and continuing to contact with Europeans in the sixteenth century. Although population size, organization, and subsistence varied across environments and regions, Mississippian societies shared many characteristics such as maize horticulture, fortified communities with large earthen mounds, social ranking, and a set of rituals and symbols concerned with fertility, ancestors, and war.

Mississippian archaeological sites contain the material remains of populous and culturally complex native societies. Monumental earthworks, rich burial treatments for a privileged few, and early historic accounts of powerful native leaders have led archaeologists to conclude that some Mississippian communities were composed of high-rank and low-rank groups whose leaders represented corporate interests (Knight 1990a; Scarry 1996). Inequities in the distribution of materials, labor, and other resources indicate that status and prestige were sometimes inherited as well as achieved. For these reasons, Mississippian social formations are said to be rank societies (Peebles and Kus 1977). Rank society is commonly defined as a kin-based social structure in which groups have unequal access to prestige, but few or no differences in access to power and economic resources (Ember et al 2002: 310; Fried 1967). Of course, rank society is a heuristic concept, not some essential quality of Mississippian populations. Access to prestige, power, and economic resources has many overlapping dimensions, and archaeologists do not yet understand the range of social variability in the late prehistoric Southeast.

Here we must introduce another frequently used (some would say abused) concept in American archaeology: the chiefdom. Mississippian societies formed political organizations commonly referred to as chiefdoms. Southeastern archaeologists use the chiefdom concept to specify the scale of political complexity in Mississippian societies because it emphasizes the material aspects of communities, identifiable as archaeological sites, and territory, identifiable by settlement patterns. The anthropologist Robert Carneiro (1981:45) defines the chiefdom as "an autonomous political unit comprising a number of villages or communities under the permanent control of a paramount chief." To minimally conform to the chiefdom concept, we expect a Mississippian population to be composed of ranked kin-groups in multiple communities or dispersed households, united into a permanent political organization, and headed by a formal or permanent political official—the "chief."

It must be remembered that the chiefdom concept depicts an idealized form of political organization, an effort by anthropologists to measure how societies differ in political organization along a scale with at least two dimensions. Political organizations differ as to their level of integration, measured by the largest group that can act as a political unit, as well as the degree of centralization, measured by how much political authority or power is concentrated in a social group (Ember et al. 2002:399). Weakly integrated, decentralized political organizations of a less complex form than chiefdoms (usually glossed as "bands" or "tribes") are restricted to independent local groups that form larger political units, if at all, only on a temporary basis without permanent officials.

There is considerable archaeological and historical evidence that Mississippian sites with earthen mounds mark the political-ceremonial centers of chiefdoms; we review this evidence in Chapter 2. The proliferation of mound centers across the Southeast after A.D. 1000 suggests that chiefdoms became widespread (Anderson 1994). We suspect that chiefdom formation heralded significant new sociopolitical changes as local families and kin groups surrendered some of their former independence to unite into larger political entities. This fundamental process, in which households and communities formed permanent political organizations with territories under a hierarchy of leadership, placed the Mississippian peoples on the path to complex society. Identifying the varying forms and scales of this expansion in political and social integration is the subject of our study.

It is clear, however, that the chiefdom concept, as currently applied in southeastern archaeology, fails to capture the sociopolitical variability within Mississippian societies. Some of the late Mississippian communities encountered by the Spanish, such as the sixteenth-century Chickasaws, appear to have had weakly integrated and decentralized political organizations; perhaps these groups were at the less-complex end of the chiefdom scale or were not chiefdoms (Johnson 2000:89–90). It is equally evident that some site clusters and mound centers in the Mississippian world might be better characterized as "presumptive chiefdoms," (Milner and Schroeder 1999:97) because the archaeological indicators of rank found at larger sites are either not present (Lorenz 1996) or remain undocumented. At the upper end of the complexity scale, the Cahokia site in Illinois is several times larger than any other Mississippian settlement, and may represent the remains of an archaic state (Pauketat 2004). Faced with a complex mosaic of sociopolitical diversity, recent efforts to understand variation and change in Mississippian political formations have focused on the scale of sociopolitical development (Scarry 1999), the degree of social ranking present in communities (Fisher-Carroll and Mainfort 2000), and the economic, political, and ideological means by which leaders acquired and consolidated their power (Emerson 1997; Muller 1997; Pauketat and Emerson 1997; Scarry 1996).

In this study we are concerned with the forms and scales of Mississippian political organizations, and how we may recognize the archaeological correlate for Carneiro's autonomous political unit, which we refer to as a "polity." The Mississippian polity is the largest organization that can act as a permanent political unit. In other words, all chiefdoms are polities, and most Mississippian mound-center polities were probably organized as chiefdoms. The term "chiefdom" is so deeply embedded into the intellectual history of Mississippian archaeology that it is difficult to dispense with the concept. It is necessary, however, to transcend the generalized use of the term and specify the variability of the political units often subsumed by the chiefdom concept in Mississippian studies. A more nuanced understanding of sociopolitical variability will be achieved only when the developmental histories of individual mound-center polities in a region are documented. This goal shifts the emphasis away from chiefdoms as the primary theoretical or analytical concept toward the archaeological recognition of the basic or minimal political units that composed polities.

Mississippian Political and Social Integration

To better understand Mississippian integration processes, it is necessary to create a new model that identifies the full range of sociopolitical variability in mound-center polities so that we may begin to understand the factors that influenced polity growth and decline. In a recent overview of chiefdoms, Earle (1997) proposes that the degree of political power in emergent complex societies varied with the principle sources of power available to chiefs: social (kinship), economic, military, and ideological power. Social, economic, military, and ideological forms of political power are intimately intertwined, but as Earle demonstrates, it is possible to identify separate archaeological measures for each source of power. Following Earle's lead, we propose that Mississippian leaders utilized all of these political power sources in the process of integration. Hypothetically, it should be possible to tie the specific political power source utilized by elites to different processes of integration: social integration, economic integration, military integration, and so forth. However, the regional data set available to us is inadequate to identify or measure all of these political power sources because we lack artifact samples from a full range of cultural contexts, especially households at nonmound sites. So it is not yet possible for us to specify the precise links between all political power sources and the processes of integration in the study region.

Therefore, we take a somewhat different approach, one that emphasizes the insights derived from a regional sample of mound centers. First, we define two processes of integration and formulate ways that we can measure these processes with evidence from mound-center investigations. Next, by documenting the size, location, and histories of the centers and the sociopolitical relationships between their populations, we hope to illustrate how these two integration processes developed and changed through time in the study area. Once this is done, and we have an adequate historical and cultural perspective on the problem, only then are we in a position to identify, albeit tentatively, some of the forces that drove integration.

For these reasons we restrict our study to two forms of integration that we can detect in our study area: political and social integration. The term political integration refers to the establishment of polities and associated political territories with a hierarchy of leadership. We define social integration as the formation and maintenance of a collective social identity that defined an affiliation shared by multiple kin-groups.

Our study of Mississippian political and social integration uses evidence derived from settlement patterns and pottery style distributions. The number and size of mound centers and the distances between them is used to identify variation in regional political organizations and the extent of ancient political territories. We measure the rate of political change through time by the duration of individual mound centers. A chronology for the foundation and abandonment of mound sites is used to detect power shifts between mound centers as old sites were abandoned and new sites were founded. We argue that the sharing of pottery styles indicates interaction between mound center inhabitants; the spatial distribution of shared pottery styles is our measure of the scale of social integration. Our aim is to document and understand some of the factors that influenced precolumbian sociopolitical change and variation through time in one region of the "Mississippian world" (Scarry 1999:59).

Potentially, there were at least three spatial scales of integration in the Mississippian world: local, regional, and inter-regional integration (cf. Muller 1999). Local integration was the interaction within a polity. Regional integration was the interaction between local polities within the same region. Inter-regional integration was interaction between polities in adjacent regions. Our previous research focused on important political and economic relationships between Mississippian mound centers and outlying nonmound sites (Blitz 1993; Lorenz 1996). Here, our effort to identify autonomous political units and territories is concerned mostly with mound sites. In that way we wish to expand our investigation beyond the scale of local integration to encompass the wider geographical perspectives of regional and inter-regional scales of integration. As we shall see, the ability to maintain political and social integration declined with geographical distance and placed limits on the spatial extent of polities and collective social identities.

The Significance of the Research

The political and social formations encompassed by the chiefdom concept are of anthropological importance. It was in these kinds of emergent complex societies that sociopolitical hierarchies and centralization of authority first occurred at the regional level (Johnson and Earle 1987:207). Chiefdoms occupy the scale of social complexity between small, politically decentralized

societies without strong leadership, and archaic states with large populations, social stratification based on nonkinship principles such as economic
specialization, and powerful sanctions such as armies to support a centralized
political authority. Consequently, chiefdoms vary considerably in terms of
population, territorial size, and degree of political centralization (Earle
1997). Chiefdom political centers, such as the Mississippian mound sites, fall
along a settlement scale between rural and urban. Many of the social, political, economic, and ideological underpinnings of archaic states have their
beginnings in chiefdoms. So if one is interested in the origins of government, the roots of economic specialization, the rise of social inequality, or
the variability of nascent political complexity, it is ancient chiefdoms and
their central places that hold the archaeological clues to address these issues.

As was the case with the vast majority of chiefdoms, however, the Mississippian sociopolitical formations were not necessarily on a developmental
path to statehood. Although the chiefdom is often considered an evolutionary forerunner to the archaic state, state formation is not the only reason
chiefdoms are of anthropological significance. A valuable perspective on culture process and history is gained when we identify and understand the
sociopolitical diversity that was possible in the lost world of middle-range
societies. Chiefdoms, as fully functioning and evolving political organizations independent of nation states, are not readily observable in the contemporary societies of today. Furthermore, historical documentation and ethnographic studies of chiefdoms occurred under conditions in which contact
with states may have changed native political organizations in fundamental
ways, perhaps even reducing the precontact variation that we wish to understand. Much of the early southeastern historical record lacks detail, and used
alone cannot reveal how such societies underwent organizational transformations overtime. For these reasons, anthropological archaeology is our primary source of knowledge about the long-term development and variation
of nonstate sociopolitical forms.

Organization of the Study

Our study of Mississippian political and social integration involves a series
of procedures for analyzing the archaeological data and presenting the results. This book is organized as follows. Chapter 2 provides the theoretical
background that guides archaeological efforts to identify and understand
political and social integration in Mississippian societies. In Chapter 3, we
introduce the lower Chattahoochee River region as a case study in Mississippian integration and synthesize the results of mound excavations at three
multiple-mound centers and nine single-mound centers. In Chapter 4, the

results of the mound excavations are used to create the regional cultural chronology required to determine how many mounds were in use at each center during a series of time periods.

The mound-center chronology is a prerequisite to the measurement of regional political integration in Chapter 5, in which the distances between contemporary mound centers in each time period are compared to define polity boundaries. Establishing the mound-center variables of duration of mound use, number of mounds at each contemporary center, and the distances between contemporary centers permits measures of changing polity boundaries and identification of different polity forms. Possible reasons why single-mound centers are often found as closely spaced pairs of sites are addressed, as is the intriguing pattern of mound abandonment and reuse. These phenomena are integral components of regional political integration in Mississippian societies.

Chapter 6 examines regional social integration by mapping ceramic style zones. Stylistic and spatial discontinuities between sites with Mississippian tradition pottery and sites with indigenous Woodland tradition pottery document the nonlocal origin of Mississippian populations. Ceramic style zones are compared to polity boundaries to identify the changing scales of regional social integration through time and assess the relationship between social and political integration.

Chapter 7 places polity formation, growth, and decline in the study region in an inter-regional context. Initial Mississippian polities in the region are identified as immigrant horticultural communities that interacted with indigenous populations on an expanding frontier. Inter-regional alliances and exchange networks marked the growth and decline of large polities in the region. A precipitous decline in political integration coincides with similar declines in neighboring regions. Possible reasons for the rise and decline of the Chattahoochee mound centers are evaluated and related to environmental and social changes that are inter-regional in scope.

In Chapter 8, our conclusions are summarized to provide a synopsis of political and social integration in the lower Chattahoochee River valley. Although there were specific historical contingencies that created a culture history unique to this region, as an archaeological case study, the processes of integration that we identify operated broadly in rank societies throughout the Mississippian world and beyond. Therefore, it is appropriate that we bring together several concepts that can form the basis for a new theory of Mississippian political and social integration.

Finally, there are four appendices that present detailed descriptive and quantitative data. For readers who want more information on excavation methods, cultural contexts, and artifact provenience, Appendices A and B document the archaeological investigations at the multiple-mound centers and single-mound centers, respectively. Our method of pottery classification is presented in Appendix C for those who may want to assess our empirical units or use these data for comparative purposes. Methods used to seriate the mound pottery samples are detailed in Appendix D.

2   Mississippian Political and Social Integration

In this chapter we map out the theoretical and methodological terrain that must be traversed before we can go from archaeological remains to an understanding of Mississippian political and social integration. Our effort is part of an ongoing dialogue in anthropological archaeology concerned with the origins and development of complex society. Scholars inquiring into the nature of Mississippian societies have made important contributions to this dialogue, in part due to the industrious pace of research applied to a rich archaeological record, as well as the insights derived from anthropology and ethnohistory. From these sources, archaeologists have constructed models of sociopolitical organization and found ways to evaluate the models with material evidence from extinct cultures.

Measuring Political Integration

For archaeologists to measure political integration in rank societies, a standard set of observations is required so that polity scale and form can be identified and charted across the dimensions of time and space. Minimally, we need to find material remains that identify ancient political units; we need to know the spatial extent of ancient political territories so that we can identify the boundaries between political units; we need to know if there were hierarchical relationships between the political units; and we need to know the relative degree of organizational complexity that characterized the political units. Let us begin with the relationship between categories of material remains and ancient political units.

Platform Mounds, Polities, and Chiefs

Perhaps the most important feature of the archaeological record for measuring political integration in Mississippian societies is the platform mound. Mississippian platform mounds are flat-topped earthen pyramids enlarged by repetitive construction episodes over extended periods. As forms of monumental architecture, platform mounds are the product of large amounts of human labor harnessed by community leaders. Archaeological sites with platform mounds mark the central places of Mississippian polities where leaders exercised their political authority. We will not attempt a detailed review of the extensive literature on the forms and functions of Mississippian mounds (e.g., Knight 1981a; Lindauer and Blitz 1997; Payne 1994; Steponaitis 1986). Instead, we need only highlight the evidence that permits archaeologists to link these impressive monuments to Mississippian political integration. Specifically, what is the connection between platform mounds, polities, and formal offices of leadership such as chiefs?

Platform mounds support the remains of buildings larger in size and different in function than nonmound buildings. Archaeologists interpret these buildings as "public" structures, elite residences, chief's houses, and mortuary temples (Payne 1994). Some platform mounds contain human remains. The people buried in mounds were segregated at death from others not buried in mounds. Thus mound burial was a privilege reserved for a subset of the total community population. At some sites, a few of these mound burials have elaborate ornaments, such as copper breastplates and headdresses, nonfunctional stone axes, and incised shell ornaments, many decorated with the recurrent symbols of a complex iconography. The position of these rare artifacts in the mound interments indicates that they were elements of dress and other personal adornments, and their restricted distribution has led archaeologists to conclude that the adornments marked high rank or leadership status (Peebles 1971). Therefore, some mounds were elite charnel houses or mortuary temples, complete with ancestral bones, wooden or clay platform remains that seem to be altars, and stone or wooden human representations interpreted as idols (Brown 1985). Mortuary and nonmortuary mound buildings were also places where valuables, food, and weapons were stored (DePratter 1991:96–119). Numerous archaeological investigations confirm these functions and activities for the precolumbian Mississippians, and Europeans observed similar uses of platform mounds in the early historic era in the Southeast.

Mississippian platform mounds served as powerful symbols of group unity and chiefly authority. For example, historic, linguistic, and archaeological evidence suggests that platform mounds were symbols of the earth associated with rejuvenation and fertility; the periodic addition of mound construction stages may have been a communal rite of world renewal (Knight 1986). Because the large size of many mounds required a group construction effort, mounds were unifying symbols for a social unit or community, but there is evidence that communal mound building was an expression of social ranking as well. From European accounts of mound use by late Mississippians and their descendents, such as the Natchez of the Lower Mississippi Valley, we know that leaders had their houses on mounds, that the bodies of chiefs and other important people were often placed in temples on mounds, and that the death or replacement of chiefly leaders required that the mound-world symbol be renewed by a new construction effort (Swanton 1911).

Such a close link between mounds and leaders suggests that these monuments, though objects of communal or corporate group veneration, also served as material evidence of a leader's ability to compel compliance to a central authority. Thus some archaeologists interpret platform mounds from a political economy perspective, in which the ability to amass and direct labor for mound construction was under the control of chiefly elites or leaders as a form of corvée labor (Haas 1982:214–215) or tribute extraction (Steponaitis 1978:444–449). It should not be surprising that mounds could represent both collective and individual interests because in all chiefdom societies, chiefs are the symbolic embodiment of the well being of their followers (Johnson and Earle 1987:235–236). Indeed, the architecture and associated activities of North American platform mounds show patterned changes through time between the inclusive and open concerns of community and the exclusive and closed requirements of ranking (Lindauer and Blitz 1997).

By extending the direct historic analogies back into the precolumbian past, archaeologists may infer that Mississippian mound-building episodes punctuate periodic political events related to the succession of chiefly office (Anderson 1994:126–129). The continuous additions of mound construction stages over time intervals greater than a human lifetime imply that these monuments were the product of an institutionalized or formal office of leadership and not merely the temporary achievements in the life of a single individual (Blitz 1993:84–85). Thus there is a direct relationship between the political tenure of chiefs and the construction of platform mounds in Mississippian societies. If a sequence of major mound stages represents the efforts of a series of chiefly office holders, then it follows that the cessation of mound building marks the termination of the institution of chief at a mound center (Hally 1996:95–97). This means that sites with earthen mounds were the seats of chiefly authority, and in that sense functioned as political "capitals" (Payne 1994:17).

Drawing on southeastern historical accounts of mounds and mound architecture, cross-cultural comparative studies of chiefly capitals, and the Mississippian archaeological record, Claudine Payne found that despite a diversity of size and complexity, Mississippian capitals shared specific characteristics of structure. She concluded that (1) capitals were the largest settlement in the polity, and were marked by earthen platform mounds; (2) capitals contained a chief's house, which stood on the largest and tallest (main) mound; (3) buildings on main mounds were larger than non-mound buildings; (4) mortuary temples (buildings with human remains) were placed on platform mounds at sites with two or more mounds; (5) mortuary temples were placed on a mound that was smaller or not as tall as the main mound; and (6) mortuary temple buildings and chief's houses are similar in size (Payne 1994:225–227).

Settlement Models of Mississippian Political Organization

Regional settlement analysis is a pragmatic means for archaeologists to recognize relative degrees of political complexity, identify polity forms, infer aspects of political organization, and measure political integration. If we accept the interpretation that mound centers were the territorial seats of power for chiefly polities, then the location, size, and number of mound centers in a region through time permit archaeologists to address variation and change in Mississippian political organization. If mound centers were chiefly capitals, then single-mound centers and multiple-mound centers should represent polities with different organizational forms and degrees of political complexity.

As a central place that exerted political control over a territory, chiefly mound centers are at the top of a settlement hierarchy. A regional pattern of central places that differ in size and complexity is interpreted as an indicator of a sociopolitical hierarchy (Johnson 1977). An emphasis on site size, as indicated by number of mounds, provides a scale to measure the sociopolitical variability encompassed by the chiefdom concept. Now that we have reviewed the connection between platform mounds, polities, and chiefs, we may consider two contrasting models of Mississippian political change and variation that can be documented by regional settlement analysis: the simple-complex chiefdom model and the polity fission-fusion model.

In the simple-complex chiefdom model, chiefs are defined as decision makers; thus the number of decision-making levels or chiefs measures the political complexity of chiefdoms (Steponaitis 1978). In Mississippian research, a simple chiefdom is equated with a two-tiered settlement size hierarchy composed of (1) households and (2) a small mound center with one or two platform mounds. A three-tiered settlement size hierarchy of (1) households and (2) small mound sites (secondary centers) affiliated with (3) a larger, multiple-mound site (the principal or primary center) is identified as a complex chiefdom (Steponaitis 1978, 1986). The relationship between the decision-making levels and site-size hierarchy is based on the proposition that people were organized across the landscape to ensure the efficient movement of "tribute" (food, goods, and services) from productive households to elites at political centers (Wright 1984). In this interpretation, each mound center was an administrative hub for collecting tribute in a territory. Hypothetically, tribute flowed from households to a chief at a center, and in the case of a complex chiefdom, on up the chain of command, from secondary centers to the primary center (Anderson 1994:74–79; Steponaitis 1978:440–449; Welch 1991:8–19). The model incorporates a developmental "cycle" for the emergence and decline of chiefdoms; through time a simple chiefdom may develop into a complex chiefdom, and then devolve back to a simple chiefdom (Anderson 1994:1, 9–10).

The simple-complex chiefdom model has much to recommend it, but as knowledge about Mississippian chiefdoms and mound centers has accumulated over the last decade, there are reasons to think that the model is incomplete. For one thing, it has not been established that Mississippian chiefs exercised centralized control over a tribute-based economy in the manner proposed by the simple-complex chiefdom model (Muller 1997:49–50, 384). We do know that households supplied food, goods, and labor to their local mound centers (e.g., Blitz 1993; Emerson 1997; Jackson and Scott 1995; Lorenz 1996; Welch and Scarry 1995), so it is unlikely that non-mound settlements were politically autonomous (*contra* Mehrer 1995: 165–166). Interpretive caution is in order, however, because even in non-hierarchical societies, ritual obligations may stimulate household production, accelerate regional exchange, and concentrate foods and goods at "sacred locations" that do not function as regional political centers or exercise economic and political control over participating populations (Spielmann 2002:195).

We also know that at the time of European contact, powerful Late Mississippian chiefs demanded and received tribute from neighboring weaker chiefs, but the political and economic relationships between small and large mound centers are not yet understood, and may be quite variable. The spatial scale of political integration in Mississippian societies remains unclear. What was the upper limit on the territorial size of a Mississippian polity? How far could Mississippian chiefs extend centralized control over households and integrate them into a unified polity? The simple-complex chiefdom model is not sufficiently specific about how archaeologists might recognize the spatial boundaries of chiefdoms.

A "paramount chiefdom" has been proposed as an additional Mississippian political unit, based on a reading of the early Spanish accounts in which chiefs claimed tribute from distant subordinate communities (Hudson et al.

1985). No doubt chiefdoms were capable of extracting tribute from distant communities beyond the territory under direct control, but what is described in these accounts was a set of relationships between separate polities, not a single unified polity as implied by the "paramount chiefdom" misnomer. A paramount chiefdom was not a unified political organization with a territory as were simple and complex chiefdoms; it was an interaction sphere of powerful and weak chiefdoms engaged in *temporary* alliance, exchange, and warfare interactions (Blitz 1993:15–16; Hally 1994a:248–249). The problem is this: as a proposed polity form, the paramount chiefdom does not have an identifiable archaeological correlate (Muller 1997:75; but see King 2003:95–96).

In initial applications of the simple-complex chiefdom model, investigators arranged all regional mound centers into a site-size hierarchy assumed to be integrated into a single, centrally controlled chiefdom (e.g., Steponaitis 1978). As the occupational history of mound centers has become better known in several regions, however, it is now evident that not all centers were in contemporaneous use (Anderson 1994; Blitz 1999; Clay 1997; King 2003; Knight and Steponaitis 1998; Williams and Shapiro 1996). Obviously, before it can be said that secondary centers were linked in a tributary relationship to a primary center in a complex chiefdom, it must be demonstrated that the sites were occupied at the same time. Because it is possible that a regional pattern of mound centers represents a mosaic of political territories occupied at different times, the occupation histories of each mound center must be documented. More specifically, based on the premise that the duration of mound use at a center coincides with the duration of the chiefly polity that built and used the mound, the duration of mound use at each center must be dated. This research goal is not easily accomplished, so in only a few regions of the Mississippian world is it possible to identify how centers fit together as political units.

Based on the assumption that the occupation span of a mound center marked the time span of a chiefdom, recent studies in the South Appalachian area found that most chiefdoms were short-lived, and lasted no more than a century (Anderson 1994; Hally 1996; Williams and Shapiro 1996). Some centers had episodes of occupation, abandonment, and reoccupation, accompanied by the addition of mounds or mound stages at the site (Hally 1996; King 2003; Williams and Shapiro 1996). In other words, not all mounds at a multiple-mound site were in use at the same time, nor were all mound sites in a region in use at the same time.

When David Hally (1993, 1996) looked at the spacing of sites with mounds occupied in the same time period, he found a strong pattern. Contemporary mound centers were spaced either closer than 18 km or farther than 32 km from their nearest neighbor. Based on his discovery, Hally

(1994b:167) concluded, "(1) contemporaneous mound sites separated by less than 18 km belonged to the same polity; (2) mound sites separated by distances greater than 32 km belonged to different polities; and (3) Mississippian polities seldom exceeded 40 km in spatial extent." Hally noted that a 40-kilometer-diameter polity limit was a recurrent pattern in chiefdoms cross-culturally. Apparently, the maximum distance of one day's round-trip travel by foot from the political center limited effective administration in chiefdoms to between 12.5 and 18 km from the seat of chiefly power (Hally 1993:162–163,165). Because the polity boundary is fixed by the limitations of pedestrian travel, this distance limitation should apply to all mound centers regardless of size.

Hally's research has identified the spatial scale of political integration in a sample of Mississippian chiefdoms. A radius of 18 km extended out from a mound center is the maximum distance for effective polity administration. This 18-km distance measure can form the basis for recognizing Carneiro's "autonomous political unit" with archaeological data. Simple chiefdoms can be identified by the presence of a single-mound site with no other contemporary mound centers within 18 km. Complex chiefdoms can be recognized by the presence of two or more contemporary mound centers within 18 km of each other that exhibit hierarchical size distinctions (i.e., a primary-secondary center settlement pattern).

The other important insight provided by Hally's research on South Appalachian mound centers was the lack of evidence for the hypothetical chiefdom "cycling" of the simple-complex chiefdom model. Hally (1996:125) found that (1) most polities began and ended as simple chiefdoms (one-mound sites); (2) in only a few cases did it appear possible that complex chiefdoms developed locally out of an antecedent simple chiefdom; and (3) when a complex chiefdom ended, there was no clear evidence that it cycled back to a simple chiefdom.

The archaeological studies cited above indicate that the simple-complex chiefdom model cannot account for the diversity of mound-center settlement systems known to exist in the Mississippian Southeast. As a model of Mississippian political organization, it is incomplete; the developmental histories of Mississippian polities are too variable to fit comfortably into the simple-complex chiefdom cycle model of political organization and change. In response to these findings, Blitz (1999) proposed an alternative model of Mississippian political formations that could also be documented and evaluated with regional settlement analysis: the chiefdom or polity fission-fusion model. In contrast to an overemphasis on a settlement-size hierarchy in the simple-complex chiefdom model, the polity fission-fusion model focuses on a different process, the aggregation and dispersal of basic political units. The model defines a basic or minimal political unit composed of a leader or chief, a body of followers, and their representative symbol and integrative facility, a platform mound. These mound-affiliated political units came together or fused, and pulled apart or fissioned, to create mound-center polities of different forms and sizes.

In constructing the polity fission-fusion model, an analogy was drawn from historic-period indigenous societies of the Southeast, the inheritors of the Mississippian legacy. In the eighteenth-century Southeast, the basic political unit was the *okla* (Choctaw) or *talwa* (Muskogee) polity, defined as a "people" or "town" that shared a common ceremonial center (Gatschet 1969; Swanton 1928). By the eighteenth century, the placement of chief's houses and mortuary temples on platform mounds was in decline in favor of nonmound architecture called square grounds and rotundas. Archaeologists have demonstrated that these nonmound buildings were transformations of the key elements found on top of Mississippian platform mounds (Howard 1968; Hudson 1976:221–222; Knight 1989; Waring 1968). In at least one case, square grounds and rotundas were placed on top of mounds (Bartram 1995). Furthermore, the manner in which the ceremonial structures of ranked kin groups were positioned around the perimeter of historic square grounds is similar to the arrangement of mounds around open plazas at Mississippian centers (Knight 1998). Although the architecture of ritual space changed, there is a degree of conceptual continuity in central places with civic-ceremonial architecture from Mississippian times into the historic era.

Historic period *okla-talwas* of the Choctaws, Creeks, and others could exist as single, autonomous political units, which were organized as simple chiefdoms (Hudson 1976:210–211), or *okla-talwas* sometimes clustered together to form larger political entities, usually referred to as confederacies. *Okla-talwas*, as basic political units, were combined like "building blocks" to create polities of different sizes and degrees of centralized power (Blitz 1993:11–13; Muller 1997:193–196). Through this direct historic analogy, Blitz (1999) proposed that many Mississippian platform mounds were the civic-ceremonial facilities of a basic political unit, perhaps similar to the historic *okla-talwas*, and that a fission-fusion process was at work in precolumbian Mississippian times.

Mississippian societies with inherited leadership were particularly vulnerable to factionalism at times of succession to chiefly office because, with each new generation, the pool of genealogically qualified candidates increased significantly (Anderson 1994:84–93). This condition is a potential source of conflict characteristic of all kin-based, rank societies. The proliferation of legitimate, potential leaders at Mississippian centers created a political time bomb that increased the probability that succession to chiefly office would be disputed, and eventually undermine polity stability. Under these circumstances, the losing faction might decide to reject their subordinate status by leaving the center to establish their own new center elsewhere.

The polity fission-fusion model proposes that Mississippian mound centers formed this way, by the coming together and pulling apart of basic political units composed of a chief and a body of followers, which can be identified archaeologically with platform mounds. It is this basic political unit that we refer to as a mound-political unit. We suspect that mound-political units correspond to unilineal descent groups thought to form the social structure of Mississippian societies (Knight 1990a; Peebles 1971). Sites with multiple contemporary platform mounds suggest the presence of multiple constituent mound-political units, each with its emblematic earthen monument of residential or mortuary function. Viewed this way, multiple-mound sites are composite compositions of mounds built and maintained by different constituent groups composed of several mound-political units. Due to the volatile politics of factionalism, each mound-political unit was the potential nucleus for a polity. Thus mound-political units were the corporate-group building blocks that created large or small Mississippian political organizations.

We have presented two contrasting models of Mississippian chiefdoms. The simple-complex chiefdom model emphasizes one kind of process: the arrangement of mound centers into a political hierarchy based on the number of mounds at a site. The polity fission-fusion model emphasizes another process: the aggregation or dispersal of mound-political units to create multiple-mound sites or single-mound sites. The next step is to operationalize these models so we can apply them to the archaeological record in a specific case study. Then we can evaluate if or how each model contributes to an understanding of Mississippian political organization.

Mound-Center Settlement Patterns and Polity Forms

In presenting the polity fission-fusion model, Blitz (1999) identified four possible mound-center settlement patterns that could occur within the 18-km polity limit (Figure 2.1), and proposed that each settlement pattern corresponded to a polity with a specific form of political organization. Settlement pattern A is the single-mound center polity, a mound-political unit with no other centers that conforms to Steponaitis's definition of a simple chiefdom. Settlement pattern B is the primary-secondary mound center polity, a multiple-mound center and subordinate single-mound centers that conform to Steponaitis's definition of a complex chiefdom. Settlement pattern C is the multiple single-mound center polity, two or more single-mound centers with no multiple-mound center. Settlement pattern D is the multiple-mound center polity, a multiple-mound center with no secondary centers. The simple-complex chiefdom model fails to address settlement patterns C

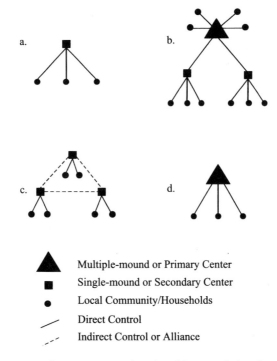

2.1. Mound-center settlement systems (reprinted by permission from *American Antiquity,* volume 64, number 4, copyright 1999 Society for American Archaeology).

and D. Not depicted here is a four-tiered settlement hierarchy, present in the unique Cahokia polity (Fowler 1978:468–471), created by adding a tier of tertiary mound centers to settlement pattern B. Cross-culturally, the four-tiered settlement hierarchy is a hallmark of the archaic state (Flannery 1998:16–21).

Unlike the simple-complex chiefdom model, the building-block model of polity fission-fusion can account for all possible mound-center settlement patterns. Potentially, several single-mound center polities like A might move to a new site where together they would create a large multiple-mound center polity like D. Subsequently, the individual mound-political units could move back apart, once again forming more A polities or C polities. In either case, these changes could occur without the polity ever creating an administrative hierarchy of secondary centers, such as found in the primary-secondary polity form B. Such a transformation of polity forms is not accounted for in the simple-complex chiefdom cycle model.

In sum, mound-center settlement pattern analysis permits us to identify and measure regional Mississippian political integration in terms of three dimensions of polity form: hierarchy, complexity, and scale (Kowalewski et al. 1983). As we have seen, the number of mound-center settlement levels or tiers above the household level is the relative measure of political hierarchy in the polity. The number of mounds (and by inference, mound-political units) is the relative measure of political complexity in the polity. All four polity forms, regardless of variation in hierarchy or complexity, have the same spatial scale or boundary conditions because effective political integration was limited to an 18-km radius from a center by the logistics of communication and transport. When we apply these measures of polity hierarchy, complexity, and scale to Mississippian settlement patterns, we can identify regional political integration. The single-mound center polity has no hierarchy of centers, and a low level of complexity (only one mound-political unit). The primary-secondary mound center polity has a hierarchy of centers and a high level of political complexity (multiple mound-political units). The multiple single-mound center polity has no hierarchy of centers (all centers have one mound) and a moderate level of complexity (at least two mound-political units within the 18-km polity boundary). The multiple-mound center polity has no hierarchy of centers and a high level of complexity (multiple mound-political units confined to a single center).

Adam King (2003:14–15) proposes that settlement patterns such as C and D in Figure 2.1 should be interpreted as a complex chiefdom and a simple chiefdom, respectively. He argues that because settlement pattern C has multiple centers, one of these mound sites must have been the political capital where polity-wide decisions were made. Although no site-size hierarchy of centers is evident, the assumption that one center was preeminent implies that the C polity had at least two levels of decision making above the local household level, and for this reason, King defines it as a complex chiefdom. King states that even though the D polity's political capital is a multiple-mound center, it represents a simple chiefdom because there is only one decision-making level above the local household level.

We disagree with King's interpretation because it ignores archaeological measures of hierarchy and complexity, two dimensions of polity form that allow us to differentiate mound-center settlement patterns. The recognition of simple and complex chiefdoms in the archaeological record depends on the presence of a site-size hierarchy and variation in the number of mounds at sites. To lump these divergent settlement patterns into the simple-complex chiefdom typology serves no useful purpose and obscures the diversity of polity forms that we wish to understand. It is best to treat settlement patterns C and D as separate, hypothetical polity forms until we have more data.

Our task is to evaluate the relationship between polity forms inferred from mound-center settlement patterns and the two contrasting models of Mississippian regional political integration. To identify Mississippian mound-center polity forms and document how they changed through time requires specific information. One must know the number of contemporary mound centers in a region and the number of contemporary mounds at each center. This means that episodes of mound construction and use at each mound center in a region must be dated as accurately as possible. Such a comprehensive knowledge of regional mound centers is very difficult to obtain because, among other reasons, mounds are big, they are sometimes hard to date, and the required fieldwork is time consuming and expensive. Also, mounds are sometimes destroyed before archaeologists can examine them, so the record is incomplete for some regions. Consequently, few such regional analyses have been undertaken in the Southeast.

The first procedural step in our case study of regional integration in Mississippian societies is to examine the mound-center settlement patterns in the lower Chattahoochee River valley of Alabama and Georgia in order to identify variation and change in political organization over the course of six centuries. By measuring mound-center settlement hierarchies, the number of contemporary mounds, and the nearest-neighbor distances between contemporary mound centers in the region, it is possible to identify the scale and form of polities. Once contemporary mound centers are identified, a static mound-center settlement pattern becomes a dynamic archaeological record of polity change and variation through time, and a measure of regional political integration in Mississippian societies is achieved.

Measuring Social Integration

Mississippian polity change and variation was due to a variety of economic, social, political, military, and ideological factors. Polities were politically autonomous, but they were not isolated. Mississippian mound centers existed in a geopolitical landscape composed of interaction spheres of competing polities engaged in various forms of alliance, exchange, and warfare, such that the history of any one polity was strongly affected by interactions with nearby polities (e.g., Steponaitis 1991; King 2003). While we have outlined methods to identify the temporal and spatial dimensions of Mississippian political integration, we need complementary methods to identify the temporal and spatial scale of social integration. Specifically, an understanding of social integration requires a measure of regular and long-term interactions between the inhabitants of mound centers at the regional and inter-regional scale.

One such approach has been to record the distribution of similar forms of the highly crafted stone, shell, and copper artifacts that compose the Southeastern Ceremonial Complex (SECC) (Brain and Phillips 1996). SECC artifacts—ornaments and other ritual paraphernalia that conveyed specific style sets of iconographic themes—circulated widely A.D. 1200–1400. Distributions of similar SECC style sets provide insights into elite interaction networks, mostly at the inter-regional scale (e.g., Muller 1999). SECC artifacts are rare, however, and the spotty distributions usually do not yield a detailed measure of regional-level interaction between centers, nor do they provide insights into the scale of nonelite interactions. For these reasons, distribution studies of more ubiquitous elements of material culture that represent the products of geographically discrete populations are required.

Interpretations of Ceramic Stylistic Diversity

Our basic premise is that populations in preindustrial, nonmarket societies that shared styles of common material culture had a greater degree of regular and long-term interaction than populations that did not share common styles. Pottery, usually found broken into potsherds, is one such ubiquitous artifact. The plasticity of clay and the additive process of forming pottery vessels created a durable medium for the expression of style. Thus the spatial distributions of shared styles of common ceramics recovered from mound centers may map onto local, regional, and inter-regional scales of social integration.

The history of mound centers presented in this study is based on a seriation of chronologically sensitive styles of utilitarian pottery, defined as decorated ceramic types (i.e., clusters of form, composition, and decoration attributes). Efforts to use individual attributes of form, composition, and decoration for this purpose proved unproductive (see Appendix C). The changing ceramic type frequencies provide chronological subdivisions and the means to assign mound-center components with similar ceramic assemblages into ceramic phases. We refer to the spatial distributions of these ceramic phase components as ceramic style zones. We propose "the prehistoric peoples who inhabited archaeological sites exhibiting a shared ceramic style must have belonged to a social group with a common history of regular and sustained interaction" (Lorenz and Blitz 2003). Put another way, the degree of social interaction and integration is reflected in the degree of ceramic stylistic similarity between sites. We also hypothesize that a high degree of ceramic stylistic similarity between sites reveals a shared or collective social identity. Therefore, ceramic style zones can measure the spatial and temporal scale of social integration.

The theoretical premises on which we base these hypotheses are neither unique nor unusual in archaeology. Both ethnographic and archaeological studies confirm that artifact assemblage similarity across dispersed communities is strongly related to geographical propinquity, a common ancestry as measured by a shared language, and a history of exchange relationships between settlements (Kirch 1991; Moore and Romney 1994; Roberts et al. 1995). However, the uses of style in social groups are complex and fluid (Conkey and Hastorf 1990; Hegmon 1992). On the one hand, there is no necessary one-to-one correlation between ceramic styles and ethnic or language groups; some studies suggest the correlation is weak at best (Shennan 1989) or that peoples with different identities may use the same ceramics (Gosselain 1998; MacEachern 1998). On the other hand, ethnographic studies of utilitarian pottery distributions demonstrate that ceramic style does correspond to a shared social identity under certain cultural conditions (e.g., DeBoer 1990; Gronenborn and Magnavita 2000; Longacre 1991; Wiessner 1983). Before a similar claim is made about archaeological style patterns, it is necessary to establish that similar conditions were probably present in the past societies in question.

In the time-space taxonomic system still used to construct the cultural-historical frameworks applied to the prehistoric Southeast (Caldwell 1958; Willey and Phillips 1958), ceramic phases that exhibit stylistic continuity with antecedent phases are considered to be the historical products of a shared ceramic tradition with considerable time depth. In this view, gradual temporal style change in ceramic traditions is attributed to cultural drift, while rapid or discontinuous style change is interpreted as disruptions due to diffusion or population replacement. At a given point in time, the spatial scale of a ceramic tradition (composed of historically related ceramic phases) is said to be the result of dissemination by group interaction or movement from a geographical point of origin (e.g., Deetz 1967:55–65).

While the taxonomic units of culture history continue to have some utility, the "learning-interaction" theory of style used to explain the cultural dynamics is too limiting (Hegmon 1992:521). With the focus on social integration, we are primarily interested in ceramic style as the communication of social group relatedness and difference, and how the changing forces of integration affected the scale of this communication. Ceramic style zones may signal social group boundaries because stylistic similarities and differences between social groups are known to vary with the degree of ethnic or social relatedness (Sackett 1985, 1990; Wiessner 1983). Wobst (1977) found that style expressed social identity by signaling or enforcing within-group conformity and demarcating between-group social boundaries. Stylistic similarity between groups also varies with the form of social interaction; competitive groups may create distinctive style boundaries in an attempt to define affiliation, while mutually cooperative groups may share styles more freely (Hodder 1985). From this style as communication perspective, artifact styles that materialize social group affiliation are likely to form distributions that reveal networks of social interaction (Braun 1985).

If style communicates, then it may signal different "messages" to different target audiences. Wiessner (1983) interprets style as "emblemic" when used to signal group identity and boundaries, and "assertive" when communicating individual status. Sackett (1985, 1990) identifies style as "isochrestic variation" or socially learned choice by artisans that is often rather inactive as communication in comparison to "iconographic style," which functions more overtly to transmit information. The information content of style may be latent and inclusive or manifest and exclusive depending on the circumstances of social interaction. Even style as isochrestic variation may rapidly take on iconographic or emblemic significance at social group boundaries where competition heightens awareness of group identity (Sackett 1985:158). The use of style as communication is more active and situational than the earlier conception of style as the passive unfolding of long-term interactions that reveal culture history.

With the formation and proliferation of mound centers in a region, we would expect a corresponding increase in the scale and scope of social integration as polities incorporated localized groups and formed political organizations composed of non-kin. Under these conditions, emergent elites had a need to create new institutions to attract followers and counter the tensions of kin-group factionalism. One way this more inclusive level of social integration was accomplished in ethnographically known societies was through the amplification of group rituals that linked non-kin in dependent relationships of ceremonial obligation and increased community solidarity (Durkheim 1933; Fortes 1953). We do not imply that increased integration erased social divisions, but rather that new ideological efforts were implemented to expand an idealized collective identity to a larger scale. Polity formation carried with it an imperative to produce collective social identities that could transcend localized kin-group loyalties (as well as mask or deflect tensions generated by emerging distinctions of rank and privilege). Indeed, style as collective social identity could be defined as a process of ideological (as opposed to social) integration and certainly the processes are intertwined, but our focus on polities as composites of interacting social segments inclines us to emphasize style as a measure of social integration.

As an increased spatial scale of political and social integration linked formerly independent local groups together, it would reduce the need for local boundary expression through style, so ceramic style diversity would be expected to decrease at the single community level; conversely, a decreased spatial scale of integration would increase local boundary expression, and ceramic style diversity would be expected to increase at the single community level (Braun 1985; Hodder 1982). At the regional and inter-regional scale, a spatial pattern of geographically confined style zones, each zone encompassing clusters of local communities with shared ceramic styles, indicates a shift toward greater integration within zones and the marking of boundary distinctions between zones (Masson 2001).

Mississippian Social Integration and Ceramic Style Zones

In Mississippian societies, current evidence suggests that utilitarian pottery was locally produced in households and distributed through local reciprocal exchange networks (King 2003:95; Muller 1997:305). Utilitarian ceramic style zones reveal the spatial extent of these localized reciprocal networks, which represent interaction spheres surrounding mound centers. The spatial distribution of mound centers and their affiliated smaller sites, in turn, appear as regional settlement clusters separated by "buffer zones" (Hickerson 1965) with little or no settlement (Hally 1996; Muller 1999; Scarry 1996). We hypothesize that the interstices between Mississippian utilitarian ceramic style zones represent social and political frontiers, boundaries that impeded the transmission of styles via local reciprocal networks (Lorenz and Blitz 2003). Open interaction, balanced reciprocity, and a high degree of social integration created a high frequency of shared utilitarian ceramic styles within style zones. Frontiers between ceramic style zones demarcate boundaries between groups with distinct social identities, barriers to communication that created restricted interaction, negative reciprocity, and a low frequency of utilitarian ceramic styles shared between style zones.

Thus far, we have proposed that utilitarian ceramic style zones were interaction spheres maintained by the reciprocal exchange networks of non-elites; the temporal-spatial scales of these zones fluctuated with the expansion or contraction of political and social integration. There were also elite interaction networks, however, that disseminated ceramic styles distinct from the common utilitarian pottery. Mississippian ceramic assemblages sometimes contain highly decorated serving wares. These serving fine wares often occur in low frequency or are absent in nonelite ceramic assemblages. Higher frequencies of serving fine wares are found in special-use or elite contexts such as platform mounds or as grave goods. These distribution patterns suggest that serving fine wares, while not restricted to a specific social rank, were valued containers used in diacritical displays of conspicuous consumption. From the style as communication perspective, it is probable that highly valued serving fine wares conveyed different stylistic "messages" than did the common utilitarian pottery: an "assertive" or "iconographic" use of style concerned with the demarcation of individual social status (Sackett 1985; Wiessner 1983).

Mississippian polity formation may have created frontiers that inhibited the spread of nonelite reciprocal networks, but as the SECC artifacts reveal, elites participated in interaction spheres that were distinct from those of nonelites. Elites competed for access to prestige goods, which circulated widely at spatial scales that were more extensive than utilitarian reciprocal networks. Possession of prestige goods legitimated, sanctified, and otherwise affirmed elite status. The stylistic content of prestige goods, including serving fine wares, may have conveyed "supralocal" symbols or an "international style" that signaled an individual's connection to nonlocal, elite networks (Blanton et al. 1996; Peebles 1971). We propose that the spatial distributions of Mississippian serving fine ware styles can be expected to cross the frontiers between utilitarian ceramic style zones to reveal a prestige ceramic style zone. The sharing of prestige ceramic styles at a spatial scale that bridges different utilitarian ceramic zones may reveal the existence of an elite social identity concerned with other, distant elites.

As outlined above, there are reasons to expect that polity formation will increase the scale of social integration, collective identity, and the sharing of ceramic styles. However, this does not mean that a ceramic style zone must be spatially equivalent to a polity boundary. The historical processes of group interaction and population movement created the spatial distributions of both shared ceramic style and polities linked through fission-fusion, but the scale of ceramic zone and polity boundary need not be the same. The spatial relationship between polity and ceramic style zone is an empirical question best approached as an archaeologically testable hypothesis.

In Mississippian studies, there have been relatively few attempts to compare the temporal-spatial distributions of Mississippian polity boundaries and ceramic style zones (Hally 1994a, b; King 2003). More regional studies are needed so that the spatial scales of both political and social integration in Mississippian societies can be identified, compared, and charted through time. The analysis of pottery style distributions as a measure of social integration complements and parallels the study of mound center location, size, and duration as a measure of political integration. Therefore, the second procedural step in our case study of Mississippian regional integration is to compare the stylistic similarities and differences of utilitarian pottery samples secured from dated mound contexts, identify ceramic style zones with these data, and then compare the mapped style zones to the reconstructed polity boundaries. Those decorated ceramic types that were shared or not shared across style zone frontiers should provide clues to the scale, intensity, and reciprocal character of social interaction. Once this is accomplished, we can detect interaction between polities, compare polity boundaries to ceramic style zones, and measure social integration. When these comparisons are made for a series of time periods, we will be in a position to evaluate the relationship between scales of social and political integration, and document how these relationships changed over time in the Mississippian societies of the lower Chattahoochee River region.

Polity Origins, Growth, and Decline

Once detected in the archaeological record, expansion and contraction in the scales of social and political integration in a region requires explanations for the origins, growth, and decline of polities. While the evidence we can muster to address these issues is limited, there are archaeological signatures of some important causal factors, such as population movement and interaction between centers. In the chapters that follow, we review such topics as the origins of the centers as the result of population movements and the decline of centers due to social, political, and environmental factors. Therefore, the third procedural step in our case study is to compare the scales of social and political integration documented in the lower Chattahoochee River region to other regions of the Southeast in order to detect similar rise-and-decline patterns and formulate models that help us understand why such broad similarities occur.

3   Archaeology of the Mound Centers

Excavations into the platform mounds along the lower Chattahoochee River have taken place numerous times over many years for various reasons. One early digger, F. W. Miller, was an artifact collector motivated either by curiosity or profit (Brandon 1909). Harvard-educated C. B. Moore (1907) developed a dilettante's enthusiasm into serious scholarship, and yet his research seldom went beyond illustrated catalogs of finds. By the middle twentieth century, however, practitioners of an avowedly scientific and anthropologically oriented archaeology considered description of the ancient remains a means to a greater end: culture history and process. Archaeology of the mound centers was no longer the hobby of individuals acting alone; teams of trained archaeologists supported by museums and universities now conducted the excavations.

Two museums played central roles in the mound-center excavations. The first of these, the Columbus Museum, is a public museum in Columbus, Georgia, with a long-term commitment to archaeological research. The museum sponsored mound excavations by Joseph R. Caldwell (1955) and Frank T. Schnell (Schnell et al. 1981). The museum's resources were limited, however, and important mound investigations were never published. In the early 1960s, reservoir construction threatened several mound centers. The River Basin Surveys (RBS) of the Smithsonian Institution initiated a federal program of "salvage archaeology." Two RBS archaeologists, Harold A. Huscher and Robert W. Neuman, conducted mound excavations. The urgency of the rescue work required more resources, and so David L. De-Jarnette of the University of Alabama and Arthur R. Kelly of the University of Georgia directed additional mound excavations (Kellar et al. 1961; Kurjack 1975). Despite the energetic efforts of Huscher and Neuman, funds for analysis and publication never materialized. The RBS was discontinued in 1969, and the extensive records and site collections were stored at the Smithsonian Institution.

The Lower Chattahoochee River Region as a Case Study

We chose the lower Chattahoochee River valley as a case study of Mississippian political and social integration for specific reasons. Numerous mound excavations had taken place there. Not only did the number and size of the lower Chattahoochee mound centers imply a range of possible polity forms, but also ceramic style traditions in the region were diverse and changed dramatically through time and across space. These conditions suggested to us that the lower Chattahoochee River was a dynamic political and social environment that could provide the data we needed to address regional integration.

This study is based on a thorough analysis of all known excavations of platform mounds along the lower Chattahoochee River that date A.D. 1100–1650. During 1996–2000, we examined excavation records and materials at the Columbus Museum and the Smithsonian Institution. We applied a standardized artifact classification to all excavated materials to facilitate site comparisons, seriated pottery types to construct a relative chronology of mound centers, and acquired additional radiocarbon assays to assign the mound occupations calendar dates.

In this chapter we provide a synopsis of the mound-center excavations. Because our research is the primary documentation for previously unpublished excavations at several mound centers that are now destroyed, an extended report on these sites is appropriate. Therefore, a detailed presentation of excavation methods, artifact provenience, and pottery classification is available in the appendices. In keeping with our research goals, the emphasis is on mound excavations and chronology, but other site characteristics are discussed to place the mound building in a wider cultural context. Before we turn to the mound excavation synopsis, it is useful to place the sites in a regional environmental setting and cultural-historical context.

The Region and the Archaeological Sequence: A.D. 700–1650

Information on the region's natural environment is available in detail elsewhere (Knight and Mistovich 1984; Schnell et al. 1981), so we will not repeat it here, but we must mention certain physiographic characteristics relevant to our concern with settlement distributions. Arising in the southern Appalachian Mountains, the Chattahoochee River flows southwest across northern Georgia. As it enters the Gulf Coastal Plain, the river forms the boundary between Alabama and Georgia. The lower Chattahoochee is that portion of the river from the Fall Line south to the Flint River confluence (Lake Seminole); from the confluence south the river is known as the Apalachicola. The Fall Line is an ecotone that divides the Gulf Coastal Plain from the upland Piedmont region. Here the river (now altered by reservoirs) once passed over rocky shoals and falls. Flowing south, the river bisects several east-to-west trending physiographic zones defined by geological strata and soils (Figure 3.1). Mound centers and archaeological phases are not equally distributed across these zones, perhaps due to varying natural resource potentials. As other researchers have, we subdivide the lower Chattahoochee River region into Northern, Central, and Southern zones (Schnell and Wright 1993). These settlement zones are heuristic designations used to subdivide site distributions in this spatially extensive region, and generally conform to boundaries between physiographic zones. In Figure 3.1, A–B is the Northern zone, C–D is the Central zone, and E is the Southern zone.

A regional sequence of ceramic phases, defined by pottery types, ordered by stratigraphic superposition and seriation, and assigned estimated time spans by radiocarbon dating, provides the cultural chronology for our study. The details of this sequence are presented in Chapter 4; the brief outline below provides a guide to the results of the mound-center investigations.

Wakulla (A.D. 700–1000) This ceramic phase identifies a time span when an indigenous, pre-Mississippian population occupied the Southern zone, without mound-center polities or other evidence of rank society. Wakulla Check Stamped is the dominant pottery type.

Averett (A.D. 900–1300) This ceramic phase identifies a time span when an indigenous population erected two mounds near the Fall Line in the Northern zone. Averett Plain is the diagnostic pottery type.

Rood I (A.D. 1100–1200) This ceramic phase identifies a time span when Mississippian peoples of nonlocal origin established fortified mound centers throughout the valley. High frequencies of the Moundville Incised pottery type are the diagnostic characteristic.

Rood II (A.D. 1200–1300) This ceramic phase spans the time of the first multiple-mound center in the Central zone. High frequencies of the Cool Branch Incised pottery type and the initial appearance of the Lamar Plain pottery type are the diagnostic characteristics.

Rood III (A.D. 1300–1400) A ceramic phase that marks the time when regional integration and mound building peaked in the Central and Southern

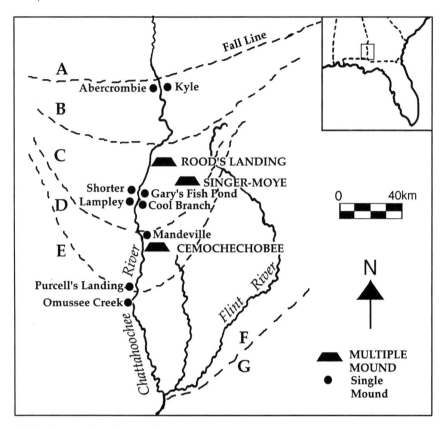

3.1. Relationship of mound centers to physiographic zones: (A) Lower Piedmont, (B) Fall Line Sand Hills, (C) Chattahoochee Red Hills, (D) Fall Line Red Hills, (E) Dougherty Plain. The Pelham Escarpment (F) and Tallahassee Highlands (G) form the southern boundary.

zones. Pottery types from the preceding phase continued in use, but in changing frequencies of popularity.

Singer (A.D. 1400–1450) A ceramic phase characterized by a replacement of previous pottery styles by new styles originating outside the valley; mound centers were restricted to the Central zone. The Fort Walton Incised and Lamar Plain pottery types were codominant, and the Lamar Complicated Stamped pottery type appeared for the first time.

Bull Creek (A.D. 1450–1550) These pottery styles identify a time when only three small mound centers were in use in the Central and Southern zones. Fort Walton Incised and Lamar Complicated Stamped were the dominant pottery types.

Stewart (A.D. 1550–1600) This ceramic phase represents the time when a multiple-mound site in the Central zone was the only center in the region. High frequencies of the Lamar Complicated Stamped pottery type and the initial appearance of the Rood Incised pottery type mark this phase.

Abercrombie (A.D. 1600–1650) This ceramic phase permits us to recognize the interval when regional mound centers were used for the last time by peoples ancestral to members of the Creek Confederacy. The initial appearance of the Abercrombie Incised pottery type marks this phase.

The Multiple-Mound Sites

Unlike the single-mound centers, which are found in all three of the settlement zones, the multiple-mound sites are present only in the Central zone. The Rood's Landing and Singer-Moye sites, each with eight mounds, are among the largest mound centers in Georgia, surpassed in the volume of earth moving only by the Etowah, Macon Plateau, and Kolomoki sites. The Cemochechobee site, with three mounds, is a much smaller center.

The Rood's Landing Site (9SW1)

Rood's Landing is a multicomponent site in Stewart County, Georgia. In contrast to the usual situation in which the largest mound centers have attracted the most extensive investigations, the occupational history of the largest lower Chattahoochee center, Rood's Landing (9SW1), is less well known than its roughly equal-sized rival, Singer-Moye, or the much smaller Cemochechobee site. In Payne's (1994) site-size classification of Mississippian mound centers, Rood's Landing falls into the Medium-Large class. Within a 6-ha area, there are eight flat-topped pyramidal mounds (Figure 3.2). Mounds A, B, C, D, and E are arranged around an open area or plaza. The two largest mounds, A and E, have ramps facing each other across the plaza, an alignment that suggests the two mounds were in contemporaneous use for some span of time. Mounds F, G, H, and C are peripheral to the compact plaza group, an arrangement that could be interpreted as later additions to an established site plan. The corners of the less-eroded mounds are oriented to the approximate cardinal directions; corners or sides oriented in this manner were the preferred arrangement in the Mississippian world (Payne 1994:143). Two ditches or dry moats mark the northern side of the site. The ages and original dimensions of the moats are unknown;

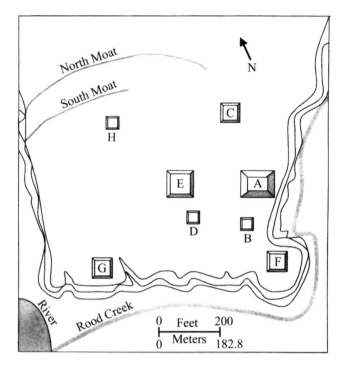

3.2. Plan of Rood's Landing site, 9SW1, contour interval 3 m.

they are now as much as 3 m wide and at least 200 m long. Oddly, both moats appear to terminate abruptly without completely enclosing the northern site perimeter.

The only significant excavation results at Rood's Landing are those of Joseph Caldwell (1955), working for the Columbus Museum of Arts and Crafts (now the Columbus Museum). Assisted by David Chase and Frank T. Schnell, Caldwell placed excavation units in Mounds A, B, D, and F. All of these mounds were constructed of sequential clay or sand stages in typical Mississippian fashion and produced evidence of burned buildings. The most extensive effort was expended on the Mound A summit, where the excavators uncovered the remains of burned buildings representing the final mound occupation (Figure 3.3). Excavations in Mounds B, D, and F were smaller in scope (see Appendix A).

Great quantities of large potsherds were uncovered in and around the buildings on the final stage of 7-meter-high Mound A, leaving no doubt that they were generated by food-consumption activities at the summit precinct. Food remains were also abundant. Artifacts other than potsherds were less numerous: ground stone discoidals, greenstone celt fragments, pottery

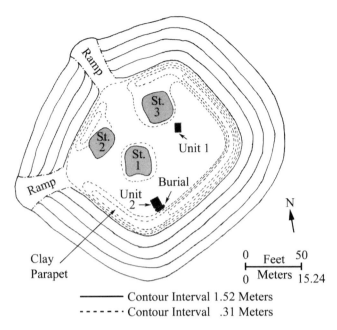

3.3. Plan of features on Mound A, 9SW1 (redrawn from Caldwell 1955).

smoking pipes, and sherd disks (artifacts of unknown function ground from potsherds and sometimes interpreted as gaming pieces or spindle whorls). Small quantities of ground hematite, red ocher lumps, and fragments of sandstone grinding slabs or anvils indicate pigment production. Found adjacent to Structure 1 was "a pottery phallus, life size and modeled in detail with considerable care. Presumably, it was a fertility symbol, and may have been used in rites which took place on top of the mound" (Caldwell 1955:31). The pottery penis, broken at one end, may have been part of a larger object; a tiny hole that runs the length of the shaft mimics the urethra.

The abundant potsherds and midden debris led Caldwell to conclude that the Mound A buildings were residences, but he thought that Structure 1 "might have been of a sacred character: it was built on a separate low elevation, it was more elaborately made than the others, its form is unlike that of any building which has been discovered to date, and after being burned it was covered with a low mound" (Caldwell 1955:28). Mounds, as earth symbols, have been linked to concerns with fertility (Knight 1986), thus the burned and buried buildings on Mound A may be expressions of purification and world renewal cycles.

The unique pottery phallus on Mound A may be invoked in support of the fertility-renewal theme, but mound-building cycles may be triggered by political events, especially a crisis precipitated by the death of a leader (Anderson 1994; Hally 1996). So it is interesting that a funeral, not the burning and covering of Structure 1, was the final event on Mound A; a grave containing an adult male, a child, and a pottery vessel intruded through the fired daub from Structure 1 on the south summit corner (Caldwell 1955:31). This was the only burial discovered on the mound.

In his 1955 report, Caldwell assigned the ceramic samples to three periods of occupation at Rood's Landing. He defined the assemblages from the final Mound A and final Mound B summit occupation levels as representative of a "Later Period." Pottery from the lower levels of Mounds A and B, and all pottery from Mounds D and F were assigned to a "Middle Period." An "Earlier Period" component was confined to the premound level beneath Mound D.

Caldwell's Earlier, Middle, and Later periods are equivalent to our Rood I, Rood III, and Stewart phases. Based on associated pottery (and radiocarbon dates from Mound A), Mounds A, D, F, E, and H were present in the Rood III phase (A.D. 1300–1400) and three other mounds were possibly present. Only Mounds A and B are known to have later building episodes, confined to the terminal construction stages. So perhaps the site reached its maximum size as a political center in Rood III phase times. Afterward, mound construction and occupation ceased at several mounds, including the preeminent Mound A. The termination of occupation on Mound A in the Rood III phase suggests that the site ceased to be a chiefly center for a period of time. Following a hiatus of 150 years, the site again became a political center in the Stewart phase (A.D. 1550–1600) when Mound A was reoccupied and Mound B was also in use. This reoccupation period must have been brief because only a single occupation level was established on Mound A before the summit structures were burned, a funeral took place, and Mounds A and B were once again abandoned. Thereafter, the site was never again a chiefly center.

The Singer-Moye Site (9SW2)

The Singer-Moye site is located in Stewart County, Georgia, 28 km east-southeast of Rood's Landing, the nearest-neighboring mound center. Unlike other lower Chattahoochee River centers, the site is located in an upland setting several kilometers from the river. Within 13 ha, there are eight earthen mounds and associated habitation areas (Figure 3.4). Like Rood's Landing, Singer-Moye is classified as Medium-Large in Payne's (1994) site-size ranking of Mississippian centers. Mound A, at 13 m high the tallest platform mound at the site, has corners oriented to the approximate cardinal directions. For the lower platforms B, C, D, and F, the sides (not

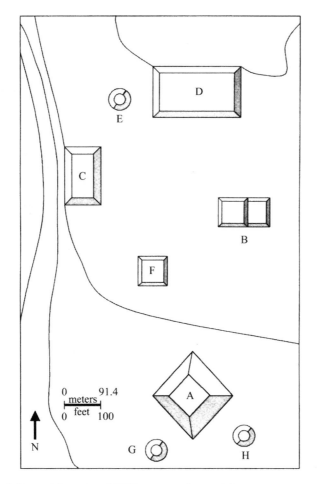

3.4. Plan of Singer-Moye site, 9SW2, contour interval 3 m.

the corners) align to the approximate cardinal directions. Mounds E, G, and H are low and rounded in outline; E and H cover the remains of "earth lodges" (square wattle-and-daub buildings with surrounding earthen berms). Unique for the site, the Mound B summit has two levels. Mounds B, C, D, E, and F are arranged around an open space that may be a plaza. A second possible plaza is bounded by Mounds B, F, A, and H.

Under the direction of Frank T. Schnell, assisted at various times by Margaret C. Russell, Donald Gordy, Vernon J. Knight Jr., John H. Blitz, and other archaeologists, excavations were conducted at the site from 1967–1972, in 1989, and again from 1991–2002. Excavations have been placed in Mounds A, C, D, E, and H (see Appendix A). A trench into the multistage

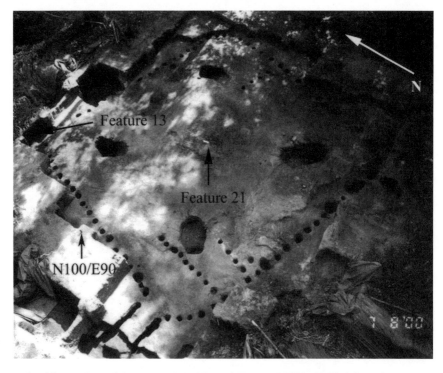

3.5. Oblique view of Structure 2H, Mound H east, 9SW2, 2000 (photo by permission of Margaret C. Russell).

Mound C revealed the oldest identified mound construction. Another early occupation occurred beneath Mound H, where a deep trench uncovered midden, numerous post molds, remains of wall-trench houses, and a 20-meter-long palisade segment. Later, a sequence of square, wattle-and-daub earth lodges was established here, then mounded over and abandoned to create the low Mound H (Figure 3.5). Cut marine shell, a marine-shell bead, stone discoidals, red and yellow paint pigments, mica fragments, sherd disks, food remains, and potsherds were found in a midden (Feature 13), a central hearth (Feature 21), and other portions of the Mound H earth lodges. Another square earth lodge was discovered at Mound E, where walls and floors were covered with contrasting red and white clays.

The most elaborate remnant building at Singer-Moye was Structure A1, located on the final-stage summit of Mound A (Figure 3.6). It was a 12-x-12 m structure that included such associated remains as two copper fragments, mica sheets, stone discoidals, portions of 14 smoking pipes, and a painted

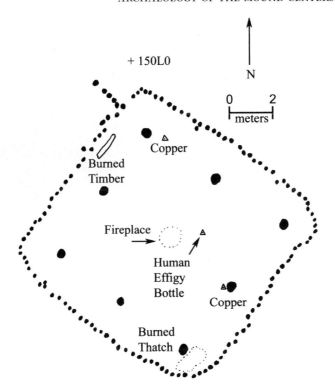

3.6. Structure A1, Mound A, 9SW2.

fragment of a human effigy bottle (Figure 3.7). Like the earth lodges at Mounds E and H, Structure A1 was associated with food remains and smashed pottery, so we think these mound buildings were elite residences.

After Structure A1 burned, a clay cap was deposited directly over the destroyed building. Because the clay cap did not extend over the entire summit, the specific purpose of this activity was to seal off the building remains and so consecrate the place. This ritual act of "building burial" is the same situation that marked the final use of Rood's Landing Mound A, where the centrally placed building on that mound, Structure 1, was also covered with a low clay cap after it burned. Unlike the termination ritual at Rood's Landing Mound A, however, no human burial was encountered on the Singer-Moye Mound A summit (much of which remains unexcavated). Because Mound A is the preeminent mound at Singer-Moye, the burning and covering of Structure A1 probably closely coincides with the abandonment of the site, or at least, its continuation as a chiefly center.

Based on multiple radiocarbon assays and ceramic seriation, Mound C

0   Centimeters   5

3.7. A polychrome-painted ceramic human head from an effigy bottle, Structure A1, 9SW2 (photo by permission of the Columbus Museum).

dates to the Rood I phase (A.D. 1100–1200), Mounds H and E were in use during the Rood III phase (A.D. 1300–1400), and the final use of Mounds D and A was in the Singer phase (A.D. 1400–1450). We have no evidence for mound building in the A.D. 1200–1300 time span (Rood II phase), nor do we have artifact samples from Mounds B, F, and G, or the lower levels of mounds A and D. While much of the mound construction history remains to be documented, we can at least establish a range for the number of confirmed and possible mounds in use at the site during each phase. During the Rood I phase, one mound is confirmed (C) and five mounds were possibly present. In the Rood III phase, two mounds are confirmed (H, E) and five were possibly present. In the Singer phase, two mounds are confirmed (A, D) and three mounds were possibly present.

The Cemochechobee Site (9CY62)

This multiple-mound site, located within the Chattahoochee Red Hills physiographic zone in Clay County, Georgia, had an extensive habitation

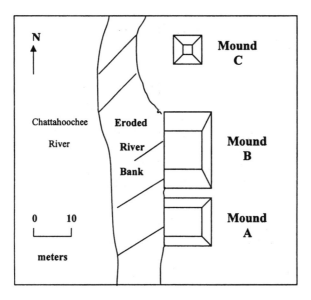

3.8. Plan of Cemochechobee site, 9CY62 (redrawn from Schnell et al. 1981).

area and three adjacent platform mounds designated A, B, and C (Figure 3.8). Most of the site is now either badly damaged or destroyed. Much smaller than Rood's Landing and Singer-Moye, Cemochechobee is in the Very Small class of Payne's (1994) site-size ranking of Mississippian centers. Like the other two multiple-mound centers, Cemochechobee is situated in the Central zone. Also like other Mississippian mound sites in the Central zone, there was no antecedent Late Woodland period founding population present before Early Mississippi period people occupied the site.

The Cemochechobee mounds were extensively excavated in 1976–1977 by archaeologists from the Columbus Museum as part of an archaeological salvage project. The stratigraphic history of mound construction and use was documented in detail (Schnell et al. 1979, 1981), so we offer only a brief overview here. The mounds were oriented to the approximate cardinal directions. Mound A was constructed in five stages to a final size of 22-x-21 m and 2.4 m high. Mound B was constructed in 10 stages to a final size of 24.1-x-28.5 m and 2.8 m high. The smaller Mound C was constructed in only two stages to a final size of 2.6-x-3.5 m and only 67 cm high. Mound A was the southernmost of the three mounds and adjacent to Mound B, which in turn was just five meters south of the smallest mound, Mound C. Mounds A and B began as separate construction events, but in the later history of each mound they converged, so that the final mound summit was shared by both mounds. In contrast, Mound C was built during the later stages of Mound B and may have replaced Mound A in function.

The mound excavations at Cemochechobee uncovered a complex sequence of construction stages with the remains of buildings thought to function as elite residences, specialized mortuary facilities, and communal meeting places. Several high-status burials contained copper, marine shell, and ground stone artifacts indicative of the Southeastern Ceremonial Complex (SECC), an elaborate iconography that flourished in the Mississippian Southeast A.D. 1200–1400.

As the result of a detailed reexamination of stratigraphy and pottery samples, together with new calibrations of radiocarbon dates (see Appendix A), we estimate that the Cemochechobee multiple-mound center was occupied in the Rood II phase (A.D. 1200–1300), one-quarter of the time span hypothesized by the excavators. Mound A was the first mound erected, and then Mound B was built, followed by construction of Mound C.

The Single-Mound Centers

Our synthesis of research conducted at archaeological sites with a single platform mound begins with centers at the northern end of the lower Chattahoochee River valley, just south of the Fall Line at Columbus, Georgia, in the Fall Line Sand Hills physiographic zone. Proceeding north to south through the valley, we consider each center in turn. All single-mound centers are in the Very Small class in Payne's (1994) site-size classification of Mississippian centers.

The Abercrombie Site (1RU61)

The Abercrombie site (1RU61) is a single platform mound (now badly damaged, if not completely destroyed) surrounded by an extensive multicomponent habitation area, in the Fall Line Sand Hills physiographic zone, Russell County, Alabama. Together with the Kyle site, only 1.6 km east on the Georgia side of the river, Abercrombie is one of two Northern zone mound centers. These two sites exemplify a tendency for single-mound centers in the region to form spatial clusters of paired centers, a settlement pattern we interpret in Chapter 5.

In 1967, Frank T. Schnell of the Columbus Museum conducted the most extensive investigation of the 1.8-meter-high mound (see Appendix B). A 15-meter-long trench dug from the mound edge to the center revealed multiple construction episodes (Figure 3.9), but perhaps due to the limited horizontal exposure, no building remains were detected (although fired daub was present). Two poorly preserved burials were also found. Domestic debris was present such as midden with abundant potsherds, animal bones, ash, and

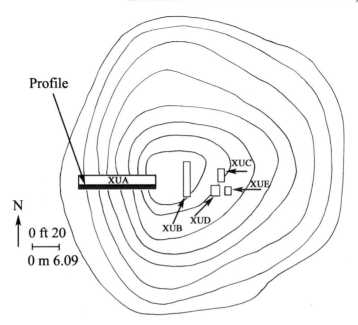

3.9. Plan of Abercrombie mound, 1RU61, contour interval 25 cm.

charcoal, but also less common materials such as ground stone slabs and red ocher used to make paint pigment, unidentified shell, and smoking pipe fragments. The upper portion of the mound had been plowed down and spread over the earlier mound remnant.

Abercrombie mound was established as an Averett phase monument (A.D. 900–1400). After several construction episodes, the mound was abandoned for as much as 300 years. Despite the plow damage, it was possible to determine that the mound was reoccupied briefly early in the era of European contact during Abercrombie phase (A.D. 1600–1650), then abandoned for a final time. We agree with others who conclude that Abercrombie is the probable site of Coweta/Cabeta burned by the Spanish in 1685 (Huscher 1959a:32; Worth 2000:273–274). Despite the lack of Euro-American artifacts from the mound deposit, the ceramic assemblage from the final mound stage is entirely consistent with a 1685 date for termination of mound construction at Abercrombie.

The Kyle Site (9ME3)

The Kyle site (9ME3), in Muscogee County, Georgia, was the location of a platform mound destroyed many years ago, prior to modern scientific investigation. What we know about Kyle mound comes from the cursory comments of local observers and artifacts retrieved by antiquarians. Kyle may be the "oblong mound" that Hawkins (1980) saw in 1799, about 4 km below a creek that matches the location of Bull Creek (Hurt 1975:17; Worth 2000:274). Peter Brandon (1909) first observed the flat-topped mound in 1888, when it was 7.6 m high and 15.2 m in diameter. Reduced in size by river erosion, Brandon found that "practically nothing" remained by 1909. So the original Kyle mound dimensions and strata are now unknown. By examining associated artifacts, however, we can estimate when the mound was built and used.

We examined eight whole pots dug from the mound by antiquarians many years ago (see Appendix B). Based on the relative stylistic dating of the pots, the mound was used in the Averett phase (A.D. 900–1300) and again in the later Abercrombie phase (A.D. 1600–1650). These are the same phases associated with the nearby Abercrombie mound. Kyle mound is at or near the site of Kasihta, an important Creek town established in the early 1600s (Worth 2000:273–274).

The Shorter Site (1BR15)

Proceeding south of the Abercrombie and Kyle sites, there are no single-mound centers until we pass south of Rood's Landing, enter the Central zone, and arrive at the Shorter site (1BR15) in Barbour County, Alabama. Located in the Chattahoochee Red Hills physiographic zone, the Shorter site was a single mound surrounded by a 2-ha area of multicomponent artifact debris, 760 m northwest of the river (Kurjack 1975:Figure 20). Walter F. George Lake (Lake Eufaula) has inundated the site.

A University of Alabama crew under the direction of David L. DeJarnette extensively excavated the mound, renumbered 1BR15X1, in 1960–1961. Kurjack (1975) reported the excavation results, so we need only review those data that concern the mound's construction history. At the time of excavation, the mound was about 40 m in diameter and 4 m high (Figure 3.10). As revealed in the north profile at the L4 grid axis (Figure 3.11), the mound was constructed in three major episodes: the primary mound, the secondary mound, and the tertiary mound. Shorter is intriguing because the tertiary or final mound stage represents a reoccupation and subsequent modification of a Middle Woodland period mound by Late Mississippi period peoples. As we discovered from the review of Abercrombie and Kyle sites, mound reoccupation is by no means unique in this region. Mandeville Mound A, a site discussed below, is also a Middle Woodland period mound with a final Mississippian construction stage.

Although the original excavators incorrectly assigned all mound construction to the Late Mississippi period, we now know that was true only of the final tertiary stage (see Appendix B). Based on the associated pottery types,

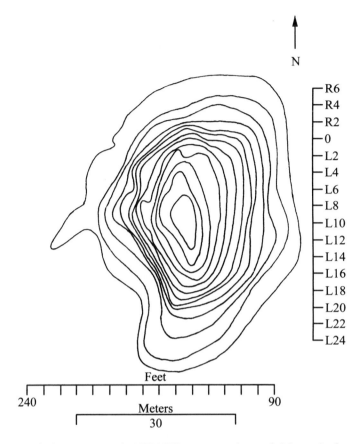

3.10. Plan of Shorter mound, 1BR15X1, contour interval 30 cm (redrawn from Kurjack 1975).

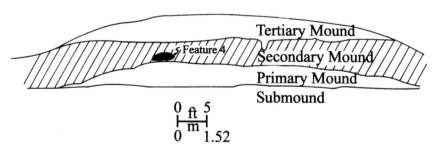

3.11. North profile at L4, Shorter mound (redrawn from Kurjack 1975).

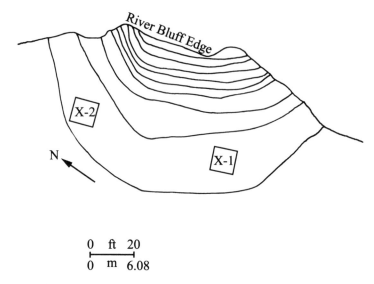

0 ft 20

0 m 6.08

3.12. Plan of Lampley mound, 1BR14, contour interval 25 cm.

we assign the Shorter tertiary mound assemblage to the Bull Creek phase, and in the absence of any radiocarbon dates, estimate that the component dates to A.D. 1450–1550.

The Lampley Site (1BR14)

South of Shorter, on the same side of the river and still within the Central zone, the next Mississippian mound center is the Lampley site (1BR14). Prior to inundation by Walter F. George Lake, the Lampley site consisted of a single platform mound situated on a high bluff above the river. Unfortunately, there is relatively little known about the site (see Appendix B).

Only a narrow strip of mound 3 m high and 15.2 m long remained intact in 1962, when Harold A. Huscher of the RBS placed two 3-x-3 m (10-x-10 ft.) units into the mound remnant (Figure 3.12). We were unable to find any description of mound strata. Daub was present, so we may infer that the mound contained architectural remains.

The cursory investigations at Lampley fall short of what are required to date the full range of mound construction and use. The number of mound construction stages is unknown. Huscher's units penetrated no deeper than one foot, so the available pottery sample most likely dates to the terminal mound occupation. We have no radiocarbon dates for Lampley. Based on the associated ceramic types, we assign the Lampley mound to the Bull Creek phase (A.D. 1450–1550).

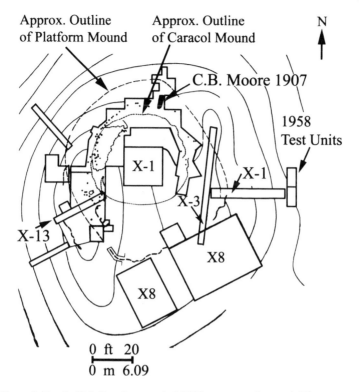

3.13. Plan of Gary's Fish Pond mound, 9QU1, contour interval 25 cm.

The Gary's Fish Pond Site (9QU1)

South of the Lampley site, and still in the Central zone, the next subject in our survey of Mississippian single-mound centers is the Gary's Fish Pond site (9QU1) in Quitman County, Georgia. This mound center is on the eastern side of the river, in the Chattahoochee Red Hills physiographic zone. Bulldozing for fill dirt to build a fishpond damaged the center of the mound sometime in the 1950s. The remnant mound was completely excavated by Harold A. Huscher of the RBS between 1958 and 1962. When Huscher arrived to begin investigations, the remnant mound appeared as a low rise 76–90 cm above the surrounding field and about 45 m in diameter (Figure 3.13). Comparison with C. B. Moore's (1907) measurements indicates that the bulldozer had reduced mound height by 70 cm and spread this material out from the mound center.

Through a series of trenches, test pits, and horizontal stripping, Huscher uncovered a very complex sequence of occupation (see Appendix B). The first occupation was beneath the mound remnant on the premound ground surface. Here, Huscher found a single grave containing a flexed adult buried with smashed pottery and a clay bead. Also on this surface were small pit features containing charred nuts.

After midden accumulated on the premound surface, the first of three mound stages was constructed. The initial mound stage (Mound 1) was a circular platform, 12 m in diameter and about 1 m high, composed of sandy fill and faced with yellow clay. Around the perimeter of Mound 1 was a line of large-diameter post molds, remnants of a wooden wall that enclosed the mound (Figure 3.14).

Built superimposed over Mound 1 were Mound stages 2 and 3, two rectangular platforms of yellow clay that expanded the mound to a final dimension of 24-x-27 m. Plow and bulldozer damage to the summits of the three mound stages removed evidence of mound-top structure patterns, but scattered post molds, small corncob-filled features (i.e., "smudge pits," a common feature at Mississippian sites thought to function as smudges to smoke hides or drive away mosquitoes), and artifacts indicate that the summits were occupation surfaces. Besides the ubiquitous potsherds, smoking pipe fragments, and sherd disks, there was evidence of intense production of mineral pigments for paint.

Based on radiocarbon dating and associated pottery, we can assign the five stratigraphic levels to ceramic phases. From oldest to most recent, the sequence is: premound surface (Rood I and Rood II phases), premound midden (Rood III phase), and Mound stages 1–3 (Singer phase).

The Cool Branch Site (9QU5)

Continuing south on the east side of the river, the next single-mound center of the Central zone is Cool Branch (9QU5), in Quitman County, Georgia. This is a "famous" site in southeastern archaeology, even though it is mentioned only briefly in various publications (Huscher 1963, 1971; Roberts 1962, 1963; Schnell et al. 1981). The site provided the name for a well-known pottery type, Cool Branch Incised (Sears 1967), yet few archaeologists know that the site produced one of the more extensive palisade remains uncovered in the Mississippian Southeast. Excavated by Harold A. Huscher as an RBS project, Cool Branch's rectangular palisade enclosed a 4.5 ha area, with a single platform mound at the center (Figure 3.15). Now inundated by Walter F. George Lake, the site was situated on the river floodplain in typical Mississippian fashion, but one kilometer back from the main channel, a concealed position that could not easily be observed from the river.

There is no record of any investigations prior to Huscher's 1958 RBS survey, when the site was placed on the A1 priority list for excavation.

3.14. Excavation of post molds at perimeter of first mound stage, 9QU1, 1960 (RBS H60B-16-6, National Anthropological Archives, Smithsonian Institution).

Huscher returned in 1960 and placed a 30 m (100 ft.) trench (X-1) into the low mound from the apparent mound edge to the center. The mound had at least two (possibly three) construction stages. Due to leveling by plow and the method of excavation, little was learned about mound architecture or summit activities. We assume that buildings were present on the red clay mound because fired daub and clay hearth fragments were recovered. Mound artifacts include arrow points, a ground sandstone slab or anvil, a

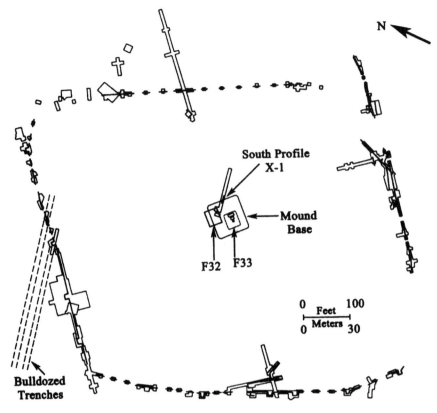

3.15. Plan of Cool Branch site, 9QU5 (Blitz and Lorenz 2002:Figure 5 reprinted by permission of the Southeastern Archaeological Conference).

sandstone abrader, a ceramic smoking pipe, sherd disks, and a large sample of potsherds. After the trench was completed, the mound remnant was bulldozed down to a level just above the contact point between the mound remnant and the premound surface. Upon exposure of this surface, the outline of the red clay mound was clearly visible as a 279 m² (55-x-55 ft.) platform.

Cutting down through the red clay mound, the remains of two large wattle-and-daub buildings were found on the premound surface. One premound structure, dubbed "Hematite House" (Feature 32 in Figure 3.15; Figure 3.16) had large quantities of broken, abraded, and powdered hematite used to produce red ocher pigment. Adjacent to Hematite House was a second structure designated "Spud House" (Feature 33 in Figure 3.15; Figure 3.17). Three features were found in Spud House: a fired-clay hearth, a 1.5-meter-deep rectangular tomb (Feature 47) containing the remains of an

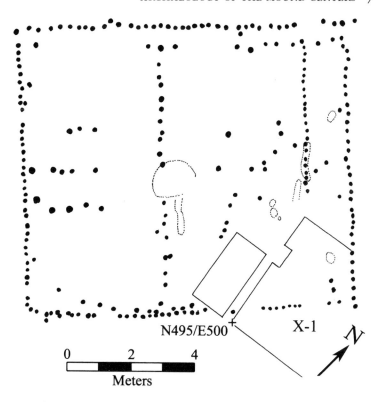

N495/E500

X-1

N

0   2   4

Meters

3.16. Plan of Hematite House, 9QU5.

undetermined number of adults associated with mica sheets and a ground slab of greenstone, and a raised clay platform that was interpreted as a "dais or altar" (Huscher 1963:2). In the immediate vicinity of the clay platform, broken into pieces by the weight of the bulldozer, were two elongated spatulate celts of highly polished greenstone (Figure 3.18). This nonutilitarian form of celt, or "pole spud," is a panregional style found at other Early-to-Middle Mississippi period sites (Pauketat 1983). The Spud House tomb is very similar to a premound tomb found at Cemochechobee, which contained an elongated spatulate celt identical in form to the Cool Branch celts (cf. Schnell et al. 1981:38–39, Plate 4.1).

   To summarize, the premound architectural plan paired two large contemporaneous buildings. Activities in the premound area generated food remains and broken pottery, which found their way into middens deposited around the buildings. Hematite House, the focus of intense red ocher production, comes closest to that class of specialized Mississippian buildings often designated "chief's house," or an elite residence. We interpret Hema-

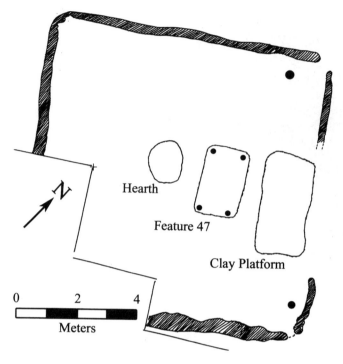

3.17. Plan of Spud House, 9QU5.

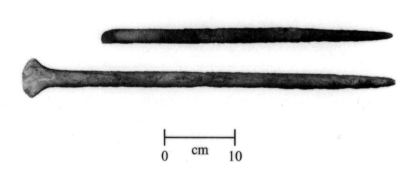

3.18. Celts found in Spud House.

3.19. Harold Huscher examines the palisade line, 9QU5, 1961 (photo by permission of Margaret C. Russell).

tite House as the residence of a local leader, and perhaps it served the additional function of communal meeting place. From the specialized nature of the associated features, we infer that Spud House had a mortuary function, although the Feature 47 burial may have been only the terminal activity in the structure. Such complementary pairings of special buildings and elite residences are known from other Mississippian sites (Lindauer and Blitz 1997; Payne 1994). Mound construction began at Cool Branch when the red clay mound was superimposed over the remains of Hematite House and Spud House.

Although our study is concerned with platform mound excavations, the off-mound work at Cool Branch provides important clues about the single-mound center community. The Cool Branch inhabitants expended far greater labor on palisade construction than they did on mound construction. The palisade walls formed a four-sided enclosure or stockade. To construct the palisade walls, posts 15–20 cm in diameter were set roughly 30 cm apart within long wall trenches (Figure 3.19). Perhaps two-thirds of the stockade was uncovered.

It is impossible to estimate palisade wall height because the depths of

3.20. Excavation of a bastion at 9QU5, 1961 (RBS H61-L9-12, National Anthropological Archives, Smithsonian Institution).

posts and wall trenches were not routinely recorded. The walls had been plastered with red clay daub, masses of which were recovered from post molds and wall trenches. Presumably, withes were woven between the gaps in the wall posts, but because the walls never burned, no impressions in daub were found to provide construction details. Wall-trench outlines of tower bastions, each 3-x-3 m, protruded outward from the curtain wall at 35 m intervals (Figure 3.20). Small-diameter posts were found at the interior corners of some bastion features.

Mississippian bastions were platforms for archers defending the wall, the regular spacing interval dictated by the effective distance of flanking cross-fire with the bow (Lafferty 1973:136). The Cool Branch bastion interval is replicated at other fortified Mississippian sites (Payne 1994:Table 4–21). Ten bastion outlines can be identified in the field maps. Huscher estimated that the stockade had six bastions to a side or 24 bastions in all. Parallel and intersecting wall trenches along the western and southern sides of the stockade indicate multiple walls, which suggest a double-walled enclosure, rebuilding episodes, or possible entranceways. By projecting excavated wall alignments across unexcavated areas to complete the enclosure, Huscher estimated a total palisade length of 853 m. If the additional wall lengths of 24 bastions are added, then Huscher's estimated total wall length is 1.06 km. Based on the 30 cm spacing of wall posts, this would mean that at least 3,300 posts were used in stockade construction. It has been estimated that it would take 15 adults working 8-hour days for 23 days just to cut, haul, and set the upright posts for a 600-m Mississippian palisade (Blitz 1993:121–123).

Based on two radiocarbon assays and the associated pottery, the premound and mound (and palisade) are Rood I phase (A.D. 1100–1200).

The Mandeville Site (9CY1)

The next mound center in the Central zone is Mandeville (9CY1), a multicomponent site with two Middle Woodland period mounds, and an associated habitation area in Clay County, Georgia. Mound A is a well-known example of a Middle Woodland platform mound, constructed in the Mandeville phase, A.D. 1–300 (V. Knight and Mistovich 1984:218–219; cf. Smith 1979). Like the previously mentioned Shorter mound, however, the final stage of Mandeville Mound A represents a Mississippian reoccupation and use of a much older monument. At the time of the 1959–1962 University of Georgia excavations (Kellar et al. 1961), Mound A was a 73-x-52 m truncated pyramid about 4.2 m high. The site now lies beneath Walter F. George Lake. We need only be concerned with the Mississippian component here.

The final Mississippian mound stage was a 42.6-x-24.3 m rectangle of red clay and brown sand piled one meter thick on the summit. Although the excavators referred to the final stage as a "cap," they detected an "apron-like" mantle of soil that extended out from the northern side of Mound A, and this too proved to be of Mississippian age (Kellar et al. 1961:12). No structure features were found on the eroded summit, but a building was probably once present because the final stage contained daub. The only other artifacts of probable Mississippian age from the summit were three pottery disks and two ceramic pipes. So there are few clues about mound summit activities, and there are no radiocarbon dates for this component.

Based on the associated pottery sample, the terminal mound stage on Mandeville Mound A was constructed in the Rood I phase (A.D. 1100–1200).

The Purcell's Landing Site (1HE3)

This site, at the ecotone between the Fall Line Red Hills of the Central zone and the Dougherty Plain of the Southern zone, is the location of a destroyed Mississippian mound. Almost all we know about the mound comes from just two sources. C. B. Moore (1907:446) dug into four mounds at or near Purcell's landing. To judge from Moore's cursory description, three of the mounds were not Mississippian platform mounds. The fourth mound, located at the edge of the riverbank, had been partially destroyed by flood erosion. Moore's crews found nothing in the mound except layers of rock and clay.

Robert W. Neuman (1959), while participating in the RBS work in the region, described and photographed two shell-tempered pottery vessels recovered from the rock-and-clay mound excavated by Moore. A local resident retrieved the vessels in 1929 and, shortly thereafter, the last of the mound remnant sloughed off into the river. The two pots, one mundane and the other extraordinary, are the only direct evidence for dating the mound. The common vessel is a standard Mississippian globular jar with loop handles (Figure 3.21, c). The other vessel described by Neuman is a variant of the Mississippian tripod bottle form in which the spheres mimic bottle gourds, and a human-head effigy surmounts the bottle orifice (Figure 3.21, a, b).

Based on the presence of the shell-tempered, loop-handled jar, we estimate that the mound was constructed sometime after A.D. 1100, when shell-tempered jars of this form first appeared in the region, and before A.D. 1350, after which they are absent from regional assemblages (a very late ca. A.D. 1600 reappearance of a shell-tempered jar form with wide-strap handles is an exception not applicable here). This dating range is probably accurate, but hardly precise. Shell temper is relatively uncommon after A.D. 1200, however, so our best guess at a phase affiliation for mound construction is early in the sequence, probably Rood I phase (A.D. 1100–1200).

The Omussee Creek Site (1HO27/101)

The Omussee Creek site, located in the Southern zone, is the southernmost Mississippian mound center in the lower Chattahoochee River region. From the Omussee Creek center south 59.3 km to where the Curlee (8JA7) and Chattahoochee Landing (8GD4) sites are clustered at the Chattahoochee–Flint River confluence there are no recorded Mississippian mound centers. This stretch of territory was a political and social frontier between lower Chattahoochee mound-center polities and those on the upper Apalachicola River, a situation we document in Chapter 6.

In 1959, an RBS crew directed by Robert W. Neuman conducted excava-

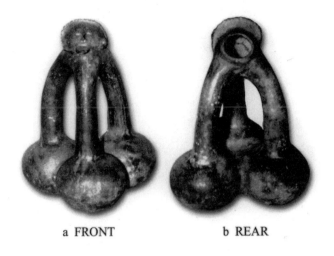

a FRONT   b REAR

c

|_____|
10 cm

3.21. Pottery from Purcell's Landing mound, 1HE3 (photo by permission of Robert W. Neuman; Newman 1959: reprinted by permission of the Florida Anthropological Society).

tions along the undamaged west and south end of the mound (Figure 3.22). Neuman determined that the mound had four major construction stages, labeled Mounds 1–4, each stage composed of sandy fill and a brightly colored clay surface. The four mound stages are clearly delineated in the east profile (Figure 3.23). Neuman mentions a low ridge of clay that demarcated the summit perimeter of Mound stage 1. This feature appears similar to the "clay rampart" feature that Caldwell found built around the perimeter of Mound A at Rood's Landing.

Although there is evidence that buildings once stood on the mound stages (several post molds are visible in Figure 3.23), no structure patterns were uncovered. Stone artifacts were not abundant. Grinding slabs, cobble ham-

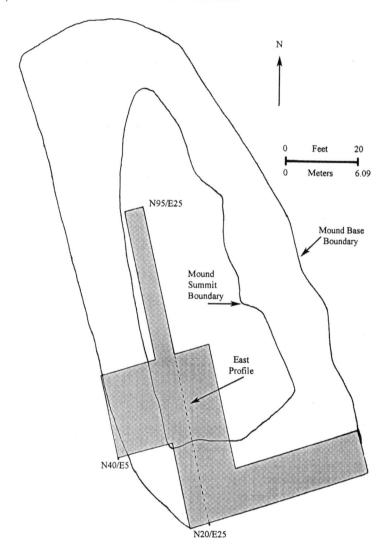

3.22. Plan of Omussee Creek mound, 1HO27.

mer stones, smoothing pebbles, ground and faceted hematite chunks, and prepared red ocher mark all stages of red pigment production, but in lesser quantities than was found at Cool Branch and Gary's Fish Pond. Cut marine shell, including a section of conch columella, and a quartzite microdrill may indicate shell bead manufacture, although no beads were recovered. Other mound finds include ceramic smoking pipes and sherd disks. On the exposed

3.23. East profile of Omussee Creek mound, 1959 (photo by permission of Robert W. Neuman; Neuman 1961:Figure 1A, reprinted by permission of the Florida Anthropological Society).

portion of the premound surface, several pit features were found that contained pottery, animal bones, mussel shells, and charred corncobs.

Based on the frequency of ceramic types associated with each construction stage, we estimate Mound stage 1 dates to the Rood III phase (A.D. 1300–1400). Mound stage 2 is undated. Pottery in Mound stage 3 and Mound stage 4 replicates styles common farther south in Florida that date to the Late Fort Walton I period (A.D. 1450–1550).

4 The Cultural Chronology: A.D. 1100–1650

With the pottery and radiocarbon samples secured by mound excavations, reviewed in the previous chapter, we can now construct a chronology of mound centers for the region. This chronological ordering of centers builds on the efforts of other archaeologists. Caldwell's (1955) work at Rood's Landing identified an early Moundville-like component with abundant shell-tempered pottery, followed by a middle component with pottery similar in style, but grit tempered, and a late component with Lamar Complicated Stamped and Fort Walton Incised pottery types that appeared related to the component found at the Bull Creek site in the 1930s (Ledbetter 1997a). Caldwell's three-part sequence was correct in broad outline, but it was overshadowed by William Sears's (1956) report on the Kolomoki site. Sears muddied the archaeological waters by incorrectly attributing the dramatic mound burials and flamboyant pottery finds at Kolomoki to the Mississippi period (Pluckhahn 2003).

With publication of the Cemochechobee report (Schnell et al. 1981), a detailed chronology based on stratified and radiocarbon-dated excavations of Mississippian mounds became available. Unfortunately, the 18 radiocarbon dates ranged widely from A.D. 690 to A.D. 1500, and yet the mound ceramic assemblages showed few changes, a clue that the actual occupation span was less than what was implied by the dates. It remained unclear how the Cemochechobee site and the Rood phase related to other regional mound sites because comparative data were lacking. Although the Mississippi period archaeological sequence was later subdivided with additional phases (Schnell and Wright 1993), much of the cultural chronology remained imprecise, largely intuitive, and unsubstantiated by published reports that quantified ceramic assemblages in stratified, radiocarbon-dated contexts. With analysis of the RBS and Columbus Museum excavations, it is now possible to significantly refine the cultural chronology, a requirement for measuring political and social integration through time.

Identifying, Ordering, and Dating the Mound Components

Our database for constructing the regional cultural chronology introduced in Chapter 3 is the pottery and radiocarbon samples from stratigraphic excavations in platform mounds. In addition to the previously published ceramic data from the Cemochechobee, Shorter, and Mandeville mounds, the database consists of samples from seven other mound sites that have received little or no previous analyses or publication: Abercrombie, Cool Branch, Gary's Fish Pond, Singer-Moye, Omussee Creek, Lampley, and Rood's Landing. Our method for constructing the regional cultural chronology was undertaken in the following manner.

First, the pottery was classified with the goal of identifying those ceramic attributes that changed through time (and across space) so that the mound provenience units associated with the pottery could be arranged into a relative chronological order (Appendix C). Previous archaeological investigations provided us with certain expectations as to which ceramic attributes would be most useful for chronology building, but we also made the classification as comprehensive as deemed feasible so that future investigators might use these data to pursue other questions. Tables of the classified pottery quantify the contents of mound provenience units (Appendixes A and B).

We did not use all of the ceramic attributes classified in Appendix C to construct the chronology. Instead, the relative ceramic chronology is based on seven decorated ceramic types: Moundville Incised, Cool Branch Incised, Columbia Incised, Lamar Plain, Fort Walton Incised, Lamar Complicated Stamped, and Rood Incised. These ceramic types were chosen because they are sensitive to changes in temporal and spatial variables, are sufficiently abundant in the samples, can be unambiguously sorted as potsherds, and facilitate comparison to relative ceramic chronologies in adjacent regions. We classified 52,558 potsherds for this study, but because decorated pottery is always a small portion of any assemblage, the named decorated types used in the chronology are approximately 7 percent of this total. Based on their presence in household middens as well as platform mound contexts, it is likely that these ceramic types had a utilitarian function in the ancient societies. Pottery types and attributes that represent special-purpose use contexts (i.e., fine-ware beakers and bottles) are identified in Appendix C, but we did not use these to construct the cultural chronology because low frequency or rarity renders them subject to sampling error. Therefore, we expect the seven decorated ceramic types to be less susceptible to the vagaries of sampling, and that the resulting chronology will be broadly applicable to both mound and nonmound contexts.

Once the pottery from mound excavations was classified, we selected pottery samples from 21 mound provenience units at 10 different mound centers and produced a seriation constructed from ceramic type-frequency data. The provenience samples were selected because they contain 50 or more potsherds classified as one of the seven decorated ceramic types. Because various researchers utilized somewhat different excavation methods to collect the pottery, it is appropriate to consider if these provenience samples are comparable. Some excavators used screens to sieve the soil while others did not. Although use of screens might be expected to affect the size of potsherds recovered in excavation, there is no reason to expect that screened and unscreened samples would differ in the frequency of recovered ceramic types (cf. King 2003:100). Furthermore, the fact that all samples are from platform mounds should reduce variation in pottery form and function due to different behavioral contexts of pottery use (a greater concern if mound and nonmound samples are compared) and adds to our confidence that the mound provenience samples are comparable.

Frequency Seriation of Ceramic Types

In the frequency seriation, pottery samples from the mound provenience units are arranged in increasing or decreasing frequency of decorated ceramic types around the sample of maximum abundance. It is assumed that the highest frequency of a ceramic type corresponds to a time when the ceramic type achieved maximum popularity of use. Mound provenience units with similar frequencies of decorated ceramic types are assumed to be closest in time and are grouped together on a graph, and the resulting pattern is assumed to represent the waxing and waning of ceramic type use through time (the dimension of space may also affect the ordering). Our frequency seriation histogram (Figure 4.1) reveals a relative order in decorated ceramic type frequencies from the 21 mound provenience units that does not violate the available evidence for stratigraphic superposition and conforms to changes in associated radiocarbon dates. The bottom of Figure 4.1 represents mound pottery samples from provenience units associated with the earliest radiocarbon dating ranges (all radiocarbon dates calculated at two sigma with a 95 percent confidence interval), while the top portion of Figure 4.1 represents mound pottery samples with the most recent radiocarbon dating ranges.

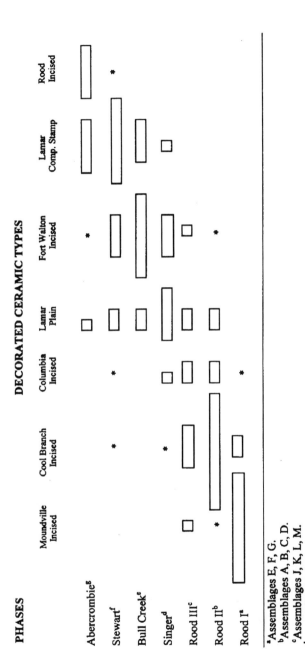

DECORATED CERAMIC TYPES

PHASES

Moundville Incised Cool Branch Incised Columbia Incised Lamar Plain Fort Walton Incised Lamar Comp. Stamp Rood Incised

Abercrombie[g]

Stewart[f]

Bull Creek[e]

Singer[d]

Rood III[c]

Rood II[b]

Rood I[a]

[a]Assemblages E, F, G.
[b]Assemblages A, B, C, D.
[c]Assemblages J, K, L, M.
[d]Assemblages N, O, P, Q.
[e]Assemblages R, S.
[f]Assemblage H.
[g]Assemblage I.
*Frequency is less than five percent.

4.1. Ceramic seriation for the lower Chattahoochee River region, A.D. 1100–1650.

Because we wished to identify mound provenience units that shared similarities and differences in ceramic assemblages, we conducted multivariate statistical analyses of the ceramic type-frequency data from the 10 mound sites to create the seriation. The techniques of cluster analysis and multidimensional scaling helped us to group similar mound pottery samples into ceramic phases with statistical confidence. The methods and results of the cluster analysis and multidimensional scaling are presented in Appendix D.

Radiocarbon Dates

Twenty-eight radiocarbon dates associated with the mound pottery samples, including seven previously unpublished dates, permitted us to assign calendar dates to the ceramic phases. At the late end of the cultural chronology, a few Euro-American artifacts known to date to the late seventeenth century have been found in Abercrombie phase contexts in the habitation area adjacent to the mound at site 1RU61 (Knight 1994b; Kurjack 1975). To assign calendar dates to the other ceramic phases, we must refer to the associated radiocarbon samples. Over the last 40 years of archaeology in the lower Chattahoochee valley, a total of 37 radiocarbon samples have be submitted for dating 16 Mississippian mound provenience units from seven sites. Table 4.1 summaries the 37 radiocarbon dates by ceramic phase. Thirteen of these 16 provenience units were used in the ceramic seriation while the other three radiocarbon-dated provenience units were omitted from the seriation due to small sample size (< 50 decorated potsherds). Of the total 37 samples, nine samples produced Middle Woodland period dates from secondary contexts in premound levels, and are excluded from further consideration. The remaining 28 radiocarbon dates from 14 mound proveniences from six sites fall within the post-A.D. 1000 time span of concern here. Seven of these dates from the Cool Branch, Gary's Fish Pond, Abercrombie, and Singer-Moye mound centers are previously unpublished.

Figure 4.2 graphs the sample dating ranges. The context of each sample is presented either in the mound excavation summaries or is available in the references cited. Following current recommendations of radiocarbon laboratories, time estimates are reported in the two-sigma range. Of course, the actual occupation span for the ceramic phases may have been considerably less. We consider the overlapping portions of the dating ranges for multiple samples from each phase to be the most parsimonious means available to us to further restrict the estimated time spans.

The Ceramic Phases

Aided by the results of frequency seriation, cluster analysis, multidimensional scaling analysis, and radiocarbon dating, we created ceramic phases that serve

Table 4.1. Radiocarbon Dates from Lower Chattahoochee River Mound Centers.

Site	Sample	Context	Material	14C (BP)	+	Phase	cal A.D. + 2	Figure 4.2***
9QU5	Beta-130241	premound	wood	850	50	Rood I	1040–1280	CB PM
9QU5	Beta-130242	mound	wood	770	50	Rood I	1210–1300	CB MD
9QU5*	SI-260	palisade	wood	1610	140	Rood I**	110–680	
9QU5*	SI-261	premound	wood	660	280	Rood I	790–1710	
9CY62*	UGa-2000	premound B	wood	1050	60	Rood II	880–1040	CEMO 1.1
9CY62	UGa-2041	premound B	wood	970	60	Rood II	980–1210	CEMO 1.2
9CY62	UGa-1942	premound B	wood	750	60	Rood II	1180–1310	CEMO 1.3
9CY62	UGa-1707	mound A I	wood	940	60	Rood II	990–1230	CEMO 1.4
9CY62	UGa-1995	mound A II	wood	960	60	Rood II	980–1210	
9CY62*	UGa-1946	premound B	wood	630	120	Rood II	1180–1470	
9CY62*	UGa-1847	premound A	wood	400	60	Rood II	1420–1640	
9CY62*	UGa-1996	mound A III	wood	1100	60	Rood II	790–1030	
9CY62	UGa-1939	mound B I	wood	790	60	Rood II	1160–1300	CEMO 2.1
9CY62	UGa-1944	mound B II	wood	1000	70	Rood II	900–1190	CEMO 2.2
9CY62	UGa-1945	mound B IV	wood	900	60	Rood II	1010–1260	CEMO 2.3
9CY62	UGa-1998	mound B IV	wood	960	80	Rood II	960–1250	CEMO 2.4
9CY62	UGa-2001	mound B IV	wood	870	90	Rood II	1000–1290	CEMO 2.5
9CY62*	UGa-1997	mound B IV	wood	1240	95	Rood II	630–1000	
9CY62	UGa-1941	mound B VI	wood	760	60	Rood II	1180–1300	CEMO 3.1
9CY62	UGa-1849	mound B VI	wood	720	70	Rood II	1190–1400	CEMO 3.2
9CY62	UGa-1848	mound B VI	wood	520	60	Rood II	1300–1460	CEMO 3.3
9CY62*	UGa-1948	mound B VII	wood	1020	60	Rood II	900–1160	
9SW2	Beta-153709	premound C	wood	770	60	Rood I**	1170–1300	SM C
9SW2	UGa-356	mound E	wood	675	80	Rood III**	1210–1420	SM E
9SW2	Beta-154049	mound H	wood	720	40	Rood III	1260–1310	SM H

Continued on the next page

Table 4.1. *Continued*

Site	Sample	Context	Material	14C (BP)	+	Phase	cal A.D. + 2	Figure 4.2***
9SW2	UGa-357	mound A	wood	560	60	Singer	1290–1440	SM A2
9SW2*	Beta-153710	premound H	wood	1210	60	Rood III	680–980	
9QU1	Beta-154048	premound	nut	620	40	Rood III	1290–1420	GFPPM
9QU1	Beta-154047	mound 3	corn	160	40	Singer	1420–1520	GFP M3
9QU1*	SI-262	premound	nut	1240	120	Singer	600–1020	
9QU1*	SI-263	mound	wood	530	120	Singer	1270–1640	
9SW1	Beta-2270	mound A 1	wood	690	60	Rood III**	1240–1400	RL A1
9SW1	Beta-2271	mound A 1B	plant	260	70	Stewart	1420–1660	RL A1B
1RU61	Beta-157589	mound 1	bone	680	70	Averett**	1170–1320	ABE M1
1RU61	Beta-2272	village	corn	160	90	Stewart**	1390–1660	ABE MV
1RU61*	Beta-2266	mound	wood	2000	370	Averett**	B.C. 880–A.D. 770	
1HO27*	Beta-154046	premound	shell	1650	50	Rood III	20–240	

Notes:

*These dates are incompatible with either stratigraphic positioning or associated ceramic assemblages.

**These proveniences do not include ceramic samples used to construct the seriation.

***These are abbreviations for provenience samples in Figure 4.2.

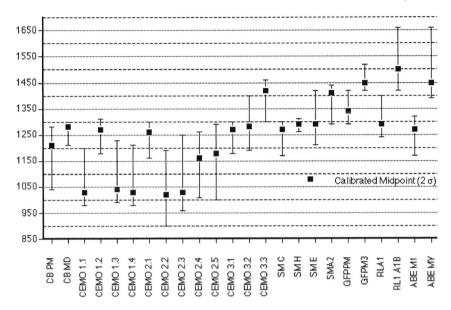

4.2. Plot of radiocarbon dates (two-sigma calibration) from late prehistoric-protohistoric mound centers, lower Chattahoochee River region.

as our chronological framework for dating mound construction and use for the interval from A.D. 1100 to A.D. 1650. Five distinctive ceramic assemblage groups exhibit temporal and spatial characteristics that we designate as the late prehistoric ceramic phases for the lower Chattahoochee River region: Rood I (A.D. 1100–1200), Rood II (A.D. 1200–1300), Rood III (A.D. 1300–1400), Singer (A.D. 1400–1450), and Bull Creek (AD. 1450–1550). The last two ceramic assemblage groups occurred after the initial contact of native populations with Europeans: the Stewart (A.D. 1550–1600) and Abercrombie (A.D. 1600–1650) ceramic phases. Although we have ordered these ceramic phases as a lineal sequence, the associated radiocarbon dating ranges indicate that some phase time span estimates overlap. Furthermore, ceramic phases have differing spatial distributions. Even so, we consider the ceramic seriation of stratified samples strong evidence of a relative sequential order. The ceramic phases are summarized below, and problems encountered in reconciling the relative dating of ceramic seriation with the absolute dating of radiocarbon are discussed. The diagnostic assemblages used in the Figure 4.1 frequency seriation are designated A-I. Two ceramic phases introduced in Chapter 3, Wakulla and Averett, were not included in the frequency seriation because these components are pre-A.D. 1000 in origin. The Wakulla and Averett phases play a role in the cultural dynamics that produced mound-center polities in the region, however, so we discuss these phases at length in Chapters 5 and 6. In the following discussion, the ceramic type frequencies presented are percentages of the total decorated assemblage (plain pottery removed from consideration).

Rood I Phase (A.D. 1100–1200)

Based on the associated radiocarbon dates, the Rood I phase represents the initial Mississippian occupation in the lower Chattahoochee River region. The Rood I pottery samples used in the frequency seriation are from the Cool Branch premound (G), Cool Branch mound (F), and Mandeville Mound A cap (E). The Rood I phase is a redefinition the old Rood phase concept as put forward by Schnell et al. (1981). Rood I phase pottery is a regional variant of the widespread Middle Mississippi ceramic tradition, readily identified by the predominance of arcade-incised handled jars. As such, the Rood I phase has no historical relationship to the ceramic traditions of the Wakulla and Averett phases that precede it in the valley. In Rood I phase ceramic assemblages, shell-tempered Moundville Incised dominates over the grit-tempered equivalent, Cool Branch Incised, and only trace amounts (< 5 percent of decorated pottery) of Columbia Incised and Fort Walton Incised are present. Plain wares are predominantly tempered with crushed mussel shell (40–60 percent of plain wares), with grit tempering in the minority. The premound D level at Rood's Landing reported by Caldwell (1955) and the premound C levels at Singer-Moye both fit the decorative assemblage and plain ware temper characteristics for a Rood I phase component, but fewer than 10 decorated potsherds (all Moundville Incised) make up each of these small samples, so we did not include them in our seriation.

Rood II Phase (A.D. 1200–1300)

The next grouping of mound pottery samples, positioned above the Rood I phase samples in the Figure 4.1 seriation histogram, is designated the Rood II ceramic phase. The Rood II phase pottery samples used in the frequency seriation are from the Cemochechobee mound center (A–C) and the Gary's Fish Pond premound surface (D). Mound pottery samples can be further subdivided into three subphases of occupation, Cemochechobee 1–3, based on stratigraphic superposition and minor variation in ceramic type frequencies.

The Rood II pottery is another regional variant of the Middle Mississippi ceramic tradition, but manifests ceramic type frequencies that differ from the Rood I phase, most notably by a higher frequency of grit-tempered pottery. Grit-tempered Cool Branch Incised dominates Rood II phase ceramic types (68–77 percent) with only trace amounts of shell-tempered Moundville Incised (2–7 percent) present. In contrast to the Rood I phase,

Columbia Incised (4–12 percent) is present in all three of the Rood II Cemochechobee subphases. Lamar Plain (2–12 percent) makes its initial appearance in the region and increases in frequency through the Cemochechobee 1–3 sequence. Fort Walton Incised is present in trace quantities (< 5 percent).

From the perspective of a relative chronological ordering of decorated ceramic types, the Rood II phase fits the frequency seriation graph above Rood I in Figure 4.1. On this basis alone, it is possible to propose that the Rood II phase follows the Rood I phase sequentially in time. We make this claim with two caveats. First, we have no archaeological example of a Rood II component found overlying a Rood I component in stratigraphic superposition. Second, the associated radiocarbon dates for the Rood II phase range from A.D. 1000–1350, which raises the possibility that it was contemporary with the Rood I phase. Therefore, the two phases could represent regional variation in contemporary ceramic assemblages of a shared pottery tradition. If, however, we further compress the dating range of the Cemochechobee site radiocarbon samples through stratigraphic ordering and overlapping ranges of multiple samples, as discussed in our review of the Cemochechobee excavations (Appendix A), then it is reasonable to suggest that the Rood II phase begins later than the Rood I phase. This is the parsimonious explanation for the presence of Columbia Incised and Lamar Plain in the Rood II phase assemblages and the absence (or trace amount) of these types in Rood I phase samples. From a culture history perspective, we interpret the Rood II phase pottery as the product of Rood I phase descendents.

Rood III Phase (A.D. 1300–1400)

Like the Rood I and II phases, the Rood III phase is a redefinition and subdivision of the old Rood phase concept as defined by Schnell et al. (1981). Rood III phase samples are from Singer-Moye Mound H premound (J), Singer-Moye Mound H (K), Omussee Creek (L), and Gary's Fish Pond premound midden (M). These Rood III phase components all share a very similar composition of ceramic types, but radiocarbon dating places their occupations later than the Rood II phase time span. Rood III phase pottery represents a continuation of the regional Middle Mississippi ceramic tradition styles produced by Rood I and II phase progenitors. The associated radiocarbon dates range from A.D. 1200 to A.D. 1430. Rood III phase ceramic assemblages reveal a decline in the frequency of Moundville Incised from earlier Rood I phase levels (down to 5–15 percent), and a concomitant increase in Columbia Incised (10–15 percent) and Lamar Plain (5–10 percent). The frequencies of Cool Branch Incised (15–20 percent) are higher than the Rood I phase frequencies for this type (5–10 percent), but much lower than the Cool Branch Incised frequencies found in the Rood II phase (68–77 percent).

Singer Phase (A.D. 1400–1450)

The Singer phase, a designation given by Schnell and Wright (1993) to the major component at the Singer-Moye center, follows the Rood III phase in time. Radiocarbon dates associated with Singer phase pottery samples from the terminal stage of Singer-Moye Mound A (O) and from the upper mound level 3 at Gary's Fish Pond (P) provide a relatively tight dating range. Singer phase ceramic types represent a distinctive break with the arcade-decorated handled jars of the Middle Mississippi tradition; the former dominance of Cool Branch Incised is largely replaced by a codominance of zone-punctated carinated bowls (Fort Walton Incised) and noded, pinched, and appliquéd rims on simple jars (Lamar Plain). In the Singer phase, Fort Walton Incised and Lamar Plain compose 20–36 percent of the decorated assemblage, Moundville Incised disappears, and Cool Branch Incised and Columbia Incised are found in trace amounts. It is during this post–Rood III interval that Lamar Complicated Stamped makes its first appearance as a minority type (1–11 percent), a useful chronological marker. The Singer phase begins a significant cultural shift, a time when the ceramic styles of two different traditions, Fort Walton and Lamar, eclipsed the long continuity of the antecedent Middle Mississippi tradition in the region. However, the type Lamar Complicated Stamped, so closely associated with the Lamar ceramic tradition, does not overtake Lamar Plain in popularity until the succeeding Bull Creek phase.

Bull Creek Phase (A.D. 1450–1550)

The Bull Creek classification, first described as a focus (McMichael and Kellar 1960) and then later a phase (Schnell 1981), was identified in Depression-era excavations at the nonmound village site of that name in the Northern zone near the Fall Line (Ledbetter 1997a). Over the last several decades, the Bull Creek classification has been applied to post-Rood phase regional components that contain Lamar Complicated Stamped and Fort Walton Incised associated together. The cultural dynamics that produced this combination of traditions remains unknown, but the fact that the phase bridges the prehistoric-to-historic period transition is perhaps germane to these changes.

There are no radiocarbon-dated mound pottery samples for this phase. While the Lampley and Shorter mound samples (R–S) do contain assemblages dominated by Fort Walton Incised and Lamar Complicated Stamped, these mounds are located in the Central zone over 50 km south of the Bull Creek site. The significant distance between these sites and Bull Creek may explain why percentages for the two ceramic types show an inverse relationship. At the Lampley and Shorter mounds, Fort Walton Incised is high in frequency (47–57 percent) and Lamar Complicated Stamped is relatively low in frequency (22–24 percent). In contrast, the Bull Creek village site has very high percentages of Lamar Complicated Stamped (45–60 percent, plain pottery included) and low percentages of Fort Walton Incised (< 4 percent) (Ledbetter 1997a:148–160). Farther south, pottery from the uppermost mound levels 3 and 4 at Omussee Creek reveals a similar pattern taken to the extreme. Although not dated with radiocarbon, these mound levels have a very high percentage of Fort Walton Incised (73–78 percent) and Lamar Complicated Stamped is virtually absent (0–1 percent). Indeed, the Omussee Creek 3–4 assemblage is best aligned with similar assemblages at sites of the Late Fort Walton I period in Florida.

Clearly, Lampley, Shorter, and Omussee Creek assemblages are very different from the Bull Creek site assemblage, the "type site" of the Bull Creek phase. We think that a time-transgressive pattern in the dissemination of the two ceramic types from areas of origin outside of the lower Chattahoochee River valley may explain the differences between the Bull Creek, Lampley, Shorter, and upper levels of Omussee Creek components. We examine this and other spatial dimensions of the ceramic data in Chapter 6. We note that the antecedent ceramic types of the Middle Mississippi tradition— Moundville Incised, Cool Branch Incised, Columbia Incised—are absent or found only in trace amounts (probably due to stratigraphic mixing typical of mound fill), while Lamar Plain declines in frequency (8–16 percent) at the three mound sites compared.

Stewart Phase (A.D. 1550–1600)

While almost all of the mound construction at the Rood's Landing site probably dates to the Rood sequence, the majority of the excavation sample is a Stewart phase component from the terminal stages of Mound A (H). Schnell and Wright (1993) suggest that the higher frequency of incised/ punctuated decoration in the Mound A component is significantly different from the Bull Creek phase (as defined by components at the Bull Creek site) to warrant the separate Stewart phase distinction. Our reanalysis of Caldwell's Mound A pottery samples found high frequencies of Lamar Complicated Stamped (which is also true of the Bull Creek assemblage) and a decrease in the frequency of Fort Walton Incised when compared to the preceding components at Lampley, Shorter, and Omussee Creek. We interpret these assemblage differences as a continuation of the time-transgressive spatial patterns detected in the previous ceramic phase: the Lamar ceramic tradition (complicated stamping), with a time-space dissemination from north to south, overtakes that of the Fort Walton ceramic tradition (zoned punctated), with a time-space dissemination south to north, to produce the fusion of traditions found in the Stewart ceramic phase. Also, a bold-incised, burnished, and carinated bowl, known as Rood Incised, makes its first appearance in the valley in low frequency.

Bracketing the Stewart phase with a dating range is imprecise because we have only one radiocarbon date. Our rationale for the beginning date of A.D. 1550 is that it is consistent with the radiocarbon estimate and the position of the Stewart phase component (H) following the Bull Creek phase components (R–S) on the frequency seriation graph. Our estimate of A.D. 1600 as an ending date for the Stewart phase is based on the absence of artifacts of European origin, which are rarely encountered in the interior Southeast prior to that date (Smith 1987).

Abercrombie Phase (A.D. 1600–1650)

The last ceramic phase marked by mound building in the region is designated Abercrombie (Knight 1994a, b; Kurjack 1975). Abercrombie components are associated with Kyle and Abercrombie, the final mound centers occupied in the lower Chattahoochee River valley at the end of the protohistoric period. At the better-documented Abercrombie site, the Abercrombie ceramic assemblage is found in the terminal mound-building stage (I) and in the adjacent habitation area. The Abercrombie phase decorated pottery assemblage is similar to the Stewart phase decorated pottery assemblage at Rood's Landing, but with higher frequencies of the bold-incised, burnished type Rood Incised and lower frequencies of Lamar Complicated Stamped to the point where each type is codominant. Lamar Plain declines to < 5 percent and Fort Walton Incised all but disappears to trace amounts. The other ceramic characteristic of the Abercrombie phase is the (re)appearance of shell-tempered pottery in the regional sequence. Abercrombie Incised, a burnished, shell-tempered equivalent of Rood Incised, is present as a minority type in the terminal mound stage at Abercrombie mound. As other researchers have, we guess-date the end of the Abercrombie phase at ca. A.D. 1650 based on the age of associated trade materials found in off-mound contexts at Abercrombie (Knight and Mistovich 1984:225).

Summary

The frequency seriation of decorated ceramic types, ordered by cluster analysis and multidimensional scaling, resulted in the delineation of ceramic phases as a practical means to construct temporal and spatial units of observation and measurement from the rather prosaic but informative potsherds in the ancient mounds. We suggest that the similarities between mound pottery samples that we group together as ceramic phases are the result of peoples living during the same time interval who made pottery in a shared style, and that each style has a measurable spatial distribution that we refer to as a ceramic style zone. In this chapter we have emphasized the temporal dimensions of these data. We will have more to say about the spatial aspects of ceramic style distributions and what these may reveal about the social and political interactions between the inhabitants of the mound-center polities in later chapters. The relative ceramic chronology is enhanced by numerous radiocarbon dates that permit the construction of a regional cultural chronology for the interval A.D. 1100–1650. Armed with this chronology, we are now in a position to determine when regional mound sites were founded, expanded, abandoned, and sometimes reoccupied as political centers over the course of several centuries. Our ability to trace the history of mound-center occupation and use is a prerequisite to identifying variation in regional polity forms and detecting political changes, and it is these topics that we address in the following chapter.

5   Archaeological Measures of Political Integration

With analysis of mound excavations and construction of a cultural chronology, we are now in a position to identify variation in Mississippian polity forms and measure political integration in the lower Chattahoochee River valley over the course of six centuries. In order to do so, we use a mound-center chronology, the distances between contemporary centers, and the number of mounds found at centers. With this evidence we measure the spatial extent of polity territories and determine if centers formed a political hierarchy. These data are then compared to the political models of Mississippian polities presented in Chapter 2. The possible political significance of two intriguing cultural patterns, paired mound centers and mound reuse, are also discussed.

Previous Interpretations of Mound-Center Settlement Patterns

Before we examine the settlement data in more detail and identify polity forms, we must consider two interpretations of regional Mississippian political organization proposed by previous researchers based on analysis of mound-center settlement patterns. Each interpretation makes a specific claim about the relationship between the size and location of Mississippian mound centers and forms of political organization. Both interpretations are based on the simple-complex chiefdom model.

Gail Schnell (1981) was the first to comment on the sociopolitical implications of the apparent regional settlement hierarchy during the Rood phase, which was then dated A.D. 1000–1400. Two factors were emphasized in her study: a settlement pattern of multiple-mound centers and single-mound centers, and burials with a cache of ritually "killed" fine-ware beakers in Cemochechobee Mound A. Citing the works of Peebles (1971, 1978) and Service (1962), Schnell argued that the apparent settlement hierarchy and status distinctions of the Rood phase matched the expectations for a prehistoric chiefdom. She concluded that the Rood phase mound centers were an example of a complex chiefdom, in which Cool Branch, Mandeville, Omussee Creek, and Cemochechobee were "subsidiary centers, more or less equally spaced apart at any given time, which owed allegiance to one of the two major Rood phase centers" (Schnell 1981:24) (i.e., Rood's Landing or Singer-Moye). Schnell did not attempt to define specific polity boundaries.

John Scarry and Claudine Payne (1986) constructed a spatial model to identify Mississippian chiefdom territories and applied their model to the "Fort Walton area," which included the lower Chattahoochee River valley. They analyzed the size and distribution of Mississippian mound centers with the XTENT algorithm (Renfrew and Level 1979). The XTENT method is based on the assumption that the spatial extent of a center's political control is directly proportional to the size of the center. Scarry and Payne devised a measure of center size based on a cumulative mound volume index for the total number of mounds at each center. To apply the XTENT method, Scarry and Payne had to assume that the centers in their regional sample were contemporaneous and that the relative size of the centers did not change through time (assumptions that they admitted were idealized for the purpose of model construction). The results of their spatial analysis produced a regional map composed of hypothetical large and small polities, expressed as circular territories, which they subsequently modified to conform to the configuration of linear river valleys.

Scarry and Payne concluded that there were two independent Mississippian polities in the lower Chattahoochee River valley: a large polity composed of Rood's Landing, Singer-Moye, and affiliated smaller centers, and a smaller polity centered on the Omussee Creek center that conformed to Steponaitis's definition of simple chiefdom. Although Scarry and Payne proposed that the large polity was a complex chiefdom, neither they nor Schnell adequately addressed the obvious problem presented by the close proximity of the roughly equivalent centers of Rood's Landing and Singer-Moye, a situation that does not conform to Steponaitis's definition of complex chiefdom. Also left unexplained was the curious pattern presented by closely spaced pairs of centers.

Mound-Center Chronology and Distribution

To understand the settlement pattern, we needed something unavailable to earlier researchers: an accurate mound-center chronology. The duration and number of platform mounds in use at each of the 12 Mississippian mound centers in the lower Chattahoochee River valley is summarized in Table 5.1. We assigned mound sites to seven time periods based on the estimated time spans of the associated mound ceramic assemblages defined as ceramic phases. In evaluating the accuracy of the mound-center chronology, the limitations of the data used to construct the ceramic phases, discussed in Chapter 4, should be kept in mind. In addition, the accuracy of the mound-center chronology may be limited by the fact that some mound ceramic assemblages are relatively small samples due to site destruction, the limited scale of excavation, or lack of associated radiocarbon dates.

Table 5.1 reveals that mound centers are unevenly distributed in time and space. Certain temporal and spatial patterns in these data should be emphasized. First, eight of the 12 mound centers, comprising more than 90 percent of the cumulative mound building in the region, are located in the Central zone. Second, while mound centers were absent for more than one period in the Northern and Southern zones, they were used in the Central zone for all periods except Period VII, at the very end of the mound-building tradition. Third, the duration of use for mound centers was relatively short. Finally, not only were mound centers frequently abandoned after a single time period of use, but also centers were often reoccupied and used again after long intervals of abandonment.

With the mound-center chronology in hand, we compare the mound-center settlement data to the four hypothetical polity forms introduced in Chapter 2. Specifically, we evaluate the agreement between the observed mound-center settlement patterns, the implied polity forms, and the two contrasting models of Mississippian political organization: the simple-complex chiefdom model and the polity fission-fusion model. Also, we assess how well the mound-center settlement data match the regional political models proposed by Schnell, Scarry, and Payne.

In our analysis, we employ Hally's (1993) spatial model of Mississippian chiefdoms, and assume that the termination of mound building marks the end of the site's function as a polity center, same-time period mound sites closer than 18 km belong to the same polity, and same-time period sites farther apart than 18 km belong to different polities. According to Hally's model, a single-mound site separated from other mound centers by distances more than 18 km can be identified as a simple chiefdom, and two or more mound sites separated by fewer than 18 km can be identified as a complex chiefdom if the centers form a site-size hierarchy (i.e., a primary-secondary center polity). In complex chiefdoms, the number of mounds at each same-period center is used to identify a hierarchy of mound centers.

In Chapter 2 we concluded that the scale of mound construction is related to the process of political integration. Centers with a bigger scale of contemporary mound construction had a greater labor input by a larger population, and presumably, a more complex political form as chiefs or

Table 5.1. Number of Mounds in Use and Duration of Mound Use for Seven Time Periods, Lower Chattahoochee River Region.

SITES	A.D. 1100–1200	A.D. 1200–1300	A.D. 1300–1400	A.D. 1400–1450	A.D. 1450–1550	A.D. 1550–1600	A.D. 1600–1650
Kyle	(1)	(1)					1
Atercrombie		1					1
*Rood's Landing			5–8			2	
*Singer-Moye	1		2–7	2–5			
Shorter					1		
Lampley					1		
Gary's Pond				1			
Ccol Branch	1						
Mandeville	1						
Cemochechobee		3					
Purcell	1						
Omussee			1		1		

* undated Mississippian mound(s) at site.
(1) number of mounds possible, but unconfirmed.

leaders exercised control over labor allocation. Because platform mounds were the symbols of corporate groups, which we refer to as mound-political units, multiple-mound centers represent the composite constructions of multiple mound-political units united into some form of political union; each mound-political unit is a segment of the total population served by the center (Blitz 1999; Lindauer and Blitz 1997). Therefore, the number of same-period mounds at a center provides a relative scale of political integration and organizational complexity at the central place, and indicates the site's relative political importance in a region. The presence of a mound-center size hierarchy within an 18-km polity boundary is a measure of the degree of political hierarchy present in a polity. We further hypothesized that the different spatial arrangements of regional mound centers reflect the fusion and fission of mound-political units into various polity forms, accomplished by repeated mound center foundation, abandonment, and re-occupation.

Settlement Data Limitations

Two factors may limit the accuracy of the regional mound-center settlement data: undiscovered mounds and undated or inadequately dated mounds. There may be Mississippian platform mounds in the study area still undiscovered. Given the extensive archaeological surveys in the region over the last 50 years, it is unlikely that multiple-mound sites or large mounds have escaped detection. This remains a possibility for small platform mounds, however, especially if altered by plowing or erosion. Two mound sites, now destroyed, cannot be dated. The Woolfolks site (9CE3), one kilometer south of the Kyle mound center, had two conical mounds destroyed long ago (Brandon 1909:195; Jones 1999:182; Moore 1907:449). The habitation area of the site is multicomponent and includes ceramics that date to the A.D. 1100–1650 interval (Huscher 1959a). From the limited descriptions, the form and content of the mounds do not conform to Mississippian platforms. A mound may have existed at the mouth of Kolomoki Creek, although this possibility is unconfirmed (Frank Schnell, personal communication, 2000). This possible mound was located on or near a multicomponent habitation area (9Cy87) with Mississippian ceramics (Belovich et al. 1982: 298–303). There is no reason to assume that the destroyed mounds at 9CE3 or 9Cy87 were Mississippian platforms, but in the absence of dates this possibility cannot be ruled out. If any of these sites were Mississippian centers, they were sufficiently far from multiple-mound centers to be independent polities.

The duration and number of platform mounds in use at each center and the distances to nearest-neighbor mound sites can be illustrated as a series of chronological maps. Dating problems at specific sites are addressed below.

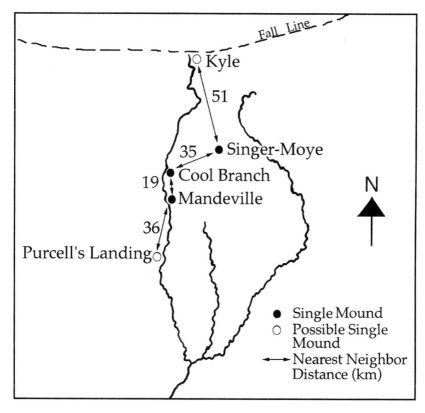

5.1. Period I mound centers, A.D. 1100–1200, with nearest-neighbor distances in kilometers.

Period I, A.D. 1100–1200

Mississippian centers were first established in Period I. The two ceramic phases are Rood I and Averett. There are three confirmed mound centers and two possible mound centers (Figure 5.1). In the Northern zone, the single mounds at Kyle and Abercrombie, separated by only 1.6 km, both have Averett phase (A.D. 900–1300) affiliations. All we can say about Kyle is that mound use could be in Periods I and/or II. For reasons stated below, we do not think Abercrombie mound was established at this time.

In the Central zone, Cool Branch and Mandeville were single-mound center polities with Rood I phase components. Both the Singer-Moye and Rood's Landing sites present interpretive problems because not all of the mounds have been sampled, and early mound-building episodes may lie undetected beneath the massive mound stages of later periods. At the Singer-

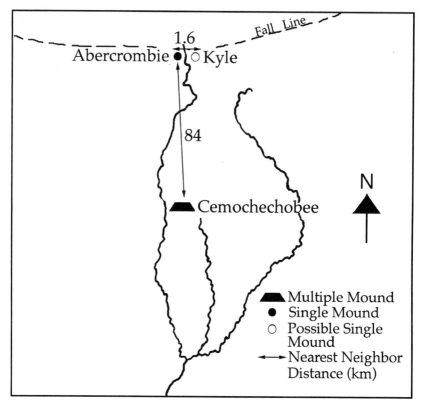

5.2. Period II mound centers, A.D. 1200–1300, with nearest-neighbor distances in kilometers.

Moye site, Mound C was in use. Rood's Landing has a similar early component (premound D), but no mound building is documented at the site at
this time. So while we do not know how many mounds were in use at Singer-
Moye and Rood's Landing in this initial period, these two sites are too far
from other centers to represent primary-secondary center polities.

The poorly documented Purcell's Landing center was probably established
at this time as an isolated single-mound polity. Farther south, mound centers
were absent in the Southern zone.

Period II, A.D. 1200–1300

Period II marks a decline in the total number of occupied centers. Mound
construction and use is confirmed at two centers and possible at two other
sites (Figure 5.2). Averett and Rood II are the ceramic phases. In the Northern zone, occupation of the Abercrombie center is confirmed. Mound use

at Kyle is possible in Period II, but unconfirmed. To repeat, our Averett ceramic samples do not permit fine chronological resolution. However, the two-sigma dating range for the single radiocarbon assay from the Averett phase mound at Abercrombie spans this period, and the low-frequency presence of Cool Branch Incised places construction after A.D. 1100. The Kyle-Abercrombie paired settlement cluster could represent a multiple single-mound center polity if they were occupied simultaneously in Period II. More likely, these are sequential occupations of a single-mound center polity, with Kyle occupied in Period I, and Abercrombie occupied in Period II.

In the Central zone, Cool Branch and Mandeville were abandoned by this period. Mound use at Purcell's Landing is possible in Period II, although it is unconfirmed. No Rood II phase component is identified at Rood's Landing or Singer-Moye; it may yet be found at one of the unexcavated mounds. The Cemochechobee center was founded, first as a single-mound center, and by the end of the period, three mounds had been built; no more than two mounds were in use at any one time. Mound centers were absent in the Southern zone.

Period III, A.D. 1300–1400

During Period III the pace of mound building reached a regional zenith, even though it was confined to three centers (Figure 5.3). By this period the Averett phase had ended, leaving no occupied mound centers in the Northern zone. In the Southern zone, Omussee Creek was an isolated single-mound center. In the Central zone, Rood's Landing was a large political center with five-to-eight mounds in use. Twenty-eight km away, another center, Singer-Moye, had two-to-seven mounds in use. All three centers were sufficiently far apart to be independent polities with no affiliated secondary centers.

Period IV, A.D. 1400–1450

Period IV ushered in a time of diminished mound construction, limited to the Central zone at two centers: Singer-Moye and Gary's Fish Pond (Figure 5.4). Both sites are widely separated. We think Rood's Landing and Omussee Creek were abandoned at this time, and the balance of political power shifted to Singer-Moye, which became the largest center in the region. Singer-Moye was a multiple-mound center polity with no single-mound subordinate centers. Gary's Fish Pond was a single-mound center polity. Singer is the ceramic phase of this period.

Period V, A.D. 1450–1550

In Period V, the scale of mound construction was low (Figure 5.5). In the Central zone, the Lampley and Shorter centers are only 2.4 km apart, and

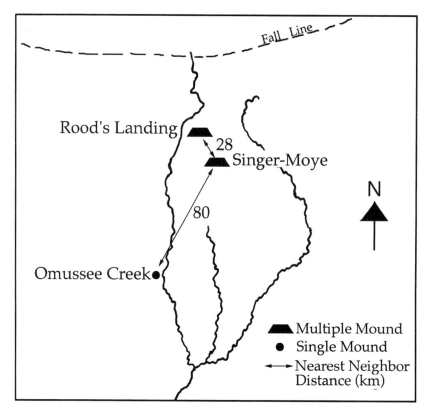

5.3. Period III mound centers, A.D. 1300–1400, with nearest-neighbor distances in kilometers.

each site had a single mound. If these centers were occupied simultaneously, then the two sites conform to the hypothetical multiple single-mound center polity. Farther south, Omussee Creek was reoccupied to become a single-mound center polity. Bull Creek is the ceramic phase at Lampley and Shorter, while Omussee Creek has a divergent ceramic assemblage similar to sites of the Late Fort Walton I period in Florida.

Period VI, A.D. 1550–1600, and Period VII, A.D. 1600–1650.

Around A.D. 1550 (Figure 5.6), a multiple-mound center polity was re-established at Rood's Landing, where the old abandoned Mounds A and B were reoccupied. This component is the Stewart phase. Although Rood's Landing was the only polity in the valley, the new political center did not last long, and by Period VII it was no longer in use. In the early seventeenth century, the long-abandoned single mounds at Kyle and Abercrombie were

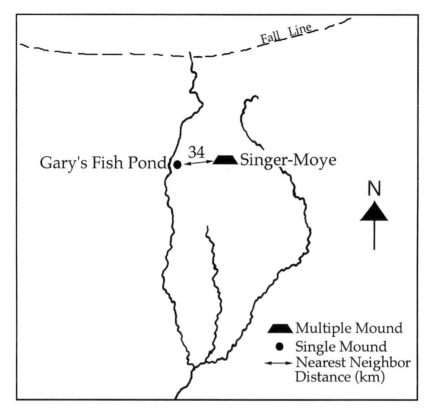

5.4. Period IV mound centers, A.D. 1400–1450, with nearest-neighbor distances in kilometers.

reoccupied (Figure 5.7). Kyle and Abercrombie are 1.6 km apart, so once again we have a spatial cluster of paired mounds. The two centers conform to the hypothetical multiple single-mound center polity, but as was the case with the revitalized polity at Rood's Landing, the renewed use of the Kyle and Abercrombie mounds was short-lived. Kyle is the possible site of seventeenth-century Kasihta, and Abercrombie is the possible site of Coweta, burned by the Spanish in 1685. Soon thereafter, the native inhabitants ceased to construct platform mounds.

To summarize, 28 platform mounds were constructed in the lower Chattahoochee River valley from A.D. 1100 to A.D. 1650. In Period I, mound centers consisted of a single mound, but a multiple-mound center polity, Cemochechobee, was established in Period II. It is not known if the large multiple-mound centers of Rood's Landing and Singer Moye began as single mound centers or multiple-mound centers, but in the case of multiple-

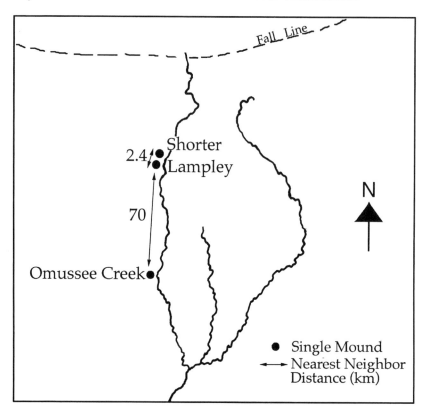

5.5. Period V mound centers, A.D. 1450–1550, with nearest-neighbor distances in kilometers.

mound Cemochechobee, the site began as a single-mound center polity. The most intensive mound construction occurred in Periods III–IV, when political integration and complexity climaxed in the region. Mounds and mound-political units were concentrated at a few sites, especially the large Rood's Landing and Singer-Moye centers. After Period IV, fewer mounds were built, the mounds were smaller, reuse of abandoned centers increased, and polity forms were simpler. The general trend through time is one of dispersed small centers in Period I, followed by aggregation into multiple-mound centers in Periods II–IV, and then again dispersal into fewer, smaller centers in Periods V–VII. The two largest sites, Rood's Landing and Singer-Moye, are distant from other mound sites. Smaller sites are either widely dispersed across the landscape or are separated by only a few kilometers.

From the observed mound-center settlement patterns, we have inferred different polity forms. The regional polity forms were diverse in implied or-

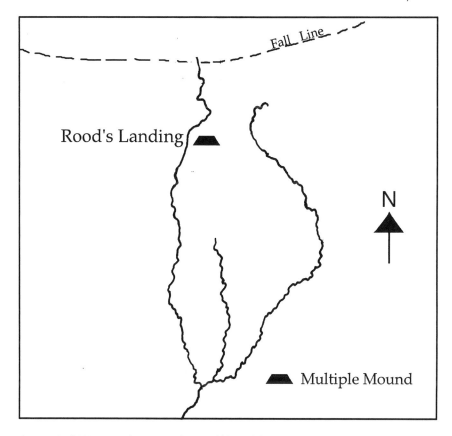

5.6. Period VI mound centers, A.D. 1550–1600.

ganizational complexity and duration of occupation. Between A.D. 1100–
1650, we see an ever-changing assortment of political territories. Mound-
center settlement patterns diagnostic of the single-mound center polity
and the multiple-mound center polity are clearly represented in the region.
The hypothetical multiple single-mound center polity may be indicated by
the Kyle-Abercrombie paired settlement cluster in Period VII and by the
Lampley-Shorter paired settlement cluster in Period V.

With a new perspective gained from a mound-center chronology, we find
that the evidence does not support the models of Mississippian political organization proposed by Schnell, Scarry, and Payne for the lower Chattahoochee River valley. Without a detailed chronology, these researchers interpreted the regional pattern of multiple-mound centers and single-mound
centers according to the simple complex chiefdom model: an integrated, hierarchical settlement system with one or two primary centers and several

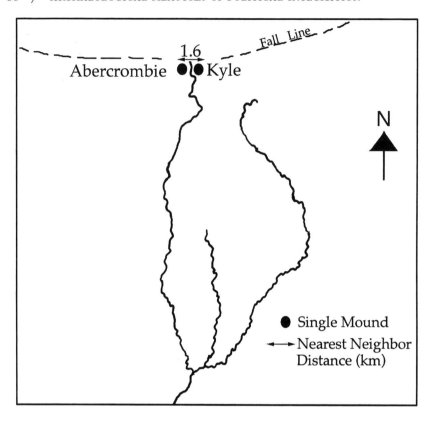

5.7. Period VII mound centers, A.D 1600–1650.

subordinate secondary centers. Once same-period mound centers are identified, however, we can replace this static interpretation of mound-center
settlement patterns with a dynamic historical record of individual centers,
and follow the growth and decline of polities over time. The primary-
secondary center polity, diagnostic of a complex chiefdom, is not apparent
in the settlement patterns. Instead, the pattern of political change is one
of aggregation and dispersal of mound-political units. Political power was
achieved not by the regional extension of an administrative hierarchy of secondary centers controlled by a primary center, but by the concentration of
multiple mound-political units at a single central place.

The reconstructed polity forms lend additional support to the perception
that a Mississippian chief's political power and control declined with distance from a mound center. This spatial limitation to political control in
chiefdoms not only permits the recognition of polity boundaries but also
suggests there were spatial limits to political integration beyond which Mis-

sissippian polities could not expand. We propose that the basic political dynamic of six centuries consisted of oscillations between dispersed and concentrated political power in which the fission-fusion of mound-political units created polities with different degrees of complexity. In the lower Chattahoochee River region, political integration assumed at least two, possibly three, different polity forms without ever establishing a hierarchical network of administrative centers.

The polity fission-fusion process we have detected in the changing polity forms implies that political power was more centralized in the era of multiple-mound polities prior to A.D. 1450 and more decentralized after A.D. 1450. Why was there a diminution in mound building after A.D. 1450? Why did the mound-political units aggregate at multiple-mound centers in one period and disperse into polities with only one mound in another period? Why were mound centers abandoned? Where did the people go? Over and over we see the abandonment of old centers followed by the foundation of new centers. Do these centers share a common historical relationship? Did people move from an abandoned center to a new center nearby? The answers to these questions are elusive, of course, and involve circumstances that are difficult to document with archaeological data. One avenue of inquiry into these cultural dynamics is to examine the phenomenon of closely spaced or paired mound centers.

Paired Mound Centers

Maps of all the mound centers (Figures 1.1, 3.1) reveal that centers often cluster together in pairs separated by only a few kilometers. Single-mound centers separated by 7 km or less are Abercrombie-Kyle, and a cluster of four sites: Cool Branch–Gary's Fish Pond–Lampley–Shorter. Single-mound Mandeville forms a closely spaced pair with multiple-mound Cemochechobee. The paired center pattern continues farther south on the Apalachicola River in Florida, where two Fort Walton mound centers, Cayson and Yon, are paired with each other on opposite sides of the river. Other Apalachicola River platform mounds of uncertain date, but at sites with Fort Walton components, also form closely spaced pairs (i.e., Curlee–Chattahoochee Landing and Pierce–Cool Spring). Why do single-mound centers so often occur as clustered pairs? Because the mound sites do not form a hierarchy, the spatial arrangement cannot be attributed to the efficient administration of regional tribute flow by a centrally controlled political economy (i.e., Steponaitis 1978; Welch 1991). Even in a primary center–secondary center polity with a tributary form of production, clustered centers would be less efficient than evenly spaced centers. So when a site hierarchy of contemporaneous centers is absent, we must seek other explanations for the mound cluster pattern.

The clustered or paired-center settlement pattern, widespread in the Mississippian Southeast, has not gone unnoticed by others. Mark Williams and Gary Shapiro (1990) called these sites "paired towns," and proposed that paired towns were created by sequential population movement between two closely spaced sites. In other words, occupation of the centers was not coeval, but alternated between two neighboring mound sites over time. Movements were thought to be sparked by local resource depletion or by new chiefs who relocated the civic-ceremonial center close to a local support group upon succession to office. The environmental explanation for mound center abandonment is strengthened by a model of Mississippian agricultural practices in eastern Tennessee, which suggests that large settlements would move every 50 to 150 years due to soil depletion and crop failures (Baden 1987).

Hally (1996:114–115) claimed that local resource depletion was an unlikely motivation for moving the location of mound building such a short distance. In the South Appalachian area, Hally found several clear examples where a mound center used in one phase was abandoned, and in the subsequent phase, a new mound center was established nearby. Hally (1996:114) observed, "If platform mounds and the buildings they supported were important symbols of chiefly continuity and legitimacy, it seems unlikely that they would be periodically and voluntarily abandoned, especially at the time of peaceful succession." If power shifted from one faction to another and the succession was contested, however, then "abandonment of the old mound and construction of the new mound [at another location] may have been symbolic acts to emphasize the commencement of a new chiefly lineage" (Hally 1996:115).

There were historic-era polities that formed when one polity abandoned its center and joined another polity as refugees seeking protection from the attacks of a more powerful foe. Paired centers, as an example of the hypothetical multiple single-mound center polity, may have originated in this manner, if the refugee group built its own mound center near the host polity (Willis 1980).

Turning to the lower Chattahoochee paired mound centers, is it possible to identify specific fission-fusion processes with the archaeological data? As a first step toward this goal, we propose three kinds of temporal relationships between closely spaced mound centers: sequential mound occupation, simultaneous mound occupation, and discontinuous mound occupation. Because we are concerned with a site's function as a political center, the dates of mound use are our measure of occupation.

By sequential mound occupation, we refer to population movement between two nearby centers; center A was abandoned and the A population moved to found a new center, B, nearby. We can identify this event archaeologically if mounds at center A and center B have sequential phase components; the center B mound component should be the ceramic phase that immediately follows in time the ceramic phase at center A. Because sequential mound occupation is a proposed historical relationship in which center A is the ancestral settlement of center B inhabitants, we expect a continuity of ceramic style sufficient to indicate participation in a shared ceramic tradition. Pottery samples at sequentially occupied mound centers should fall close together on ceramic seriation graphs, and the relative order of the samples in time should indicate the direction of the sequential movement between centers.

Simultaneous mound occupation is when mounds at paired centers A and B were in use at the same time. To recognize this situation archaeologically, paired centers A and B should have same-period components. This is our criterion for identifying the hypothetical multiple single-mound center polity.

Discontinuous mound occupation is identified when mound components at paired centers A and B exhibit a temporal discontinuity, perhaps the length of one or more time periods or ceramic phase intervals. This pattern would occur if center A were abandoned, and after a temporal hiatus, a new population entered the vacant area and established new center B near the abandoned A site.

Based on the dating of regional centers located fewer than 7 km apart, the following kinds of temporal relationships are identified. In the Northern zone, Kyle and Abercrombie are single-mound centers 1.6 km apart on opposite sides of the river just south of the Fall Line. Because of the small sample size at Kyle (i.e., 8 whole pottery vessels), we cannot use changing frequencies of ceramic types to compare the two sites. Both mounds have an Averett component (A.D. 900–1300). So it appears we have an example of paired centers with simultaneous mound occupation. Yet the available radiocarbon date and presence of Cool Branch Incised places the Averett component at Abercrombie mound in Period II (A.D. 1100–1200), whereas the poorly dated Kyle mound could be either Period I and/or Period II. While we cannot rule out the possibility of an Averett polity composed of two single-mound centers, we think it is more likely that this is a sequential occupation, with occupation at Kyle in Period I, then movement from Kyle to Abercrombie in Period II.

Kyle and Abercrombie were later reoccupied; both have Abercrombie components (A.D. 1600–1650). We cannot detect any potential chronological difference between these components, so the two centers conform to the hypothetical polity composed of multiple single-mound centers in Period VII. As we shall see below, there is a historic Creek oral tradition about these two sites that may provide an insight into the situation.

In the Central zone, the single-mound centers of Cool Branch and Gary's

Fish Pond are 2.4 km apart. Cool Branch mound is Rood I phase, A.D. 1100–1200. The premound surface and midden at Gary's Fish Pond have superimposed Rood II phase (A.D. 1200–1300) and Rood III phase (A.D. 1300–1400) components. Mound construction commenced in the Singer phase (A.D. 1400–1450). A temporal hiatus exists between mound abandonment at Cool Branch and mound construction at Gary's Fish Pond. The Gary's Fish Pond–Cool Branch pair is an example of discontinuous mound occupation.

Gary's Fish Pond and Lampley are 3.6 km apart. The final mound stage at Gary's Fish Pond is a Singer phase component. Because Lampley mound is a Bull Creek phase (A.D. 1450–1550) component that immediately follows the Singer phase in time, we interpret the Gary's Fish Pond–Lampley pair as an example of sequential mound center occupation with population movement from Gary's Fish Pond to Lampley.

Lampley and Shorter are 2.4 km apart. Both centers have Bull Creek phase components in Period V. Although both mounds were occupied sometime in this 100-year time span, the Shorter and Lampley ceramic samples differ in relative ceramic frequencies (a higher ratio of Lamar Complicated Stamped to Fort Walton Incised at Shorter). We know that as a general temporal trend, the relative frequency of Lamar Complicated Stamped increased in the region over time, which places Shorter later in the relative ceramic chronology. So we think the Lampley-Shorter pair represents a single-mound polity at different points in time: a sequential population movement from abandoned Lampley to newly established Shorter.

Mandeville and Cemochechobee are 6.4 km apart. The Rood II phase component at Cemochechobee immediately follows the Rood I phase component at Mandeville in time. This relationship fits our expectations for a sequential mound center occupation, with population movement from the older Mandeville center to the new Cemochechobee center.

Finally, we must address the unusual proximity of the two largest centers, Rood's Landing and Singer-Moye. Williams and Shapiro (1990:Figure 30) included the two sites as examples of "paired towns." The two sites are 28 km apart, considerably farther than the other paired sites discussed above, and too far apart to be one polity. The two centers were both occupied in Period III, but by Period IV, power shifted to Singer-Moye as Rood's Landing declined or ceased to be a political center altogether. Due to the spatial proximity and shared material culture, we suggest that the two sites are linked in a developmental relationship, the nature of which eludes us. The polity fission-fusion process may be implicated in these changes. One possibility is that mound-political units relocated from Rood's Landing to Singer-Moye.

Of six paired center arrangements, four are sequential mound occupa-

- Grated Locatelli - container
1 lb. Ricotta Cheese (Reg. or Low fat)
- Shredded Mozzarella
- 2 boxes ziti   1 lb box

tions. Such a relationship is consistent with a rapid abandonment-resettlement event as posited by the resource depletion and contested succession hypotheses, although we have no data with which to test these propositions. One pair is a discontinuous mound occupation, so no direct historical relationship is implied. The Kyle-Abercrombie pair is the only possible example of the hypothetical multiple single-mound center polity. If Kyle-Abercrombie is a case of simultaneous mound occupation, then the relationship between the two sites is more consistent with the expectations of the refugee group hypothesis. Such a conclusion is quite tentative, perhaps unwarranted, primarily because the available chronological controls may be too imprecise for the task at hand.

Despite these limitations, there is sufficient evidence to identify mound-center abandonment with subsequent population movement to found new political centers as a fundamental process of Mississippian political formations. Site foundation, abandonment, resettlement, and the accompanying shifts in regional political power created the mound-center settlement patterns. In each time period, new centers were founded and old centers were abandoned. Within the limitations of our dating methods, the abandonment-resettlement process appears to have been a rapid one. We have no direct proof that people at one center moved to another center, but the abandonment of some centers coincides with the appearance of new ones nearby, so we think population movement is the most likely interpretation. We cannot confirm what specific factors drove the polity fission-fusion process that we have proposed, but we have offered evidence of when, where, and how the process took place. For these reasons, we conclude that the polity fission-fusion model is a better interpretation of the observed settlement patterns than the simple-complex chiefdom model.

Mound Reuse

The phenomenon of paired centers leads us to a neglected issue of Mississippian mound building and political change: mound reuse. By mound reuse, we mean the reuse of an older, abandoned mound by a new mound-political unit. While periodic addition of construction stages to mounds under continuous use is the norm in the Mississippian world, some platform mounds exhibit radical temporal discontinuities in sequential mound-building episodes. Discontinuity in mound use for decades or even centuries, followed by reoccupation and addition of new stages, is documented at many Mississippian mound sites (Hally 1996; King 2003; Williams and Shapiro 1996).

Despite the fact that mound reuse is well documented, few archaeologists have commented on the political significance of mound reuse (Blitz 1994;

Hally 1996). Mound reuse is a dramatic illustration of the relationship between sanctity, legitimacy, leadership, and the act of mound building. It is useful to briefly consider once more the political and symbolic implications of mound building in order to place the mound reuse phenomenon in proper perspective.

Although platform mounds served as corporate group or communal symbols in Mississippian societies (Knight 1986), they were also materializations of chiefly sanctity and authority. In kin-based ranked societies, ancestor worship, principles of descent, and invocations of the supernatural are a fundamental source of sanctified authority. Early southeastern historical descriptions and modern archaeological discoveries of high-status burials, idols, special-purpose architecture, and concentrations of prestige goods at mound precincts support these assumptions (Lindauer and Blitz 1997). Some platform mounds served as the location of chiefs' houses and some platform mounds supported mortuary temples that held the bones of revered ancestors and former chiefs. Thus the mounds were physical manifestations of sanctity and authority. One strategy for status-striving individuals to extend their authority and influence was control of the ideological resources associated with the sacred mound precinct. To construct a platform mound was an essential step in validating claims to chiefly sanctity and authority. As monuments, platform mounds were a material "document" with a symbolic message that could be transmitted across generations and transcend the limitations placed on cumulative historical knowledge in nonliterate societies.

Mound Reuse and Native Oral Traditions

Population movement and subsequent mound building at new centers played a crucial role in the formation and replication of Mississippian sociopolitical systems. It should not come as a surprise, therefore, that population movement, encounters and conflicts between newcomers and indigenes, and building mounds are central themes in native southeastern oral traditions. A common form of origin myth in the native Southeast is the emergence-migration story. Emergence-migration stories recount how ancestral groups emerged from the earth or its symbolic representation, a mound, and/or journey to a new homeland and build a mound (Wheeler-Voegelin and Moore 1959). As myth, these narratives are explanations and endorsements of cultural values as well as ideological efforts to justify power relationships, expressed in allegorical form. As oral tradition, they may also incorporate "remembered history" (Vansina 1986).

Emergence-migration stories have multiple meanings, but one function is to promote claims to a territory. Statements of rank and order are frequent in these stories as well. For example, named ethnic groups or clans sometimes migrate to or from a territory or emerge from a mound in a specified order (Swanton 1928:108–111, 1931:11). In other cases, these rank-order relationships are expressed in the junior-senior social idiom in which groups travel together under the leadership of "brothers" (Swanton 1931:27–29, 33). In some versions, claims of historical relationship between separate groups are made, and explanations are provided for the fission process that split them apart (Swanton 1931:11–37). Sometimes this fission and separation is presented as a division between junior and senior, original and newcomer, or little brother and big brother, and therefore this ordering implies concepts of social ranking. At least one narrative even provides an explanation for what stimulated the migration process. In the early 1700s, the keeper of the Natchez temple told the French settler Antoine-Simon du Pratz that his people migrated to their present location to escape the domination of a tyrannical chief (Swanton 1911:182–184).

An earlier generation of archaeologists, working with a very short chronology for Eastern Woodlands culture history, made the naive attempt to connect historic southeastern emergence-migration myths with prehistoric artifact complexes. Later, an influential critique of this effort in southeastern archaeology rejected any role for population movement or native oral tradition in Mississippian archaeology (Smith 1984). This position is shortsighted, however, for it closes the door to insights derived from an indigenous perspective. While it is inappropriate to force native oral tradition into a chronicle akin to Western concepts of historiography, and attempts to correlate oral traditions with the archaeological record are usually inconclusive (Mason 2000), the native southeastern emergence-migration myths are very instructive about the polity fission-fusion process.

In the stories, the fission process spreads groups of leaders and followers over the landscape in an Exodus-like search for a homeland. This is one variation of the social dynamics proposed in the polity fission-fusion model, in which each migrating group established a new mound, and in doing so, chartered a new mythic history (cf. Kopytoff 1987). The emergence-migration narratives leave no doubt that mound building was a symbol of territoriality and leadership, but more importantly, they reveal group fission and migration as a key mechanism of polity formation. Such stories express culturally specific perceptions of rank, factionalism, social competition, territoriality, and other aspects of the political process. We must realize that southeastern emergence-migration stories contain emic statements of indigenous political theory.

Mound Reuse at Mississippian Centers

This digression into native oral tradition has been necessary to emphasize the complex symbolic and political implications of the mound reuse phenomenon. In the first and most common category of reuse, relatively short-term discontinuities of mound building on the order of 100–200 years were followed by reuse and the addition of new stages. Hally (1993) documented the duration of mound use, as measured by phase intervals, at 47 Mississippian mound centers in the South Appalachian area. Most mounds show continuous use through one or two sequential phases, which Hally equates with the duration of Mississippian chiefdoms or polities. However, a few mounds skip one or two phase intervals, revealing abandonment and subsequent reuse. Examples in northern and central Georgia include the Tugalo, Scull Shoals, Dyar, and Shinholser sites. The large Etowah center also experienced episodes of mound abandonment and subsequent reuse (King 2003). In the lower Chattahoochee River region, for example, Rood's Landing was abandoned in Period IV, after it reached its zenith of mound construction activity. Subsequently, after 150 years of abandonment, Rood's Landing was again occupied during Period VI, when Mounds A and B were once more put to use.

Another category of mound abandonment and reuse is even more intriguing. Abandoned Woodland mounds became the base or core for later Mississippian mound building. In other words, the abandoned monument of an earlier cultural tradition was encapsulated by the construction of a later Mississippian platform. These episodes of use are separated by many centuries. In the lower Chattahoochee River valley, Mandeville Mound A and Shorter were Middle Woodland platforms that lay unused for hundreds of years until appropriated and rebuilt by Mississippian peoples. Similarly, the mounds at Kyle and Abercrombie were erected in the Averett phase, abandoned for at least 300 years, and then Abercrombie phase occupants added new mound stages in the early historic era.

In the case of short-term abandonment and reuse, such as the Rood's Landing example, a cultural tradition or memory may have survived to tie a people to a specific abandoned mound, but this is unlikely for the long-term examples. Clear discontinuities in cultural traditions and the extreme time spans between abandonment and reuse underscore the fact that justification claims to ancient mounds were "mythic, expedient, and independent of historical reality" (Blitz 1994).

Mound reuse in the lower Chattahoochee River region occurs at major political or cultural transition points. The addition of a new stage to the old Middle Woodland Mandeville Mound A initiated one of the first Mississippian centers in the valley. Mandeville's Rood I phase component was not an indigenous cultural development; reoccupation of the old mound was by relative newcomers to the region (Blitz and Lorenz 2002). Use of the Mandeville center was brief because only one Rood I phase mound stage was built before abandonment. So it would appear that Mandeville's status, as a political center, was quite insecure. At Shorter, mound reuse followed the decline of the large multiple-mound centers, accompanied by a new fusion of two distinct ceramic traditions of nonlocal origin. Only a single mound stage was added to the old mound before it was once again abandoned. Reuse of mounds at Rood's Landing, Kyle, and Abercrombie occurred in the unsettling protohistoric period of early European contact.

No doubt these major cultural transition points were filled with stress and insecurity, a time when individual leaders and their followers sought to forge a closer link to ancient sacred symbols. Perhaps groups that reused old mounds were newcomers asserting claims of continuity to a supposed ancestral territory, or perhaps the symbolic message was one of a new cultural order triumphant over an older order. Whatever the case, the political efficacy of reuse was appropriation and control of a sacred resource for ideological purposes.

At this point, we must address one objection to the theory that mound reuse was an effort to appropriate a symbol of sacred authority. An alternative explanation, offered by various archaeologists in informal discussions, asserts that reuse of an old mound was merely an expedient, laborsaving decision. In this view, refurbishing an abandoned mound was more "efficient" and cost effective than starting at ground level. Furthermore, the ancient mound site furnished all the required material resources for resettlement. We do not find this argument persuasive.

It is true that Mississippian mound builders sometimes took advantage of the physical landscape, even reshaping natural contours, hills, and rises (e.g., Emerald Mound, Mississippi, Brain 1978:352; and Singer-Moye Mound D). Also, a mound might be situated at a terrace edge, which exaggerated the height when viewed from a river or lower terrain (e.g., Lampley Mound). There is no evidence, however, that laborsaving was a concern to Mississippian mound builders. Indeed, the social and political context of mound building suggests quite the opposite was true, and that one goal was to expend as much energy as possible. In part, mounds were symbols of authority because they were demonstrations of the labor pool available to a chief. In their role as corporate group symbols, the height and volume of mounds expressed the demographic size, energy, and vitality of the mound-political unit that built the edifice (Blitz and Livingood 2004), sending a message about corporate group status that was surely not ignored by other interest groups.

Just as the corporate groups of other ranked societies erected totem poles or megaliths in competitive displays, perhaps the Mississippian mound builders were motivated by similar concerns. As Bruce Trigger (1990) has pointed out, ancient monument building took place in a social context quite alien to modern Western notions of labor efficiency. If laborsaving were the primary motivation for mound reuse, then we would expect smaller mounds to be preferred over larger mounds because more labor is required to add a new stage to a large mound than to a small mound. But there is no indication this was the case. For example, after a period of abandonment, the large Mound A at Rood's Landing was chosen over smaller mounds for reuse in Period VI. Also, it must be remembered that although mounds are often an impressive size, labor was expended in short, periodic building efforts that probably placed no serious burden on a community's time and energy (Muller 1997:274–275).

The efficiency argument ignores the salient characteristic of mounds as symbols. Once in place, ancient monuments endowed the landscape with power (Bradley 1993). Periodically, new peoples revitalized the old dormant mound symbolism to bolster new claims. We interpret mound reuse in the lower Chattahoochee River region and elsewhere in the Mississippian world as a political strategy to fabricate mythic histories through possession of powerful monuments in a sacred, yet geopolitical landscape, and so legitimate new social orders with appeals to sacred authority (Blitz 1994; Bradley 1998; Hally 1996; Lindauer and Blitz 1997; Prent 2003; Sinopoli 2003).

What we have detected here is no more than the native southeastern version of a common cross-cultural phenomenon. Whether it is the reuse of Neolithic henge monuments and barrows (Balter 1993; Thomas 1987), the recarving and alteration of Classic Maya monuments (Baker 1962), the establishment of Spanish churches atop the razed remains of precolumbian temples (Bauer and Stanish 2001:10), or the struggle between three world religions for the sacred mount at the heart of modern Jerusalem, the basic sociopolitical rationale is the same: appropriation of an old sacred symbol to bolster new political efforts.

Summary

Our research has been designed to measure regional political integration in a ranked, nonstate society. To achieve this goal, we evaluated two contrasting models of Mississippian political organization and change through regional settlement distributions of mound centers that functioned as central places or capitals of ancient polities. These data have been used to chart the rate of political change through time by measuring the duration of individual centers. We have identified variation in regional polity forms by measuring the number and size of the mound centers and identified polity territories by measuring the distances between mound centers. We have detected power shifts between mound centers by measuring the foundation and abandonment of mound centers.

We can now draw some tentative conclusions about political integration, polity variation, and polity change from our analysis of mound-center settlement patterns. In Chapter 2, we defined a basic Mississippian political unit composed of a leader or chief, a body of followers, and their representative symbol, a platform mound. We termed this sociopolitical organization a mound-political unit. We tried to push beyond the generalized chiefdom concept to specify the potential variability of Mississippian political organization by charting how these mound-political units changed through time in a specific region. Over the course of six centuries, we have documented when mound-political units combined to produce multiple-mound polities or remained single-mound polities, identified the polity forms created by these combinations, and gained some insights into how this was accomplished.

The simple-complex chiefdom model cannot account for the observed mound-center settlement patterns or the implied polity forms. As an explanation of Mississippian culture process, it is incomplete, and must be augmented by additional models that accommodate this diversity of political forms. The polity fission-fusion model provides an alternative explanation for changes in mound center size, complexity, and location. Mound-political units assembled and disassembled to create polities of different size and complexity. As we have seen, by this process political organizations could assume at least two, or possibly three, different polity forms without establishing the primary-secondary center settlement hierarchy of complex chiefdoms.

This is our interpretation of the observed settlement pattern changes. There might be other explanations for these patterns that we have not considered. We think the polity fission-fusion model offers a better explanation of the variable mound-center settlement patterns than does the simple-complex chiefdom model. We emphasize, however, that we have not confirmed what specific factors drove the polity fission-fusion process, but we have identified some possibilities.

Mound-center settlement patterns and polity forms like the lower Chattahoochee River examples are not unique; they are found in other regions (Blitz 1999:580–583). The lower Chattahoochee case study joins a growing body of research that reveals Mississippian political transformations rarely followed the simple chiefdom-complex chiefdom-simple chiefdom cycle (Hally 1996:125). As we have seen, once we are able to accurately date supposed secondary mound centers, what appeared to earlier researchers to be complex chiefdoms turn out to be oscillations between small centers and big centers occupied at different times. Mississippian peoples did create complex chiefdoms, but these polity forms were the political exceptions, not the rule. In the lower Chattahoochee River region and in many other areas of the Mississippian world, mound-center settlement systems fail to conform to the integrated hierarchy of centers predicted by the simple-complex chiefdom model. The absence of primary-secondary center hierarchies implies that management of regional tribute flows between centers was not the organizing principle of most Mississippian polities, nor was it the primary determinant of most mound-center distributions. Political change was more rapid and dynamic, driven by factors that created an ever-changing geopolitical landscape shaped by foundation, abandonment, resettlement, and shifts of political power between centers. Population movements were an integral part of this process. The different mound-center settlement patterns represent diverse polity forms with various degrees of political integration.

The polity fission-fusion model of political change and integration explains how Mississippian polities were reproduced through time and across geographical space by the movements and recombinations of people organized as basic political units. These basic political units were sufficiently flexible to rapidly unite or secede to create different polity forms. The utility of the simple-complex chiefdom model is more limited, focused as it is on a tributary political economy and developmental cycles between simple and complex chiefdoms. In contrast, the polity fission-fusion model can encompass all known Mississippian polity forms, but lacks the explicit link to a theory of political economy found in the simple-complex chiefdom model. The different emphasizes of the two models suggest a complementary perspective is possible once we realize that cycles between simple and complex polity forms need not follow a gradual, fixed developmental trajectory or achieve regional political integration. Which model is most informative will depend on the research questions to be addressed and the range of polity forms found in specific regions of the Mississippian world.

6   Archaeological Measures
of Social Integration

Although the lower Chattahoochee polities were politically independent, they were not isolated from one another. The polity fission-fusion process involved political power shifts from one center to another. Mound-center polities grew or declined, in part, in response to interactions with other centers. The decorated pottery found at the mound centers is one indication of such interactions.

Attributes of pottery form, composition, and decoration were patterned through time and space as social groups participated in shared traditions of material culture. It is this shared material culture that provides a window through which we can perceive expressions of collective social identities. While it is doubtful that we can know precisely what the pottery styles "meant" to the long-dead peoples who used them, we can be confident that style materialized shared perceptions, values, and cultural reference points, created and channeled by social interactions. Can we detect the temporal and spatial extent of collective social identities, just as we have for polity boundaries? Because we assume that political integration required the creation of collective social identities to provide ideological legitimacy for new sociopolitical organizations, our next research step is to measure the temporal and spatial scale of social integration.

Ceramic Style and Social Integration

In Chapter 2 we outlined the theory for interpreting the temporal-spatial scale of social integration through analysis of pottery style distributions. To summarize, we proposed that (1) the degree of utilitarian ceramic stylistic similarity between sites is correlated with the degree of social interaction and reflects shared collective identities; (2) a spatial pattern of geographically restricted utilitarian ceramic style zones indicates a greater level of integration within zones and demarcation of boundary distinctions between zones; (3) the boundaries between utilitarian ceramic style zones were frontiers that inhibited transmission of styles; (4) the temporal-spatial scales of style zones fluctuated with the expansion or contraction of political and social integration; and (5) the spatial distributions of serving fine wares are expected to cross utilitarian ceramic style-zone boundaries to create more spatially extensive prestige style zones indicative of a collective identity shared by elites.

In the previous chapter we found that political centralization was more local than regional in scale. A hierarchy of mound centers under one authority was not achieved. Instead, political integration encapsulated populations within 18 km of the local single or multiple-mound center. Despite the fact that mound centers located more than 18 km away from one another were probably politically autonomous, many of these sites shared the same ceramic assemblages as defined by seven decorated utilitarian ceramic types. If political integration was on a local scale within an 18-km radius of each mound, then what process served to integrate mound centers beyond this area of control such that they shared the same ceramic assemblages? We postulate that archaeological sites with similar ceramic assemblages represent populations created by the fission and fusion of communities through many generations (Blitz 1999; Blitz and Lorenz 2002; Lorenz and Blitz 2003). A common history of regular and sustained interaction created politically autonomous polities that shared a collective social identity.

Methods

In this chapter we attempt to measure the scale of social integration in the lower Chattahoochee River region through analysis of pottery style distributions. Three temporal-spatial units of observation are employed: (1) ceramic style zones, (2) style-zone frontiers, and (3) the presence/absence distribution of serving fine wares. The spatial distribution of mound-center components with similar ceramic assemblages, grouped into the ceramic phases defined in Chapter 4, are identified as utilitarian ceramic style zones. Using the same procedure followed in Chapter 5, nearest-neighbor distances between contemporary (same phase/period) mound centers are used to identify polity boundaries. In a chronological series of maps, the spatial scale of political integration as measured by polity boundaries can be compared to the spatial scale of social integration as measured by the ceramic style zones. Once this is done, it is possible to evaluate if or how these two processes of integration were related.

Utilitarian ceramic style zones measure the temporal-spatial dimensions of social integration, but the interstices between style zones are also informative. A frontier zone devoid of mound centers separated each utilitarian ceramic style zone. These style-zone frontiers demarcate the boundaries of contemporary ceramic phases with distinctively different vessel forms and decoration. The nearest-neighbor distance between mound centers in separate, yet contemporary, ceramic style zones measures the spatial extent of a style-zone frontier. In cultural-historical terms, style-zone frontiers separate local or regional variants of spatially extensive ceramic traditions (i.e., Caldwell 1958; Willey and Phillips 1958).

There are specific reasons why we use ceramic samples from mound centers to map ceramic style zones and style-zone frontiers. The majority of recorded nonmound sites in the region are unexcavated surface finds and thus cannot be assigned to ceramic phases defined on the basis of ceramic type frequencies. Therefore, the ceramic style zones are not defined by mapping a continuous distribution of site components for each ceramic phase. Exceptions are the Averett and Wakulla phases, defined by the presence of a single diagnostic pottery type. Because mound centers served to integrate populations dispersed in the polity's territory, it is appropriate to measure style-zone frontiers by the distance between contemporary centers in separate style zones. The resulting measure is an approximation of the boundary between style zones.

We have two measures of social integration at the inter-regional scale. First, we compare ceramic type frequencies found in lower Chattahoochee mound-center ceramic assemblages to those in the adjacent Apalachicola River region in order to identify style-zone frontiers. Second, we map the distribution of a distinctive serving fine ware shared between utilitarian ceramic style zones across style-zone frontiers.

Overview of Ceramic Style Zones

Utilitarian Ceramic Style Zones: A.D. 700–1100

It is important to examine the archaeological evidence for ceramic style zones immediately prior to the formation of Mississippian mound-center polities around A.D. 1100. Such an examination sheds light on the origins of the Mississippian way of life in the area, clarifies questions of historical relationship based on continuity or discontinuity in material culture and settlement patterns, and sets the stage for the unprecedented scale of political integration that accompanied polity formation.

From A.D. 700–1100, indigenous populations produced two discrete ceramic style zones in the lower Chattahoochee River region: the Averett phase (A.D. 900–1300) and Wakulla phase (A.D. 700–1000). The ceramic type Averett Plain is diagnostic of the northern Averett style zone and the ceramic

type Wakulla Check Stamped marks the southern style zone. The two ceramic phases are spatially distinct site distributions with ceramic assemblages
that differ in vessel shape, decoration, and temper from one another and
from Rood I, the initial Mississippian ceramic phase in the valley. As expressions of culture history, the Averett and Wakulla ceramic phases represent
Woodland ceramic traditions with deep roots in the lower Southeast.

Summarizing a more extended argument presented elsewhere (Blitz and
Lorenz 2002), there is no spatial overlap between Averett and Wakulla site
distributions (Figure 6.1, interfluvial locations away from the river are excluded due to inadequate survey coverage). The only physiographic zone
with both Averett and Wakulla components is the centrally located Chattahoochee Red Hills, which contains one Averett site and six Wakulla sites
dispersed along the river a distance of approximately 50 km north-to-south.
The southernmost Averett site (9SW124) and northernmost Wakulla site
(1BR27) are about 6 km apart. Farther south, the number and density of
Wakulla components increases dramatically. Clearly, the Chattahoochee Red
Hills is peripheral to both Averett and Wakulla settlement distributions, but
it contains the majority of post-A.D. 1100 Mississippian Rood I–III phase
components.

Because distinct and contemporaneous ceramic style zones do not overlap,
we infer that the lower Chattahoochee River valley contained frontiers: geographical and sociopolitical spaces between settlements where contact between cultural groups could be initiated or avoided (King and Meyers 2002).
The post-A.D. 1100 Mississippian Rood I phase occupations appeared without local precedent in the vacant frontier between Averett and Wakulla sites
(Figure 6.1). In the Chattahoochee Red Hills, where Mississippian components are concentrated, there was no antecedent population source for local
Mississippian emergence.

Our hypothesis of a population movement to the region by Mississippian
groups from elsewhere is strengthened by the fact that no Rood I–III phase
mound center exhibits any significant evidence for prior Averett or Wakulla
habitation as would be expected if the ceramic style changes were autochthonous transformations of indigenous parent populations. Averett ceramics
are totally absent from Rood I mound assemblages, while Wakulla ceramics
appear only in trace amounts in the lowest levels of a few Mississippian
mounds in the southern part of the valley. Some Averett components yield
small quantities of Cool Branch Incised, the common Rood phase pottery type (Chase 1963a), and radiocarbon dates indicate that Averett phase
and Rood I–II phase populations overlapped in time (Table 4.1; Ledbetter
1997b). Termination dates for the Wakulla phase in the lower Chattahoochee region are uncertain. Averett and Wakulla ceramics do not occur in
association. It is not known if the Wakulla phase and Rood I phase overlap

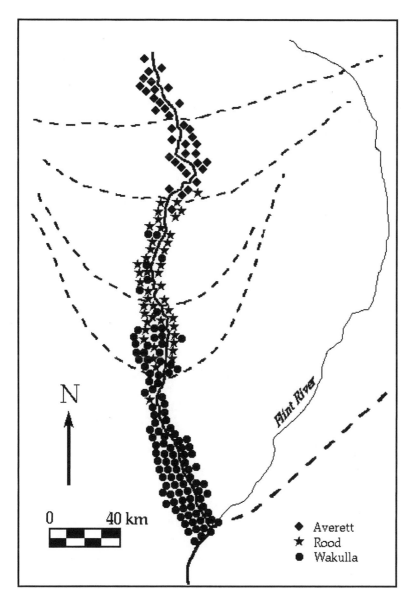

6.1. Distribution of Averett, Rood, and Wakulla components in the lower Chattahoochee River valley (Blitz and Lorenz 2002:Figure 3, reprinted by permission of
the Southeastern Archaeological Conference).

in time; the single corrected radiocarbon date yields a span of A.D. 778–1298, which is not much help here (Blitz and Lorenz 2002:124).

Utilitarian Ceramic Style Zones: A.D. 1100–1650

From A.D. 1100–1650, distinctive utilitarian ceramic style zones, identified by the spatial distribution of ceramic assemblages defined as phases or periods, are present in the lower Chattahoochee–Apalachicola River regions. We defined the lower Chattahoochee ceramic phases in Chapter 4, so we need only discuss the cross-correlation of the lower Chattahoochee River sequence with the Apalachicola River sequence.

The Apalachicola River is the continuation of the waterway below the confluence of the lower Chattahoochee and Flint rivers in Florida. The Apalachicola River region has mound-center polities that are contemporary with the lower Chattahoochee polities. The ceramic assemblages at these sites are quite distinct, however, and researchers assign them to a regional period designation or archaeological culture known as Fort Walton (Willey 1949).

The chronology of Fort Walton mound centers is imprecise. Three sequential Fort Walton periods are defined by changing ceramic type frequencies of Wakulla Check Stamped, Fort Walton Incised, and Lamar Complicated Stamped: Early Fort Walton (A.D. 1000–1200), Middle Fort Walton (A.D. 1200–1400), and Late Fort Walton (A.D. 1400–1600) (White 1982). Although there is a ceramic phase sequence for the Apalachicola River region (Scarry 1984, 1990), it is not based on published stratigraphic excavations (Marrinan and White 1998). Only the single-mound centers of Curlee (8JA7), Cayson (8CA3), and Yon (8LI2) have quantified ceramic samples and radiocarbon dates that can be used for comparative purposes with any degree of confidence (Blitz and Lorenz 2002:127–129). Of these sites, only Yon has adequate samples from mound contexts (White 1996). The greater degree of contextual evidence and provenience documentation provided by White's period sequence renders it preferable to Scarry's phase sequence for comparative purposes.

A ceramic phase sequence has been proposed for Lake Jackson, a large multiple-mound center east of the Apalachicola River near Tallahassee. The Lake Jackson I–III sequence exists as a presence-absence list of pottery types, without quantification or provenience data (Payne 1994:262–264). This unrefined chronology hinders a precise cross-correlation dating with the lower Chattahoochee and Apalachicola sequences. Nor is it possible to identify the Lake Jackson polity boundaries with the data at hand (there are undated platform mounds near Lake Jackson), even though there have been premature efforts to do so (Scarry and Payne 1986). Despite these limitations, Lake Jackson can serve as our easternmost reference point in the inter-regional comparisons that follow. Payne's Lake Jackson I–III sequence probably spans the same time interval as White's Early and Middle Fort Walton periods.

Table 6.1 presents the ceramic type frequency data that permits us to define the lower Chattahoochee–Apalachicola style zones. Style zones are ordered in the Period I–VII chronology presented in Chapter 5. The same mound ceramic samples used in Chapter 4 to create the lower Chattahoochee River seriation are employed in Table 6.1. In addition, the source for the Averett phase samples in Table 6.1 is the Abercrombie mound investigation reported in this volume. Some ceramic types identified in the Apalachicola Fort Walton ceramic samples in Table 6.1 have been translated into the ceramic-type designations used in this study.

Referring to Table 6.1, the Early Fort Walton period as defined by ceramic samples from Curlee (White 1982) overlaps in time with the Averett and Rood I phases in the lower Chattahoochee region. The Middle Fort Walton period can be subdivided into early and late temporal spans based on overlying occupation levels at the Cayson mound center that show temporal changes in key ceramic type frequencies (Blitz and Lorenz 2002:128–129; Scarry 1980). Thus the Middle Fort Walton I period is roughly contemporary with the Averett and Rood II phases, while the Middle Fort Walton II period is contemporary with the Rood III phase.

In Period IV, data are lacking for Apalachicola River components that can be correlated with the Singer phase. The Late Fort Walton period can be subdivided into early and late time spans based on temporal changes in ceramic frequencies in overlying levels at the Yon and Omussee Creek sites. In Table 6.1, the Late Fort Walton I sample is from Yon lower levels (Scarry 2000) and from Omussee Creek 3–4 reported in this volume; the Late Fort Walton II sample is from Yon upper levels (Scarry 2000; White 1996). Late Fort Walton I is contemporary with the Bull Creek phase, and Late Fort Walton II is contemporary with the Stewart phase. At the late end of the chronology, Apalachicola River components comparable to the Abercrombie phase data are unavailable.

Comparison of Utilitarian Ceramic Style Zones and Polity Boundaries

By comparing utilitarian ceramic style zones and polity boundaries, we can identify fluctuating scales of social and political integration (Table 6.2). Mound centers are grouped into ceramic style zones depicted on maps for a sequence of time spans. Some of the mound-center samples included in the style-zone maps were not part of our seriation because they did not meet

Table 6.1. Frequency (Percent) of the Most Abundant Decorated Pottery Types in Each Style Zone by Period.

Style Zone	Averett Plain	Etowah Comp. St.	MV Inc	CB Inc	Col Inc	Wakulla Ch. St.	Ft. Walton Incised	Lamar Plain	Lamar Comp. St.	Total N
PERIOD I										
Rood I	0	1	61	10	3	0	3	0	0	239
Averett	57	30	0	1	0	4	1	1	0	129
Early Ft. Walton	0	0	1	1	2	74	22	0	0	805
PERIOD II										
Rood II	0	0	4	71	10	0	2	6	0	618
Averett	57	30	0	1	0	4	1	1	0	129
Middle Ft. Walton I	0	0	9	0	0	15	74	0	0	34
PERIOD III										
Rood III	0	16	7	27	13	0	6	13	0	316
Middle Ft. Walton II	0	0	4	2	1	1	84	0	0	147
PERIOD IV										
Singer	0	5	1	4	5	0	25	30	7	1329
PERIOD V										
Bull Creek	0	0	0	0	0	0	52	15	23	127
Late Ft. Walton I	0	0	1	4	0	1	75	8	1	256
PERIOD VI										
Stewart	0	0	0	1	1	0	23	9	55	1070
Late Ft. Walton II	0	0	0	2	0	1	13	0	80	309
PERIOD VII										
Abercrombie	0	0	0	0	0	0	1	5	33	218

Type percentages are relative to the total decorated ceramics in each sample.

Table 6.2. Lower Chattahoochee–Apalachicola River Ceramic Style Zone and Frontier Sizes by Period.

Style Zone	Number of Mound Sites	Style Zone Size (km)	Near (km) Neighbor	Frontier Size (km)
PERIOD I				
Averett	1	85[a]	–	51
Rood I	4	73	30	60
Early Fort Walton	2	58	58	68
PERIOD II				
Averett	1	85[a]	–	84
Rood II	1	27	27	103
Middle Fort Walton I	2	63	63	121
PERIOD III				
Rood III	3	82	54	82
Middle Fort Walton II	2	63	63	82
PERIOD IV				
Singer	2	34	34	175
Lake Jackson III	1	–	–	175
PERIOD V				
Bull Creek	2	62	32	70
Late Fort Walton I	2	82	82	70
PERIOD VI				
Stewart	1	49	49	115
Late Fort Walton II	1	–	–	115
PERIOD VII				
Abercrombie	2	36[b]	2	–

[a]distance between northernmost and southernmost Averett sites.
[b]all known sites are encompassed by a maximum polity diameter (18-x-2 km).

the minimum of 50 decorated sherds, but nonetheless their assemblage was distinctive enough to assign them to particular style zones.

Period I: A.D. 1100–1200

To begin with the earliest time period (Figure 6.2), the Rood I phase style zone contained four contemporary mound-center occupations within the central and southern portion of the lower Chattahoochee River valley: Cool Branch, Mandeville, Singer-Moye Mound C, and Purcell's Landing. In addition, a nonmound Rood I component is present at Rood's Landing. The average nearest-neighbor distance between contemporary centers is 30 km, which exceeds the maximum radius of 18 km for the average Mississippian

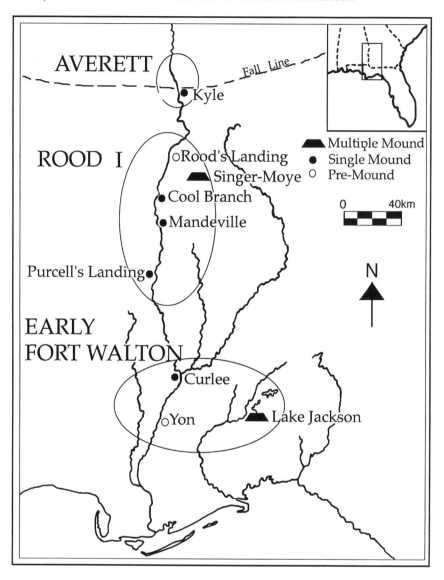

6.2. Period I ceramic style zones, A.D. 1100–1200.

chiefly sphere of administrative control. The spatial extent of the style zone is more than three times the average distance between mounds. These distances suggest that the Rood I phase mound centers were most likely autonomous polities linked in a larger interaction sphere of populations with a collective social identity as reflected by a shared ceramic style.

The southern Early Fort Walton–Rood I style-zone frontier is identified by a nearest-neighbor distance of 68 km between the southernmost mound of the Rood I phase style zone (Purcell's Landing) and the northernmost mound of the Early Fort Walton style zone (Curlee). This style-zone frontier is more than three times larger than the nearest-neighbor distance between mounds within the Rood I phase style zone. An estimated 32 km, or at least a day's walk, separates the two polity's territorial boundaries.

In the northern lower Chattahoochee River valley, people within the Averett ceramic style zone occupied the Kyle and Abercrombie mound centers at a time when the Rood I–II phase style zones were present farther south. For reasons stated in Chapter 5, we think the two Averett centers were occupied sequentially. With only one mound center per period, the size of the Averett style zone is difficult to measure based on mound-center samples alone. An Averett style zone as measured by the spatial extent of nonmound sites with Averett Plain is 85 km north-south along the lower Chattahoochee River (Figure 6.1), although it is unlikely that all these sites were occupied at the same time. The nearest-neighbor distance between the Averett Kyle center and the northernmost mound center within the Rood I phase style zone is 51 km, thus defining a northern Averett–Rood I style-zone frontier as more than twice the average distance between mound centers found within the Rood I phase style zone.

Period II: A.D. 1200–1300

The Rood II style zone is marked by high frequencies of Cool Branch Incised relative to other ceramic types (Figure 6.3). Only the Cemochechobee center exhibits this distinctive frequency pattern, with one related premound component at Gary's Fish Pond. Thus the extent of the style zone is limited to the 27 km distance between these two contemporary mound and nonmound sites. The nearest-neighbor distance between the Cemochechobee Rood II center and the northernmost contemporary Middle Fort Walton I center (Cayson) is 121 km. This is an increase in the size of the southern Rood–Fort Walton style-zone frontier compared to Period I. The northern Averett-Rood style-zone frontier also grew more extensive in Period II.

Period III: A.D. 1300–1400

The Rood III phase style zone has a similar scale of social integration as the earlier Rood I phase, with three contemporaneous mound centers distributed within an 82-km style zone (Figure 6.4). Two of these mound sites are the multiple-mound centers of Rood's Landing and Singer-Moye, located 28 km apart. The average nearest-neighbor distance of 37 km between mound centers implies continued autonomy. To the north, the Averett style zone disappeared, perhaps due to the abandonment of the northern valley by populations producing the Averett ceramic assemblages. To the south, the Rood–Fort Walton style-zone frontier was maintained.

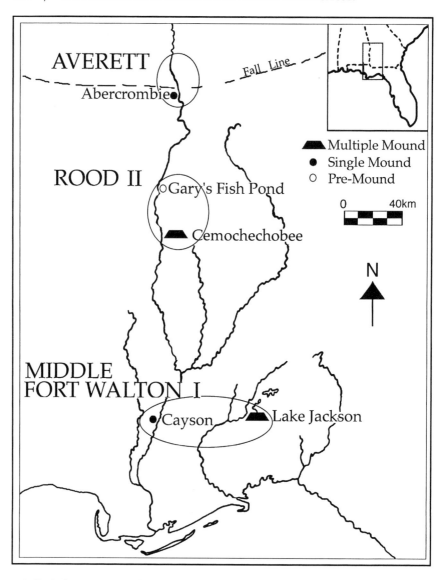

6.3. Period II ceramic style zones, A.D. 1200–1300.

Periods IV and V: A.D. 1400–1550

During this interval, mound-center distribution data and associated ceramic assemblages reveal a dramatic shifting of polities and ceramic style zones. In the Period IV Singer phase, the diagnostic Rood ceramic type Cool Branch Incised was replaced by ceramic types of nonlocal origin with geographi-

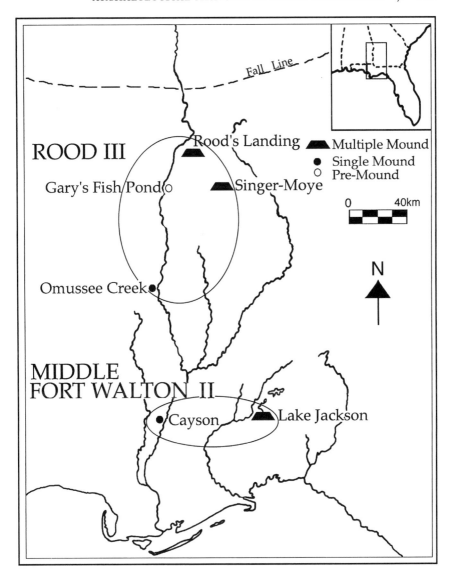

6.4. Period III ceramic style zones, A.D. 1300–1400.

cal centers of distribution (and presumably area of origin) to the northeast in Georgia (Lamar Plain) and south (Fort Walton Incised). The territory initially occupied by Rood I phase settlers around A.D. 1100 was, by A.D. 1400, either abandoned by Rood phase populations or the inhabitants stopped making the distinctive handled jars popular over the last 300 years

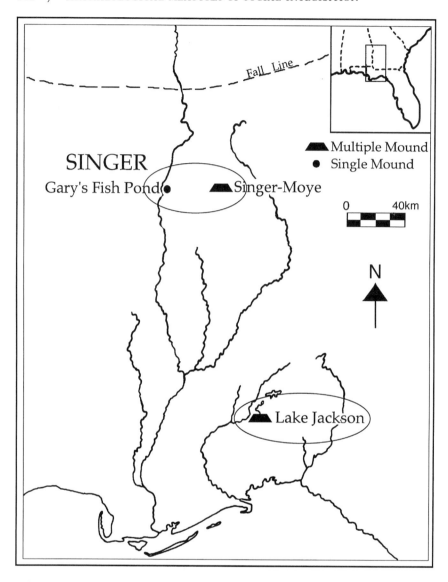

6.5. Period IV ceramic style zones, A.D. 1400–1450.

and adopted the new styles. The Singer phase style zone contracted in size to two contemporary mound centers distributed over a 34 km style zone (Figure 6.5), which is smaller than it was during the earlier Rood I–III phases. The only Fort Walton center that can be documented for Period V is the Lake Jackson site. The 175-km distance between Singer-Moye and

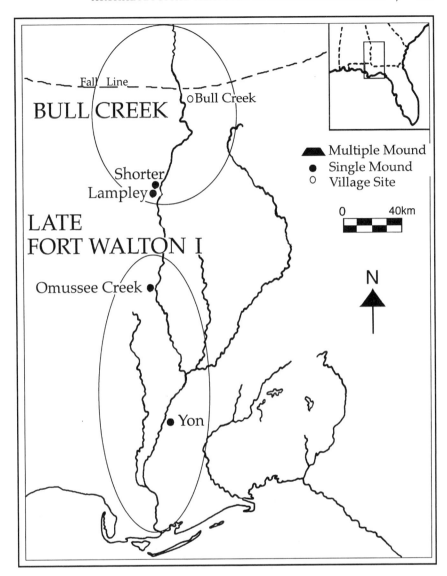

6.6. Period V ceramic style zones, A.D. 1450–1550.

Lake Jackson defines an approximate maximum size for the Singer–Lake Jackson III style-zone frontier.

In the Period V Bull Creek phase (Figure 6.6), the lower Chattahoochee River valley was occupied by three single-mound centers. Two of these, Lampley and Shorter, are 2 km apart and likely represent sequential occupations within the phase time span. Omussee Creek, the southernmost mound center in the valley, previously demarcated the southern edge of the Rood III style zone. The 70-km distance between Omussee Creek and the Lampley-Shorter mound cluster was devoid of contemporary mound centers. Bull Creek (9ME1), an excavated nonmound site, provides a rough approximation of the northern edge of the Bull Creek style zone. The Bull Creek and Shorter sites are separated by 62 km.

Fort Walton Incised became the dominant decorated ceramic type at the lower Chattahoochee centers. Lamar Complicated Stamped was second in frequency to Fort Walton Incised in the ceramic assemblages at the northerly mound centers of Lampley and Shorter. Farther south at Omussee Creek, Lamar Complicated Stamped occurred in very low frequency (Table 6.1), an assemblage composition that places this southernmost lower Chattahoochee center in the Late Fort Walton I style zone. The Omussee Creek–Lampley distance of 70 km establishes the Bull Creek–Late Fort Walton I style-zone frontier. The Lake Jackson center ceased to function as a polity center during this period (Payne 1994:264).

Periods VI and VII: A.D. 1550–1650

Use of only two centers can be confirmed in Period VI (Figure 6.7). Rood's Landing is the Stewart phase center. The distance from Rood's Landing to 9CY51, an excavated nonmound site of this period (Broyles 1963) provides an estimate of the size of the style zone. Upper levels of the Yon center date to this period, but no other Late Fort Walton II center has been confirmed. Yon and 9CY51 are 115 km apart, our best estimate of the size of the Stewart–Late Fort Walton II style-zone frontier.

In Period VII, pottery of the Abercrombie phase is spatially restricted to the two mound centers and a few nearby sites (Figure 6.8), a phenomenon attributed to severe population loss through exposure to epidemic diseases introduced by Europeans (Knight and Mistovich 1984:225). With political and social integration shrunk to the local scale, ceramic style zone and polity boundary were the same.

A Prestige Ceramic Style Zone?

In contrast to the common ceramic types used to delineate the utilitarian ceramic style zones, serving fine wares found in ceremonial contexts have a markedly different distribution pattern. A distinctive style of incised bottles and beakers, ceramic types known as Nunnally Incised and Andrews Decorated (Schnell et al. 1981), was in use throughout the lower Chattahoochee–Apalachicola River regions A.D. 1100–1450 (see Appendix C). These bottles and beakers have similar designs, occur together in mound contexts, and

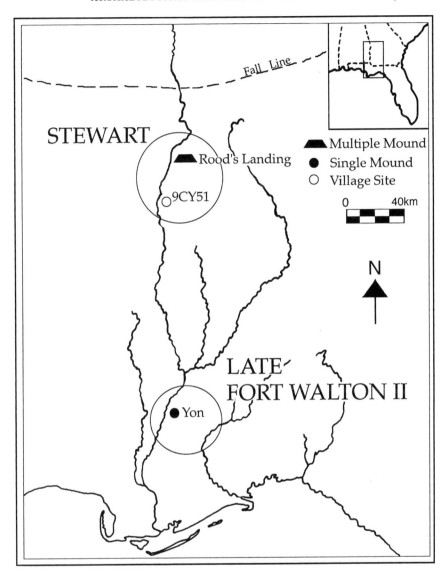

6.7. Period VI ceramic style zones, A.D. 1550–1600.

appear to be a functionally related set of fine wares for serving libations perhaps equivalent to the "black drink" ceremonials of the historic period (Hudson 1979). We did not include Nunnally Incised and Andrews Decorated in our frequency seriation due to their rarity. It is possible, however, to record the presence-absence distribution of the bottle-beaker fine wares

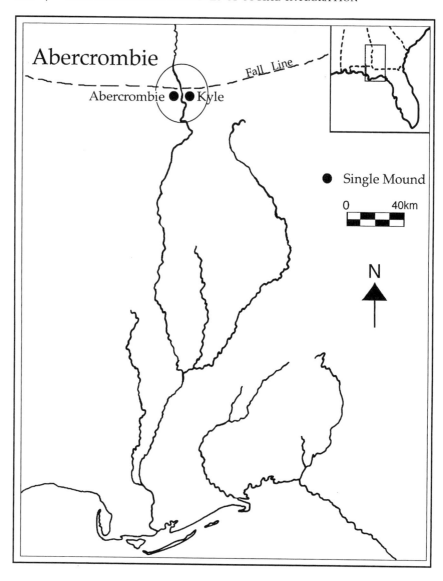

6.8. Period VII ceramic style zones, A.D. 1600–1650.

recovered at centers in the study area. As is apparent in Figure 6.9, the inter-regional distribution of the bottle-beaker fine wares crosscuts the style-zone frontiers defined by utilitarian ceramics.

We interpret the distribution of the bottle-beaker fine wares across style-zone frontiers as an example of the materialization of an elite ideology that

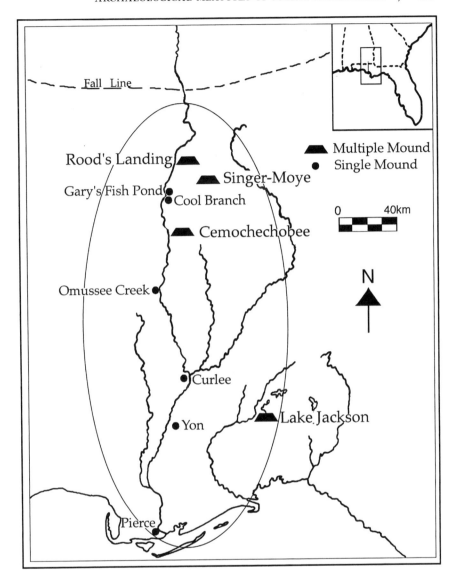

6.9. Style zone of beaker-bottle fine wares.

served to bridge social and political territories. Perhaps these vessels were used as tokens of cooperation and friendship by elites who were engaged in some form of interaction between mound centers. We stress, however, that it is not known if these elaborate pottery vessels were widely exchanged between centers or manufactured locally. Nonetheless, it is clear from the inter-regional distribution that bottle-beaker fine wares were not products of a parochial social identity as were utilitarian ceramics. Instead, these fine ware vessels were highly valued and therefore closely associated with elites whose social interactions and political concerns were not confined to the local scale (Lorenz and Blitz 2003).

Discussion

Our study reveals that political boundaries were embedded within the larger scales of social integration. Multipolity or regional-level social integration was present across the central and southern portions of the lower Chattahoochee River valley from A.D. 1100 to A.D. 1450. The distances between contemporary Rood I–III mound sites make it unlikely that centers were ever under the control of a region-wide complex chiefdom, even though they shared a common style of utilitarian pottery. This shared style was the product of local autonomous polities with similar cultural origins, replicated and disseminated by polity fission-fusion, and sustained by interaction in matters of alliance and exchange.

Style-zone frontiers mark barriers to larger-scale social integration. From A.D. 900 to A.D. 1450, interaction between populations in different style zones took a form that was not amenable to the free exchange of utilitarian ceramic styles. Averett and Wakulla phase populations shared no ceramic styles across their common style-zone frontier from A.D. 900 to A.D. 1100. Moundville Incised and Cool Branch Incised, the common jar forms of Rood I–III style zones, are found only in very low frequency in some nonmound Averett components (Chase 1963a). Averett Plain, the Averett phase diagnostic ceramic type, is not found at Rood I–III phase centers.

Interestingly, small percentages of Etowah Complicated Stamped ceramics are found in some Averett components (Table 6.1; Chase 1963a). Such a distribution suggests that Averett phase populations were more closely affiliated with peoples some distance north of the Fall Line in the Georgia Piedmont, where contemporary ceramic assemblages are dominated by complicated stamped pottery, than they were to their Rood I–II phase neighbors to the immediate south.

When ceramic type frequencies in the Rood I–III phase and Fort Walton style zones are compared, we note that Wakulla Check Stamped and Fort Walton Incised are majority ceramic types during the Early Fort Walton period, while only present in trace amounts or absent altogether in Rood I–III style zones (Blitz and Lorenz 2002). Conversely, Rood I–III ceramic types such as Cool Branch Incised are present at Early and Middle Fort Walton period sites, but in low frequencies.

Style-zone frontiers between Rood I–III phase centers and the nearest contemporaneous Fort Walton centers were several times larger than the average nearest-neighbor distance between centers in the Rood I–III ceramic style zones. The shorter nearest-neighbor distance between centers within style zones suggests more frequent or open interaction. The longer distances defining the style-zone frontiers were perhaps maintained as buffer zones to discourage raiding by other populations that did not share a collective social identity.

In contrast to utilitarian pottery, the beaker-bottle fine wares have an inter-regional distribution that crosscuts the Rood–Fort Walton style-zone frontiers. The inter-regional distribution of the beaker-bottle fine wares suggests that Rood and Fort Walton elites were linked in possible alliance partnerships or shared an emerging sense of common interests beyond local loyalties.

The relatively low level of stylistic similarity for utilitarian ceramics across style-zone frontiers implies a correspondingly low level of inter-regional social integration for the A.D. 900–1450 time span. When the distributions of mound centers and ceramic style zones are compared, our findings suggest that for some Mississippian societies it was easier to maintain a level of social integration sufficient to produce the spatially extensive ceramic style zones than it was to maintain large-scale political integration. And yet, the presence of Southeastern Ceremonial Complex (SECC) artifacts at the Cemochechobee center and the distinctive style of bottle-beaker fine wares distributed across style-zone frontiers suggest efforts by elites to achieve some form of inter-regional integration. Although we know very little about the political and social implications of these artifacts, there is some basis to propose that these items signaled the owner's aspirations to membership in a panregional elite identity. Unlike utilitarian pottery, these valued artifacts had a symbolic content that transcended local and regional concerns.

After A.D. 1450 in the lower Chattahoochee River region, there was a decline in the scale of political integration marked by a decrease in contemporary mound occupation. The Fort Walton Incised and Lamar Complicated Stamped ceramic types replaced the Rood ceramic types. Unlike the Rood pottery styles, the ceramic traditions of Fort Walton and Lamar can be traced to indigenous, pre-Rood roots in their respective geographical areas of origin beyond the lower Chattahoochee River region. In other words, the style-zone frontiers that had separated the Rood I–III phase populations from their distinct neighbors were removed. It would appear that with the collapse of the Rood polities, the spatial scale of political integration declined and the spatial scale of social integration increased, filling the political void with a cultural fusion of previously separate traditions.

Summary

Theories of style as communication, discussed in Chapter 2, shed light on the social contexts of the fluctuating ceramic style zones and frontiers we have identified. The scale of political and social integration increased in the lower Chattahoochee River region after A.D. 1100. As a result, the need for localized or community-level boundary expression through ceramic style declined, while the need for regional and inter-regional boundary expression increased. At the regional and inter-regional scale, a spatial pattern of utilitarian ceramic style zones signaled a shift toward increased levels of social integration within style zones. The relative homogeneity of utilitarian ceramic styles within style zones indicates that style served to express group similarity or an idealized collective identity.

Although utilitarian ceramic style need not have been employed as an overt message of collective identity, it was probably acknowledged as such at style-zone frontiers, where the marking of boundary distinctions between competitive (and possibly ethnically distinct) groups was easily perceived. Style-zone frontiers were geopolitical spaces where boundary distinctions between populations were emphasized, where barriers to the expansion of social integration were encountered, and where frequent, balanced reciprocal relationships between households ended.

In contrast to an emblemic style of utilitarian ceramics that communicated group status, bottle-beaker fine wares were assertive or iconographic forms of stylistic communication about individual status. Bottle-beaker fine wares were an inter-regional style that signaled the owner's link to the non-local realm of elite concerns. The bottle-beaker style spans the A.D. 1100–1450 time span when the scale of political integration peaked across the Southeast.

Beginning A.D. 1400, the replacement of Rood ceramic types with Fort Walton–Lamar ceramic types signaled a collapse of the old collective social identity associated with the Rood polities and the establishment of a new collective identity for the region. The Singer and Bull Creek phases, composed of utilitarian ceramic types that had been spatially distinct, signaled the breakdown of style as a marker of group boundary distinctions at the regional and inter-regional scale.

The precise social context of the post-A.D. 1400 style replacement remains unclear. Citing theories of style as communication, however, we hypothesize that as the scale of political integration declined, former political barriers to social integration at the inter-regional scale were lifted. Consequently, ceramic styles were more easily transmitted between potters who made utilitarian ceramics, producing the time-transgressive, north-south clinal distributions of such types as Lamar Complicated Stamped and Fort

Walton Incised. A new collective social identity was expressed in new utilitarian ceramic styles. With the decline in the spatial scale of political integration, the old symbols of elite identity no longer had political currency, and the prestige ceramic style zone of the bottle-beaker fine wares disappeared.

7 The Rise and Decline of the Chattahoochee Chiefdoms

Our research presents a unique culture history and yet polity formation, growth, and decline in the lower Chattahoochee region cannot be understood as isolated or particular developments. Similar political and social dynamics unfolded across the Southeast. There are several reasons for this: historically related population movements from ancestral areas of development, widely shared subsistence strategies, organizational patterns common to chiefdoms, and linkage to other populations in interaction spheres. These similarities were the products of cause-and-effect relationships that developed over time at scales larger than sites and regions.

In this chapter we examine the processes of political and social integration identified in the lower Chattahoochee region—polity formation, growth, and decline—from a perspective that encompasses the entire Mississippian world. Because the formation of mound centers after A.D. 1100 coincides with the appearance of a nonlocal cultural tradition in the region, we address the issue of Mississippian origins. It is our contention that many of the initial Mississippian polities throughout much of the middle and lower Southeast were the result of population movements on an expanding frontier. Specifically, we propose that movement into new regions by nonindigenous Mississippian settlers and subsequent competitive interaction with indigenous Woodland peoples was the common way that the first Mississippian polities were established in the lower Chattahoochee region and many other areas.

Next, we argue that the fission-fusion process identified in the lower Chattahoochee region was the principal mechanism of polity formation, growth, and decline throughout the Mississippian world. Not only is the lower Chattahoochee sequence of short-lived, politically unstable mound centers common elsewhere, but the proliferation of multiple-mound centers from A.D. 1200 to A.D. 1400 was synchronous with similar growth-and-decline cycles throughout the Southeast. We propose that polity formation and growth was subsidized by surplus food, labor, and valuables achieved during periods of favorable rainfall, and that drought-induced shortfalls of these resources was an important factor in the abandonment of large, multiple-mound centers in the lower Chattahoochee region and neighboring regions after A.D. 1400. We conclude that the timing of initial Mississippian settlement and the synchronous growth-and-decline trajectories are unitary phenomena when viewed from a panregional perspective.

Mississippian Origins

In the previous chapter we interpreted the Cool Branch site and other Rood I centers as the products of nonlocal Mississippian immigrants. Summarizing evidence presented at length elsewhere (Blitz and Lorenz 2002), we based this conclusion on (1) a regional discontinuity in material culture; Rood ceramic styles and wall-trench house forms have no antecedent developmental forms in the region; (2) Rood site distributions are in an area between Averett and Wakulla site distributions; Rood sites have no evidence of immediately antecedent occupations and thus reveal a demographic discontinuity with indigenous populations in the region; (3) the extraregional source territories for the Rood immigrants, while not precisely known, can be identified as regions to the north and west, based on similarities in material culture and settlement patterns; these Mississippian cultural characteristics appeared first in the source territories, especially in the central Mississippi River valley; and (4) the organizational capabilities of rank society and the ability to erect fortifications is evidence of a logistical advantage that allowed the immigrants to successfully compete with neighboring indigenous populations in the new territory. This evidence satisfies the minimum requirements for demonstrating population movements or "site unit intrusion" with archaeological evidence (cf. Krause 1985; Rouse 1958).

Our explanation for the rise of the Chattahoochee polities addresses an enduring issue: the origin and spread of the Mississippian cultural phenomenon, or what Bruce Smith (1990:1–2) calls the "analogy-homology dilemma." Is Mississippian an analogous process of multiple, local developments due to "independent and isolated cultural responses to similar challenges" (Smith 1990:2)? Or conversely, are Mississippian origins to be understood as a homologous or historically related process of migration or diffusion from core areas of development to new areas? This complex problem is compounded by the multiple meanings of Mississippian as a developmental stage subdivided into time periods (Bense 1994), a form of chiefdom organization (Peebles and Kus 1977), an adaptive or subsistence strategy (Smith 1978), a set of distinctive artifact complexes (Griffin 1967), and a cultural tradition (Caldwell 1958).

We are most concerned here with "Middle Mississippi" (Griffin 1967; Willey and Phillips 1958) or the "Mississippian Tradition" (Caldwell 1958), widely recognized in numerous archaeological cultures, variants, or phases, including the Rood I–III polities. The Middle Mississippi cultural phenomenon is a constellation of associated material and organizational elements: fortified platform mound-plaza site plans, intensified maize horticulture, specific pottery attributes such as globular jars, loop and strap handles, and use of shell temper, wall-trench buildings, a marked increase in the production of stone, copper, and shell valuables, and evidence of rank society and chiefdom political organization (Griffin 1985; Scarry 1996). Middle Mississippi sites are distributed from the central Mississippi River valley, east and south across portions the American Midwest and Southeast (Griffin 1967: Figure 5).

Following Jenkins (2003), we distinguish between emergent Mississippian and terminal Woodland. Emergent Mississippian is the autochthonous development of the Middle Mississippi cultural tradition from local, antecedent Late Woodland populations in the central Mississippi River valley from A.D. 800 to A.D. 1000 (i.e., Kelly 2000). Terminal Woodland refers to Late Woodland populations that interacted with an intrusive Middle Mississippi tradition. This latter process of culture contact is sometimes referred to as "Mississippianization" (Cobb and Garrow 1996:21–22; Pauketat 2004:119–120).

In a vigorous promotion of the analogy explanation, Smith (1984:30) contended "the development of the Mississippian cultural tradition took place relatively simultaneously over a wide geographic area, making local development a more reasonable interpretive framework than site unit intrusion." This statement is untenable given current archaeological evidence. In a study of the spread of Mississippian, David Anderson (1999:226) maps a time-transgressive west-to-east appearance of chiefdoms in the Midwest and Southeast. According to Anderson, chiefdoms are earliest at A.D. 900 in the Missouri "boot heel" and American Bottom regions of the central Mississippi River valley, appear in western Kentucky, western Tennessee, and northeastern Arkansas by A.D. 950, spread to southwestern Indiana, most of Arkansas, central Kentucky and Tennessee, northern Mississippi and western Alabama by A.D. 1000, and parts of the Atlantic Coastal Plain by A.D. 1200. Although Anderson (1999:225, 227) minimizes population movement as a causal factor, he concludes that it is likely that chiefdoms first arose in the central Mississippi River valley "and spread through a process of both competitive emulation and defensive reaction" (Anderson 1999:225).

Anderson's map is intended to show "the spread of chiefdoms," but it closely charts the spread of the Middle Mississippi tradition, a time-transgressive pattern in the distribution of sites with a similar material culture that supports the homology scenario. In addition to chiefdom organization, many of the cultural elements identified with Middle Mississippi—wall-trench architecture, specific vessel forms, and maize intensification—have antecedents in emergent Mississippian populations in the central Mississippi River valley (Anderson 1997:263–264; Blitz and Lorenz 2002:124–125). For example, wall-trench architecture appears by A.D. 1050 at American Bottom Mississippian sites (Pauketat 2004:82). Globular, collared jars and use of shell temper are present by A.D. 600–900 in southeastern Missouri (Lafferty and Price 1996). Maize intensification was under way by A.D. 800 in the emergent Mississippian populations of the American Bottom region (Fritz 1992). These distinctive Middle Mississippi cultural materials and practices are not found farther east and south until at least 50 to 100 years later.

Least readers accuse us of reifying Middle Mississippi, we only wish to highlight temporal-spatial patterns in the material signatures of this heuristic concept. Earlier researchers readily recognized these cultural elements over a large geographical area, but better dating methods now reveal time-transgressive patterns. We emphasize that there need not be single origins for any one trait. Our point is that these cultural materials and practices are oldest in the central Mississippi River valley, first coalesced into the Mississippian way of life at early centers such as Cahokia (Pauketat 2004), and are absent in locales to the east and south until later in time, when the initial Middle Mississippi variants appear in these regions.

As others have, we see a "Mississippian radiation" out from centers of emergent Mississippian development in the central Mississippi River valley, accomplished primarily through population movement (Caldwell 1958). Beyond the area of emergent Mississippian centers, local phases of the Middle Mississippi tradition are very similar over a geographically extensive area, but typically exhibit radical discontinuities in material culture and organization with indigenous Late Woodland populations.

Indeed, convincing evidence of in situ Late Woodland to Middle Mississippi developmental sequences is lacking in the many areas beyond the central Mississippi River valley where regional Middle Mississippi variants and phases are found: portions of Illinois (Delaney-Rivera 2004; Emerson 1991), southern Wisconsin and western Missouri (Stoltman 2000), southeastern Indiana (Hilgeman 2000), central and eastern Tennessee (Faulkner

1975), northeastern Arkansas (Morse 1977), northern Mississippi (Brain 1989; Williams and Brain 1983), all of Alabama (Jenkins 2003), central Georgia (Williams 1994), and parts of northern Florida (Scarry 1996).

Evidence, in the form of overlapping radiocarbon dates and ceramics of different traditions found in direct association, reveals that indigenous Late Woodland populations coexisted with Middle Mississippians in Alabama (Jenkins 2003), Georgia (King 2003), northern Mississippi (Brain 1989), Tennessee (Faulkner 1975), northern Florida (Blitz and Lorenz 2002), Illinois (Delaney-Rivera 2004; Emerson 1991) and Wisconsin (Stoltman 2000). In the cases cited above, Middle Mississippi cultural elements are found as additions to local Late Woodland assemblages (terminal Woodland, in Jenkins's terminology), or exist as spatially distinct sites that are contemporary with local Late Woodland sites. Coexistence was brief, however, as Middle Mississippi replaced local Late Woodland traditions in a time-transgressive pattern much like Anderson's map of the spread of chiefdoms. Population movement into new regions beyond the emergent Mississippian centers of development is implicated in the rapid replacement of antecedent cultural patterns.

There is a core-periphery spatial pattern to the spread of Mississippian. The Middle Mississippi tradition is distributed as a centrally located core area (i.e., central Mississippi River valley, lower Midwest, middle South, upper Gulf Coastal Plain) while on the geographic periphery (i.e., lower Mississippi River valley, portions of the lower Gulf Coastal Plain, Piedmont, and Atlantic Coastal Plain) are found the "regional traditions," variously referred to as South Appalachian Mississippian, Plaquemine Mississippian, Fort Walton Mississippian, and others (Caldwell 1958:Figure 13; Griffin 1967:Figure 5). In contrast to the cultural discontinuity, brief coexistence, and replacement that is characteristic of the terminal Late Woodland–Mississippian transition found in many locales of the Middle Mississippi core area, the regional traditions are characterized by an indigenous cultural and demographic continuity, especially continuity in material culture such as ceramic forms and decoration. Some populations in these peripheral regional traditions, such as Coles Creek (lower Mississippi River valley) and Napier/Woodstock (northern Georgia) archaeological cultures, had platform mound centers and were possibly pre-Mississippian chiefdoms formed by localized or indigenous developments (e.g., Cobb and Garrow 1996; Kidder 2002; Little 1999; Pluckhahn 1996). In other peripheral regional traditions, however, interaction and competition with Middle Mississippi populations is implicated in the creation of chiefdoms (e.g., Blitz and Lorenz 2002:130–131).

Anderson (1999:225, 227), while not ruling out population movements, suggests that the "cultural emulation and defensive reaction" motivation for chiefdom formation spread by diffusion through Late Woodland populations. If adoption of chiefdom organization were a matter of survival and resistance, it would not take 150 years to diffuse to the peripheral regions. If the spread of chiefdoms is to be explained primarily by diffusion or cultural borrowing, then we have a puzzle. Why, with the initial appearance of chiefdoms in the Middle Mississippi core area, were indigenous Late Woodland cultural traditions rapidly abandoned and replaced by the Middle Mississippi tradition, whereas when chiefdoms formed in the peripheral areas of the regional traditions, populations retained their indigenous house forms, ceramic traditions, and the like? Indeed, we doubt that this complex form of political organization could be transmitted through long-distance diffusion.

Chiefdoms appear in the core area at the same time as other Middle Mississippi cultural characteristics. As others have before us, we consider the Middle Mississippi core area beyond the central Mississippi River valley area of initial emergence and coalescence to represent the geographical expansion, settlement, and successful displacement or absorption of Late Woodland indigenous populations. Chiefdom formation in some areas, especially at the core-periphery interface, probably resulted from Anderson's "cultural emulation and defensive reaction," and resistance to expanding Middle Mississippi populations. Rather than change effected through long-distance diffusion, a more direct, localized, and ongoing contact is implicated.

It is important to remember that the analogy scenario of Mississippian emergence gained favor with the rise of processual archaeology in the 1970s. Mississippian chiefdom formation was attributed to stresses in local population-resource imbalances, resolved by agricultural intensification and organizational innovations, and conceived as a neoevolutionary stage of development out of local precursors. Thus the analogy scenario had to be argued, but this theoretical orientation created blind spots. To summarize our specific arguments against the analogy scenario:

(1) If the Mississippian cultural tradition were created by analogous causes, there would be a random spatial pattern of multiple core areas of development. Instead, the time-transgressive mapping of Middle Mississippi and the spread of chiefdoms reveal a pattern that is directional and not simultaneous.

(2) There is no evidence of simultaneous population growth and density climaxes in Late Woodland populations as expected in the analogy scenario (Anderson 1999:225). Late Woodland population densities are regionally variable and unevenly distributed (Nassaney and Cobb 1991).

(3) The chance of multiple origins for such a distinctive set of material culture traits as found in the Middle Mississippi tradition is very unlikely.

(4) There are radical material culture and settlement discontinuities throughout the Middle Mississippi core, not the continuities expected in the analogy scenario.

(5) There is evidence of Middle Mississippi coexistence and interaction with terminal Late Woodland populations throughout the core area; these archaeological cultures are not sequential developmental stages that changed gradually one into the other as interpreted in the analogy scenario.

In sum, we attribute the time-transgressive pattern for the appearance of initial Middle Mississippi polities across a large area of the Eastern Woodlands to population movements from emergent centers of development (homology), with subsequent displacement or absorption of indigenous Late Woodland populations ("Mississippianization"). Chiefdoms in peripheral regional traditions such as South Appalachian Mississippian and Fort Walton may have originated from analogous causes rooted in local material and social conditions, but these developments were augmented by homologous factors introduced through direct contact and competition with Middle Mississippi. Such circumstances are instances of secondary chiefdom formation: chiefdom formation as the result of contact with a preexisting chiefdom. Thus, on closer inspection, the analogy-homology dichotomy dissolves into a more complex history of uneven development, culture contact, and subsequent interaction (Cobb and Garrow 1996; Pauketat 2004:124–141).

The Mississippian Frontier

We are not proposing that a single migratory wave swept over the Southeast as some earlier advocates of site-unit intrusion theory once proposed. Instead, an expanding frontier of self-sufficient horticulturalists engaged in repetitive small-scale population movements is the best explanation for Anderson's time-transgressive map of chiefdom formation. We invoke the fission-fusion model of Mississippian polity development as the mechanism of population dispersal from centers of emergent Mississippian development in the central Mississippi River valley. We propose that as early Mississippian centers in western Illinois, Kentucky, and Tennessee grew in size, factionalism increased, which was resolved by fission into smaller daughter populations. These daughter populations moved along an expanding Mississippian frontier to found new mound centers with their factional leaders as chief.

Although the production of immigrants by polity fission need not suppose "population pressure," it does imply a significant rate and scale of population growth. It has long been recognized that a steady population increase occurred in areas of emergent Mississippian development (Kelly 1990:143). By A.D. 1050 growth peaked in the powerful Cahokia polity, with population estimates that range from 8,000 to over 150,000, then declined through subsequent decades due, in part, to emigration (Pauketat 2004:107, 120). The Cahokia growth-and-decline cycle was of a scale sufficient to disseminate ideas, products, and people over a large area of the Mississippian core and contribute directly to "Mississippianization" (Anderson 1997:259–264; Pauketat 2004:124–141).

If one envisions this growth-and-fission process continuing for another 100–200 years, we can easily explain the time-transgressive west-to-east spread of mound centers with evidence of the shared material culture that Pauketat, Anderson, and other archaeologists have recognized. Only short-distance moves, perhaps to an adjacent river valley, were required to produce the dispersal pattern. A common heritage and some degree of continuing contact with the parent population from whence they originated was sufficient to produce the spatial pattern we see: far-flung settlement clusters more similar to each other in material culture and organizational practices than to the indigenous populations that were already there. This scenario best fits the available archaeological evidence across large portions of the Southeast for the A.D. 1050–1200 interval, when the prevailing pattern was that of competing small polities centered on single-mound centers.

Mississippian origins in the lower Chattahoochee region fit these larger patterns. The Rood I phase is a Middle Mississippi variant, part of the historically related process of population movements on the Mississippian frontier. Averett represents a coexisting indigenous population. Rood and Averett sites are distributed as adjacent but spatially segregated territories along the river. It is not known if construction of Averett mounds at the Kyle and Abercrombie sites is an analogous development of a mound-center polity or an example of the emulation and defense reaction to the Rood newcomers, but Averett populations clearly resisted adoption of other Mississippian cultural elements. Averett populations retained their indigenous ceramic tradition and there is little evidence of interaction other than trace quantities of Rood phase ceramics at Averett sites.

Growth and Decline of Mississippian Polities

Like initial Mississippian polity formation, panregional events and processes shaped the growth and decline of Mississippian polities. From A.D. 1200 to A.D. 1400, large multiple-mound centers formed in various regions of the Southeast, including along the lower Chattahoochee River. In some areas, when these large centers appear, there are fewer single-mound centers across the landscape, as if the smaller centers were being abandoned in favor of relocation to multiple-mound centers (Blitz 1999; Clay 1997). During this time span, the SECC inter-regional artifact styles circulated across polity and social boundaries, linked with elite personages in their archaeological contexts. After A.D. 1400, numerous large centers across the Southeast went into decline or were abandoned altogether, and production of the SECC artifacts ceased (Anderson 1994:136–137). Once again, the lower Chattahoochee River region mirrors this widespread pattern. What accounts for the rapid and apparently synchronous growth and contraction of political and social integration from A.D. 1200 to A.D. 1450 in the lower Chattahoochee valley and neighboring regions?

In a study of Mississippian political change, King argues that, "anything that impacts the production of a surplus, a leader's ability to mobilize surplus, a leader's ability to perform his/her specified duties for society, or the ideological structures that justify the leader's position and ability to mobilize surplus has the potential to bring about political change" (King 2003:22). Several factors identified by King—ideology, factional competition, polity interaction, environment, population—must be considered as interacting variables that can enhance or detract from a leader's roles and responsibilities. We turn now to the archaeological record in an attempt to assess how these factors may have impacted the polity growth and decline pattern in the lower Chattahoochee River region and elsewhere in the Mississippian world.

Ideology, Factional Competition, and Polity Interaction

As was the case with initial polity formation, the fission-fusion process shaped polity growth and decline. While local demographic growth after initial Mississippian settlement is certainly implicated, polity growth and the rapid creation of multiple-mound centers required the fusion of mound-political units through alliance and resettlement. Defense and participation in the production and distribution of surpluses were likely motivations for mound-political groups to unite and create large centers. Increased ceremonials and rites of intensification, such as mound building and feasting, would have served the cause of political integration while keeping factionalism in check.

Explanations for the growth and decline of the large multiple-mound centers during the A.D. 1200–1400 interval must address the concurrent growth and decline of the SECC prestige goods. Models of chiefdom political economy view control over the production and distribution of prestige goods as an important source of political power (Earle 1997). Prestige goods and the nonlocal materials used to produce them were exchanged through interaction networks. Mississippian elites participated in these networks to gain access to the symbols used to express and manipulate the ideological underpinnings of their authority (King 2003). As social differentiation increased, so would the demand for valuables and prestige goods as validations of rank and status. If the production and distribution of SECC prestige goods aided the expansion of political integration by linking elites into interaction spheres, then the growth of certain centers might be fueled by a strategic geographical location that conferred advantages in the exchange network (Kelly 1991). Conversely, loss of access to the SECC prestige goods would weaken authority and contribute to the destabilization or even collapse of Mississippian polities (Welch 1991).

If Mississippian polity growth of the A.D. 1200–1400 period was fueled by a political economy based on the diversion of surplus food, labor, and valuables to status enhancement, then polity decline and the abandonment of large mound centers ca. A.D. 1400 might be due to shortfalls in these critical resources. In Chapter 5, factionalism and local resource depletion were identified as potential causes of the sequential movements between nearby centers. Factionalism, tied to generational or succession conflicts, and resource depletion, based on wood or soil depletion, would be expected to increase with time and population growth. These factors alone, however, cannot explain the widespread and nearly synchronous abandonment of multiple-mound centers across large portions of the Mississippian world ca. A.D. 1400 (Anderson 1999). A more pervasive factor, such as environmental change, may be at work.

Environmental Change

Anderson et al. (1995) analyzed cypress tree-ring growth patterns dating to A.D. 1000–1600 in the Savannah River valley of South Carolina and Georgia. It was discovered that periods of high rainfall correlated with the spread and growth of chiefdoms in the valley, while periods of low rainfall were associated with large-scale mound-center abandonment. To summarize, the period from A.D. 1152 to A.D. 1200 had favorable rainfall amounts with few shortfalls. The first half of the 1200s was less productive, with shortfalls in 16 of 50 years. The longest continuous span of favorable rainfall occurred from A.D. 1251 to A.D. 1358, when multiple-mound centers proliferated across the Southeast and the SECC artifacts were produced. The span of near-constant crop surplus was followed by a highly stressful 20-year period from A.D. 1359 to A.D. 1377 when 12 of 19 years would have experienced crop shortages. In the Savannah River valley, this period correlated with the large-scale abandonment of several single-mound and multiple-mound centers. An even more devastating drought period occurred from A.D. 1407 to A.D. 1476, with near continuous crop failure from A.D. 1469 to A.D. 1476, an interval correlated with abandonment of multiple-mound centers and depopulation of much of the valley.

Due to the lack of comparable studies, it is not known if the climate changes identified in the Savannah River study occurred in the lower Chattahoochee river region or elsewhere in the Southeast. It is known that appearance and spread of Mississippian polities took place during the Medieval Warming period of A.D. 1100–1300, an episode of wetter, warmer weather in the Northern Hemisphere (Lamb 1984). Subsequently, the widespread decline of the multiple-mound centers after A.D. 1400 occurred during the Little Ice Age, a period of cooler weather from A.D. 1450 to A.D. 1850 (Stahle and Cleaveland 1994). These pervasive climate episodes are consistent with the results of the Savannah River study and imply that similar climate-change patterns were widespread. One need not promote environmental determinism to acknowledge that climate change may have influenced people's decisions and impacted their abilities to expand political and social integration. Assuming that mobilization of surpluses fueled polity growth, rainfall patterns could create social opportunities or constrains for growth, and either enhance or detract from a leader's ability to mobilize surpluses (Anderson et al. 1995:272).

A Model for Mississippian Polity Growth and Decline

Let us propose a model for the impact of good-year surpluses and bad-year shortfalls on Mississippian polity growth and decline for the years A.D. 1200 to A.D. 1450. The model must also link subsistence shortfalls to the boom-and-bust pattern of SECC prestige-goods exchange. In periods of high rainfall, larger crop yields could sustain greater numbers of people in residence at a center. Surpluses could be mobilized by leaders for feasting and hosting visiting elites from neighboring polities. Alliances between polities within a river valley could have been cemented by prestige-good exchange and elite marriage, creating kinship ties between polities and allies for support in times of need. As social integration expanded at the regional scale, we would expect shared ceramic styles between nearby allied centers as collective social identities were expressed. At the inter-regional scale, a prestige-goods network, such as the SECC inter-regional styles, would best maintain polity alliances. More inter-regional alliances between mound centers would reduce the frequency of warfare. Thus, when rainfall was adequate, polities grew in size and political integration expanded in scale.

The opposite climatic scenario, extended drought periods leading to continual harvest shortfalls, could destabilize polities dependent on surpluses to subsidize political and social integration. The first impact of reduced maize surpluses would have been a reduction in a polity's ability to support a given population size. Horticultural population sizes are limited by the maximum number of people that can be supported during successive drought years when crop production does not meet population demands. To maintain large support populations in time of drought, leaders would have to find some way to supplement crop yields or face losing supporters through fission and dispersal. One solution would be to seek subsistence support from neighboring centers, but if the drought were widespread, neighboring polities would be unwilling or unable to help.

Another solution to drought-induced shortfalls would be appeals to the supernatural, with the required increases in community ceremonials. To achieve ceremonial goals, demands on household production would intensify at a time when the local support population had little to offer. As a consequence, leaders would have less surplus foods available to finance feasts and participate in the SECC prestige-good network. If alliance networks were no longer maintained, the SECC prestige goods would no longer be distributed as tokens of alliance, and marriageable spouses would no longer be exchanged between centers, thus removing the "social glue" that obligates affinal kin in different polities to support one another (Chagnon 1997:145). As alliance-exchange systems collapsed, we would expect evidence of an escalation in regional warfare between polities to supplement crop shortfalls with demands of tribute.

Consequently, the sociopolitical system would undergo rapid change as mound-political units abandoned multiple-mound centers and dispersed at a time when polity leaders needed their support. With alliance-exchange collapse, we would expect to see a dramatic decline in the presence of exotic goods encoded with SECC symbolism, a devaluing of the attendant elite ideology, and a reordering of the social boundaries marked by ceramic style zones. The dispersal of mound-political units from the large centers would produce new single-mound centers with different collective identities and none of the prestige-good symbols of a discredited elite ideology.

Lower Chattahoochee Polity Growth and Decline

The timing of mound center growth and decline in the lower Chattahoochee River region correlates with the timing of the Savannah River climate changes and with polity growth and decline patterns in surrounding regions. Multiple-mound centers formed at Moundville, Lake Jackson, and at Cemochechobee in lower Chattahoochee River regions ca. A.D. 1200. The appearance of multiple-mound centers at this time fell at the end of a long period of favorable rainfall. The span from A.D. 1200 to A.D. 1250 was marked by 16 drought years, apparently not severe enough to curtail growth. In northwestern Georgia, however, the Etowah site was abandoned from A.D. 1200 to A.D. 1250. During the A.D. 1250–1375 span of high rainfall, Etowah was reoccupied, and grew into a powerful polity. King (2003:124) argues that from A.D. 1250 to A.D. 1375, networking elites at the powerful Etowah center exchanged copper symbols for marine shell artifacts from Florida centers such as Lake Jackson, via an "SECC exchange corridor" through the lower Chattahoochee River valley.

Inter-regional styles found at lower Chattahoochee mound centers from A.D. 1200 to A.D. 1400 suggest links to specific polities. The bottle-beaker fine wares discussed in Chapter 6, while not encoded with SECC symbols, are found at Lake Jackson (John Scarry, personal communication, 2000) and Moundville (Steponaitis 1983:327–328). A headdress of copper arrows at Cemochechobee is an SECC style also found at Moundville, but not at Etowah or Lake Jackson (Brain and Phillips 1996:372–373). Clay smoking pipes of the punctated-bound style are found at Etowah, Lake Jackson, and several lower Chattahoochee centers, including Cemochechobee (Brain and Phillips 1996:382). Cemochechobee (A.D. 1200–1300) and Rood's Landing (A.D. 1300–1400), on the main channel of the river, were well placed to play a role in this interaction sphere. Like Etowah and Lake Jackson, most of the mound building at Rood's Landing dates to the 100-year period of crop surpluses and the rise of network-oriented multiple-mound centers across Georgia and the interior Southeast. At this same time, the Singer-Moye mound center appears to have been reoccupied and mound building escalated. Moreover, Etowah/Savannah Complicated Stamped ceramics appear at Singer-Moye in sufficient quantities to suggest possible alliance-exchange relationships with Etowah or related centers to the north or east. Based on these lines of evidence, the lower Chattahoochee polities, Lake Jackson, Etowah, and Moundville were probably linked in an inter-regional interaction sphere from A.D. 1200 to A.D. 1400.

While large populations were supported during the high-rainfall, high-surplus years of A.D. 1251–1358, the true population threshold was closer to the numbers of people that could be supported during the successive drought years of A.D. 1359–1377 and A.D. 1407–1476. The impact of successive years of crop shortfalls between A.D. 1359–1377 and A.D. 1407–1476 would have been devastating to polities whose growth was dependent on crop surpluses and alliance-exchange networks. Abandonment of the Etowah, Lake Jackson, Rood's Landing, and Singer-Moye centers, and decline in the circulation of SECC goods all appear to fall into the A.D. 1375–1450 span of severe drought and surplus shortfalls.

King (2003:126–131) attributes a rise in conflict to the decline in the SECC inter-regional style and abandonment at Etowah about A.D. 1375, which in turn led to a decentralization of multiple-mound centers into the single-mound centers common in the Lamar archaeological culture. In the Savannah River valley, fortifications were prevalent at sites during the late 1300s to mid-1400s, followed by abandonment of large centers and depopulation (Anderson 1994:242–245). Lake Jackson was abandoned sometime around A.D. 1450 (Payne 1994). At Moundville, SECC artifacts were no longer used by A.D. 1450, and the resident population was small (Knight and Steponaitis 1998:19–20). Even beyond these regions, the A.D. 1375–1450 interval was a time when many of the largest Mississippian mound centers were abandoned or suffered significant depopulation: Kincaid, Illinois (Cobb and Butler 2002:627); Angel, Indiana (Hilgemon 2000:227–230); Wickliffe, Kentucky (Wesler 2001:148); Winterville and Lake George, Mississippi (Brain 1978:351–352); Rembert and Mason's Plantation, Georgia (Anderson 1994:242); and other sites.

Singer-Moye, situated in an upland area away from the river, continued to be occupied after the abandonment of Rood's Landing until the mid-fifteenth century when it too was abandoned. Similar settlement pattern shifts away from the main river channel to headwater areas in the Savannah and Etowah river valleys (Anderson 1994:245, 311; King 2003:131–132) suggest a desire to avoid attack by raiders moving along river routes. Following Singer-Moye's abandonment, brief occupations appeared at the single-mound centers of Lampley, Shorter, and Omussee Creek. The ceramic tradition of the earlier era was now gone, replaced by Lamar and Fort Walton styles derived from outside the region. The post-A.D. 1450 centers show no evidence of prestige goods imbued with an inter-regional style. The old order was gone, replaced by a new collective identity, different social boundaries, and a reduced scale of political integration.

8   Research Synopsis and
        Theory Synthesis

In the preceding pages we addressed some fundamental issues in the development of complex society in the ancient American Southeast. As a research strategy, models of sociopolitical organization were evaluated with evidence generated through archaeological excavations. Our research goal was to identify forms and scales of political and social integration in the lower Chattahoochee River region during the interval from A.D. 1100 to A.D. 1650 as a case study of sociopolitical change and variation in Mississippian rank societies.

Taking a regional perspective, we focused on mound sites, the central places of polities. The number of same-period mounds at centers and the distances between same-period centers provided measures of polity complexity, hierarchy, and territory, and allowed us to trace polity forms and boundaries through time. By mapping the spatial extent of mound centers with shared ceramic styles for a series of time periods, we identified ceramic style zones and style-zone frontiers, distributional patterns that identify collective social identities and measure the scale of social integration. We proposed that the expansion and contraction of political and social integration in the study area was driven by a complex interplay of social and environmental factors such as population movement, the mobilization of surpluses, polity interaction, and climate change. An interpretive synopsis of the research findings is now in order.

Research Synopsis

From A.D. 900 to A.D. 1100, there were no mound-center polities in the lower Chattahoochee River region. The Averett and Wakulla ceramic phases, products of indigenous populations without evidence of social ranking, have distinct styles with continuity from antecedent pottery traditions. From A.D. 1100 to A.D. 1200, peoples of nonlocal origin settled in the vacant frontier between the Averett and Wakulla territories. The immigrants established at least three polities marked by mound centers. The newcomer's pottery styles (Rood I phase), architecture, fortifications, and other artifacts had no regional precedent, but faithfully replicated a regional variant of Middle Mississippi material culture previously established elsewhere. At the Mandeville site, the Mississippian settlers refurbished an abandoned Middle Woodland mound in an apparent attempt to assert a link to the past and bolster the legitimacy of territorial claims.

Indigenous populations reacted to the Mississippian pioneers by unprecedented moves toward political integration. Averett populations constructed the Kyle mound center far removed from the closest Rood I center. The Averett–Rood I frontier was relatively impermeable to shared styles, most likely an indication of an antagonistic relationship. Farther south, Wakulla-derived Early Fort Walton populations created mound-center polities on the Apalachicola River. The low frequency of ceramic types shared between Rood I and Early Fort Walton centers suggests a closed frontier between hostile, mutually distancing populations.

During the A.D. 1200–1400 interval, descendents of the Mississippian founding population abandoned some original centers and founded new ones. Climate data from elsewhere in Georgia suggest that high-rainfall conditions from A.D. 1251 to A.D. 1359 favored mobilization of surpluses by elites to support larger populations and polity interaction. Regional political integration accelerated with the establishment of the multiple-mound Cemochechobee center. Participation in the inter-regional exchange of SECC goods reflected the desire of emergent elites for access to panregional symbols that legitimated claims to authority. Regional leaders capitalized on a middleman position in an alliance-exchange network that linked them to other elites at Etowah, Moundville, and Lake Jackson.

Indigenous Averett populations had a single-mound polity at Abercrombie until A.D. 1300, when the Northern zone was abandoned. Unlike Rood I–II phase pottery styles, many Averett ceramic assemblages have complicated stamped pottery, a utilitarian style shared with mound-center polities in the upper Chattahoochee and Etowah river valleys. The Averett affiliation with northern Georgia polities may represent either a shared cultural heritage or a more expedient alliance in response to the threat from nearby Rood I–II polities.

With Averett populations gone and no occupied centers in the Northern zone, regional political and social integration peaked in Rood III times, A.D. 1300–1400. For the first time, polities in the lower Chattahoochee River region shared a single ceramic style zone. The Rood II–III phase utilitarian ceramic styles had a distinctive regional cast, yet continuity in form and decoration with the transported tradition of the founding pioneers was still evident. The multiple-mound polities of Rood's Landing and Singer-Moye, and the single-mound Omussee Creek polity shared this social identity, yet remained politically independent of one another.

Social segments that composed the polities found it to their advantage to concentrate at large centers, a strategy that may have conferred a distinct advantage in the inter-regional competition for SECC goods and other resources. The founding of the Omussee Creek polity in the Southern zone may represent a social segment that hived off from a preexisting center, not to found a subordinate administrative center, but to establish a strategic middleman location in the vacant Southern zone of the SECC exchange corridor. Such high-risk moves may have been attractive to leaders who wished to enhance their position in the exchange network.

The Rood II–III ceramic phases and the Middle Fort Walton polities to the south had distinct ceramic style zones. In contrast to the low-level sharing of a few utilitarian ceramic types, a set of highly decorated beakers and bottles bridged the utilitarian style-zone frontier to create a prestige ceramic style zone. Like the SECC goods, the beaker-bottle fine ware was an inter-regional style, possession of which sent a stylistic "message" that one was a person of means with connections beyond the local domain.

The A.D. 1359–1475 period was a time of drought-induced shortfalls in crop surpluses elsewhere in Georgia, and perhaps these effects were felt in the lower Chattahoochee River region. With the reduced ability to mobilize surpluses, the scale of mound building lessened and multiple-mound centers lost population or were abandoned across Piedmont Georgia and neighboring areas (Anderson 1994:326; King 2003:129). From A.D. 1375 to A.D. 1450, the Etowah and Lake Jackson sites were abandoned and the powerful Moundville center was depopulated (King 2003:Figure 19; Knight and Steponaitis 1998:19–20; Scarry 1999:68). Coincident with widespread polity decline was a dramatic curtailment in SECC production and exchange (Anderson 1999:223). With the collapse of the inter-regional SECC exchange, the lower Chattahoochee polities underwent dramatic political and social changes.

At the beginning of the fifteenth century, Rood's Landing and Omussee Creek were abandoned as political power (and possibly social segments) shifted to the multiple-mound polity of Singer-Moye and a new single-mound polity at Gary's Fish Pond. A reorientation in social integration was signaled by the replacement of previous pottery styles by new styles with antecedents outside the valley: the Fort Walton Incised and Lamar Complicated Stamped ceramic types. The continuation of the Lamar Plain ceramic type from Rood III suggests that this shift to a fusion of two foreign ceramic styles was not simply a population replacement but an adoption of new social identities by descendants of the old social order. The Singer-Moye site's unusual interfluvial location at the eastern edge of the region may have conferred some as yet unknown advantage during this time of political and social transition.

Between A.D. 1450 and A.D. 1550, a new round of mound-center abandonment and foundation ensued. The Singer-Moye polity collapsed and only single-mound centers were present. While Fort Walton Incised was the majority decorated ceramic type throughout the valley, Lamar Complicated Stamped was more popular in the Central zone, where centers were closer to the growing power of polities in northern and central Georgia where Lamar pottery styles were dominant. Abandoned mounds at Shorter and Omussee Creek were reoccupied, and then abandoned once more, suggesting that the lower Chattahoochee River region had become an open frontier with unconsolidated political and social integration. Reoccupation of old centers replaced construction of new centers as social segments attempted to revitalize a fragmented political and social order by reusing old monuments of authority in a mythic landscape of abandoned centers. The last mound center was abandoned about A.D. 1650 or slightly later, as populations composed of culturally disparate social groups forged new strategies of political and social integration to create the early-historic-period Creek Confederacy.

Throughout the sequence outlined above, political and social integration were clearly related processes, but exhibit different temporal and spatial patterns. Political integration was unstable, and remained decentralized at the regional level. A primary-secondary center polity indicative of complex chiefdoms never developed. Leaders at the Chattahoochee centers participated in alliance-exchange with distant polities, acquiring the panregional status symbols of a short-lived elite identity. This construction of elite identity was an attempt to extend political integration beyond polity boundaries, but such efforts could not be sustained due to unpredictable surplus deficiencies and factional competition. The same fission-fusion process that undermined the establishment of a unified regional polity ensured that social segments with a shared social identity could expand social integration to the regional level and beyond. Yet collective social identities were not immune to rapid replacement by new identities.

Theory Synthesis

Although our study revealed a culture history specific to the lower Chattahoochee region, comparable and related patterns of culture process occurred in neighboring regions. Our findings can form the basis for new theories of Mississippian political and social integration applicable throughout the Mississippian world. We are not proposing an explanation of how and why chiefdoms first emerged in the southeastern United States; the lower Chattahoochee study has more to say about the subsequent reproduction, geographical spread, diversification, and decline of chiefly polities. Nor do we wish to ignore the insights provided by the simple-complex chiefdom cycle model altogether. However, the simple-complex chiefdom cycle model emphasizes hegemonic, hierarchical, and gradual processes that do not account for the diversity of Mississippian polity forms or the continuous reformation and movement of their constituent political and social segments. The results of our study lead us to propose an alternative interpretive framework that accommodates rapid, punctuated change, and places the diverse polity forms identified in the study in a dynamic historical perspective. The new theory synthesis incorporates four concepts: (1) the fission-fusion process of segmentary organization, (2) a frontier model for the geographical spread and chronological replication of polities, (3) the production of social memory through the use of platform mounds, and (4) the interplay between environmental change and polity growth and decline. Other southeastern archaeologists have already laid the foundation for these models, and we draw on their work below.

The polity fission-fusion process is a better fit with the settlement pattern and ceramic-style nuances of the study region. Two aspects of the fission-fusion process facilitated rapid change and polity diversity: segmentary lineage organization and population movement. It is assumed that the societies in question had a kin-based segmentary organization in which lineages were grouped into larger corporate units based on concepts of common descent (Anderson 1994:87–93; Knight 1990a). Segmentary lineages can fission or come together to create organizations capable of defense or expansion into new territory (Sahlins 1961). Although Sahlins considered segmentary lineage organization to be characteristic of tribal social formations, it is found in more complex societies, where polities grow through the successively larger grouping of like segments bound together by kinship and ever-shifting degrees of political authority (Fox 1987; Southall 1956). Segmentary organization permits these redundant social units to form vertical hierarchies or horizontal heterarchies in short-term response to shifting internal and external circumstances (Fortes 1953:32–38). Because lineages compete for political authority, no one segment can maintain dominance for very long, which creates an inherent political instability resolved through fissioning (Southall 1956:257). Fissioning of social segments is accomplished by population movement, which directly produced the periodic mound-center foundation, abandonment, and reoccupation patterns detected in the study region and elsewhere.

Several archaeologists have proposed that Kopytoff's (1987) Internal African Frontier model is applicable to Mississippian societies, offering what we see as a means of expanding the theoretical scope of the fission-fusion process (Blitz and Lorenz 2002:120; King 2003:118–119). Kopytoff marshaled ethnographic and historic data to explain why similar social institutions were distributed over an enormous geographical area of Africa. In a repetitive historical process of social construction, alienated or dispossessed social groups seeking new advantages become settlers on a frontier that is "internal" or in-between the core areas of population nucleation from whence they came. Contrary to Fredrick Jackson Turner's famous thesis that frontiers create a new culture, Kopytoff (1987:10–11) sees the African frontier as an "institutional vacuum" into which frontiersmen carry a cultural inventory or blueprint brought from the mature core. Once in the institutional vacuum of the frontier, the conservative cultural blueprint is constantly revitalized by continued interaction between mature core and frontier periphery and replicated in new frontiers.

A requirement of this process of social construction and reproduction is that new frontier communities be politically independent of the mature core, which has a "limitation of power by distance" (Kopytoff 1987:28). Spatially and temporally, concentric patterns of older core polities and new frontier polities emerge. "Hence, the frontier could become a stage for the emergence of numerous new, small-scale, and independent political formations . . . some of which grew into new polities that provided the nucleus for the emergence of new societies" (Kopytoff 1987:10–11).

Applied to the ancient American Southeast, a frontier model can explain the geographical spread of the Mississippian phenomenon, the development of regional Mississippian variants, and why political and social integration often exhibit different temporal and spatial scales. Key elements of the frontier process have already been presented in this study, from the fission dynamics that ejected frontiersmen from larger groups, to the "movement in groups" with "pre-existing social models" into new territories and once there, the need to attract additional social segments, or fusion (Kopytoff 1987:16–17). Kopytoff's frontier process also contains an explanation for the ranking of social segments according to a "firstcomers and latecomers" principle in which high rank, privilege, and the exercise of authority was legitimated by claims of first-use rights by founding first comers. This senior-junior ranking rationale is well documented in southeastern ethnohistorical sources and native oral tradition (Blitz 1993:583–585).

Kopytoff (1987:17) found that local African elites, influenced by the regional political context, eventually found it useful to transcend the limitations of parochialism to acquire new legitimacy from the values, traditions, and symbols of neighboring polities. We detected archaeological examples of this need for nonlocal symbols in the sharing of bottle-beaker fine wares across ceramic style zones, participation in the SECC symbolism, and the rapid rejection of the old Middle Mississippi tradition of ceramic style in favor of a fusion of Lamar and Fort Walton ceramic types.

This observation brings us to our third component of new theory: the ideological constructs that helped create and justify the new identity, authority, and power structures that accompanied political and social integration. Identity, authority, and power were united in the active production of "social memory," defined as "the construction of a collective notion (not an individual belief) about the way things were in the past" (Van Dyke and Alcock 2003:2). Social memory is conveyed through different media, including the platform mounds that we have examined at length.

As we have seen, platforms mounds could materialize various meanings linked to territory, rank, authority, community, and other values. Once on the landscape, mounds became commemorative places "fixing social and individual histories in place" (Knapp and Ashmore 1999:13). Pauketat and Alt (2003) consider the act of mound building as an ongoing "negotiation" of identity, authority, and power through production of social memory. In contrast to Kopytoff's emphasis on the conservative replication of social values on a frontier, Pauketat and Alt view the geographical spread of platform mound construction as repetitive attempts to reconfigure values according to new circumstances, and stress that mound construction and abandonment both expressed and contested different versions of the past. A window into the content of the social memories generated by platform mound use is found in native southeastern oral traditions. Emergence-migration stories, while fraught with interpretive dilemmas when paired with archaeological evidence, do reveal native concerns with rank, territorial claims, first-use rights, and illuminate the ideological underpinnings of the polity formation process.

The final component of new theory focuses on the interplay of environmental and social conditions that enhanced or impeded a Mississippian leader's ability to mobilize the surpluses used to expand political and social integration. The implications of the Savannah River climate study suggest that crop surpluses during favorable rainfall periods underwrote the population aggregation, ceremonials, and alliances required for polity growth. Such growth and fusion produced multiple-mound centers engaged in inter-regional alliance-exchange networks. The panregional symbols acquired through polity interaction reinforced alliances, possibly reduced warfare, and validated the status of elites. Sustained droughts significantly reduced the surpluses available to leaders, depriving them of the means to fund the ceremonials needed to reduce factionalism, maintain alliance-exchange, and access status symbols. The collapse of alliance-exchange networks might lead to intensified warfare, a devaluation of elite symbols and ideology, and loss of followers through fission. If these trends could not be reversed, then mound-center decline and abandonment would occur, with possible impacts on polities in neighboring regions through emigration. The scale and scope of political and social integration would be rearranged, signaled by changes in settlement patterns and ceramic styles as new political and social boundaries were created.

In this study we have presented a specific culture history for the purpose of understanding general cultural processes. We have strived to avoid both abstract theorizing devoid of data and descriptive data presentations without a purpose. In presenting these concluding remarks about political and social integration in the ancient American Southeast, our intent has been to highlight the implications of our findings and suggest future avenues of inquiry. Many of the old mounds are now gone, drowned beneath reservoirs or scraped away by bulldozers. We still have much to learn from the sites that remain.

Appendix A
The Multiple-Mound-Center Excavations

In this appendix we present detailed overviews of all archaeological investigations at the multiple-mound sites of Rood's Landing, Singer-Moye, and Cemochechobee, including previously unpublished excavation results. Our purpose is to supplement the site synopses in Chapter 3 by emphasizing the provenience and context of the mound artifact samples and associated radiocarbon dates that we use to construct the regional chronology presented in Chapter 4.

Excavations at Rood's Landing (9SW1)

The impressive mound group known as Rood's Landing did not go unnoticed by that indefatigable pursuer of ancient southeastern artifacts, C. B. Moore (1907:448), but he was denied permission to excavate. Rood's Landing reminded Moore of the much larger Moundville site in Alabama, which it superficially resembles. In 1958, RBS archaeologists Harold Huscher and David Chase procured surface collections from Mounds E, G, and H, but no excavations took place. Archaeologist Joseph Caldwell (1955) uncovered a large area on the final stage of Mound A. Additionally, two 3-x-3 m (10-x-10 ft.) units were dug to a depth of 1.2–2.1 m below the Mound A summit. Elsewhere, two 3-x-3 m (10-x-10 ft.) units were placed in Mound B, dug to a depth of 2.3 m, and profiles recorded. On Mound D, a 3.6-meter-long looter's trench was cleaned out down to the premound level. Finally, a single 3-x-3 m (10-x-10 ft.) unit was laid out on the Mound F summit and dug to a depth of 60 cm. No substantive investigations at Rood's Landing have taken place since Caldwell's research. Caldwell's 1955 report, besides being a rather obscure publication, does not present all excavation data, nor does it mention all recovered materials. Our interpretation of the site is based on an examination of all artifacts acquired by Caldwell and the RBS effort, aided by field notes, drawings, and photographs.

Mound A Excavations

Mound A is the largest mound at Rood's Landing. Access to the 7.6-meter-high summit was gained by two ramps, each 15.2 m long, 4.5 m wide at the summit, and 7.6 m wide at the base. One ramp exits northwest to the plaza, where it faces directly opposite the Mound E ramp; the other ramp exits to the southwest. The summit of Mound A forms a 44.2-x-38.1 m platform. Upon removing the uppermost surface of the Mound A summit to a depth of one foot, Caldwell discovered the burned remains of three wattle-and-daub buildings (Structures 1, 2, 3) resting on the final occupation level, designated occupation level I (Caldwell 1955:26–32). Structures 2, 3, and the partial post mold patterns of two additional structures were arrayed around the rectangular summit, one to each side. The largest building (Structure 1) was positioned at the center of the mound summit. Near Structure 1 was an isolated post mold, 32 cm in diameter, which Caldwell interpreted as analogous to historic period "slave posts." Similar large, isolated posts are a recurrent feature of Mississippian mound architecture (Lindauer and Blitz 1997:173), and a similar feature was found at the Cemochechobee site (Schnell et al. 1981:57). Portions of occupation level I were surfaced with a "pavement" of prepared yellow clay. This same material formed a "clay parapet" or rampart, 60–90 cm high, around the summit perimeter, with openings at the ramp exits. Along the southwestern parapet segment, a line of post molds revealed that a log fence had backed the clay parapet and enclosed the mound summit. Similar parapet-fence features were uncovered at the Omussee Creek mound and Gary's Fish Pond mound.

Structures 1, 2, and 3 were constructed of wooden timbers, whole cane wattles, clay-and-Spanish-moss-daub plaster, and walls of single-set pine posts 12 cm in diameter. Structure 1, with three straight walls attached to a semicircular wall, "resembled a teardrop" in plan view (Caldwell 1955:28). It was 7.3 m in length along the northern axis. A projecting entranceway was placed at the southwest corner. There were four large interior post molds indicating roof supports and small interior posts for a partition or supports for benches (Figure A.1). No prepared fire basin was found, but a central burned area indicated the presence of a hearth. Fired daub with wood and cane impressions, charred timbers, and charred canes had fallen on the sand floor when the building collapsed. After the building burned, the floor area and charred house debris were covered by a layer of sand 25–45 cm thick to form a low mound. Structure 2 was built along the interior edge

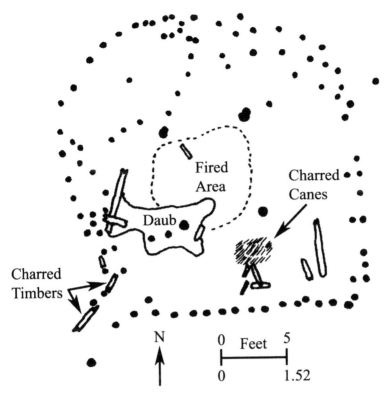

Fired Area

Charred Canes

Daub

Charred Timbers

N

0 Feet 5

0   1.52

A.1. Plan of Structure 1, Mound A, 9SW1 (redrawn from Caldwell 1955).

of the northwest parapet. It was rectangular, 6-x-2.4 m, and was subdivided into two rooms by a line of small posts. Structure 2 also had a projecting entranceway, which exited onto the clay pavement at the southwestern ramp. Structure 3, with a floor area of 64 m², was on the northern summit side. No entranceway was detected. Not all surfaces on the southern and western summit areas were excavated, but exposed portions of post mold patterns convinced Caldwell that buildings were placed at these locations as well.

Although no detailed ecofact analysis or inventory is available, Caldwell found animal bone, mussel shells, burned pine posts, charred cane withes, maize, acorns, and the beanlike seeds of *Stewartia malacodendron*, a member of the *Theaceae* or tea family.

Two 3-x-3 m (10-x-10 ft.) squares, Test Units 1 and 2, penetrated 2.1 m and 1.2 m, respectively, beneath the Mound A summit. Test Unit 1 was located east of Structure 1 and Test Unit 2 was placed between the southwestern ramp and Structure 1. These two units revealed multiple episodes of mound construction beneath occupation level I. Thin layers of hard sand or

Test Unit 1

Mound Summit

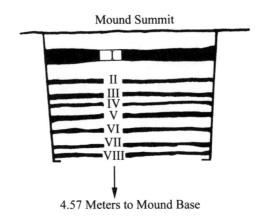

4.57 Meters to Mound Base

Test Unit 2

Mound Summit

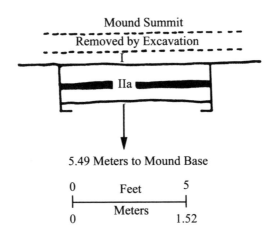

5.49 Meters to Mound Base

A.2. Profiles of Test Units 1 and 2, Mound A, 9SW1 (redrawn from Caldwell 1955).

clay, designated occupation levels II–VIII, alternated with layers of sand fill to create mound construction stages (Figure A.2). Both units produced fired daub, charred wood, and other evidence of structure remains, but low artifact densities.

Excavations in Mounds B, D, and F

Excavations on Mound B were less extensive than those on Mound A. Under Caldwell's direction, Chase placed two 3-x-3 m (10-x-10 ft.) units on the Mound B summit. The exact location of these units is uncertain, and no profile drawing of the units exists. However, Chase (1955) describes the stratigraphic sequence in his field notes. Both units revealed the same stratigraphy. Two "occupation levels" were encountered. Just beneath the modern humus deposit, occupation level I extended from 15 to 55 cm below the summit surface, followed by occupation level II, from ca. 60 cm to 2.3 m below surface. Both strata were composed of hard-packed sand interspersed with fire-reddened clay and associated potsherds, daub, post molds, and animal bone. A poorly preserved skeleton of an infant was discovered 70 cm below surface. There were no associated artifacts, nor was a prepared grave feature detected. Beneath occupation level II was a nearly sterile fill of yellow, red, and gray clay, which was still visible when the unit terminated at 2.3 m below summit surface.

At Mound D, a looter's trench was cleaned out and cut back to produce a 3.6-x-1.5 m trench. The exact position of the trench on Mound D is uncertain, but it exposed a portion of the summit and flank. A drawing of the resulting section is illustrated in Figure A.3. On the final occupation summit, just below the humus level (A), the remains of a burned wattle-and-daub structure (B) were encountered. Beneath this structure was a thick deposit of orange clay (C). Under stratum C, "the situation became more complex" (Caldwell 1955:34), and the extant profile drawing does not entirely resolve this complexity. Caldwell (1955:34) describes strata E and F in Figure A.3 as "two levels of fill differentiation, beginning near the base of the mound and rising toward the mound edge." Caldwell omits a written description of stratum D altogether, and the exact relationship between strata D, E, and F is obscured by gaps in the lines of demarcation between these layers in the profile drawing. Caldwell could not determine if strata E and F were occupation surfaces. No post molds and few artifacts were discovered below stratum B. Some of the strata probably served as surfaces for buildings, however, because charred logs were discovered at the interface of strata D and E (Figure A.3).

Interpretation of Mound D was further restricted because we were unable to find any artifacts from the Mound D excavation in the Columbus Museum collection, and Caldwell did not quantify them in his report. He does mention that the pottery associated with the stratum B house was grit-tempered plain with handles, and that pottery associated with strata D and E was the same except that "a few were shell tempered" (Caldwell 1955:35). Mound D rested on a premound midden (G), about 12 cm thick, which contained predominately shell-tempered potsherds and chipped stone. There was a decrease in the frequency of shell-tempered pottery through time from the premound midden to the top of Mound D, but we cannot quantify this change because these data are missing.

Under Caldwell's supervision, Frank T. Schnell excavated a single 3-x-3

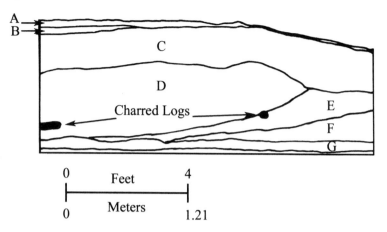

A.3. Southeast profile, Mound D, 9SW1.

m (10-x-10 ft.) unit in the center of the Mound F summit. Fired wall daub, potsherds, and a greenstone celt fragment, encountered just below the modern surface, were residues of a burned structure built on the final occupation surface of the mound. Not enough of this surface was uncovered to determine the size or form of the burned building. The excavation terminated at 60 cm below the mound summit surface without penetrating additional mound construction levels.

Artifact Provenience and Chronology

Caldwell did not present a table of artifact counts by provenience units in his 1955 report. We have analyzed all of the 1955 excavation materials available for restudy and placed the individual artifact lots into provenience groups consistent with the stratigraphic relationships and feature associations recognized by Caldwell (Tables A.1–A.5). Caldwell did not establish a site grid; units are specific to each tested mound. These provenience groups are summarized below:

A1. This provenience group is from Mound A occupation level I, the final occupation level on the summit. Excavation controls permit further subdivision into north (A1-N), east (A1-E), south (A1-S), west (A1-W), and central (A1-C) units. A1-C includes materials associated with Structure 1. A1-W includes materials associated with Structure 2. A1-N includes materials associated with Structure 3.

A2. This provenience group is from Mound A, lower levels. It includes all materials below A1 recovered in Test Units 1 and 2, including occupation levels II–VIII.

B1. This provenience group is from Mound B, upper levels, which includes occupation level I.

B2. This provenience group is from Mound B, lower levels, which includes occupation level II.

PD. This provenience unit is material recovered from the premound mound midden under Mound D.

E. This provenience unit is the 1958 RBS collection from the surface of Mound E.

F. This provenience unit is material recovered from the excavation on the summit of Mound F.

G. This provenience unit is the 1958 RBS collection from the surface of Mound G.

H. This provenience unit is the 1958 RBS collection from the surface of Mound H.

Beginning with the last occupation and working back in time, the following history of mound construction at Rood's Landing can be pieced together. The site ceased to be an important center during the Stewart phase (A.D. 1550–1650), when the buildings on top of Mound A were burned and covered with sand, a stone-covered tomb was dug, and use of the summit (A1) was terminated. A radiocarbon sample (Beta-2271) from a Structure 1 charred-wood post (Knight 1994a:381; Scarry 1984:Table 2) produced a date of two-sigma cal A.D. 1420–1660, with an intercept of A.D. 1500 (Table 4.1).

Mound A level II, at .76 cm below the final summit, also produced burned structure debris. Few artifacts were recovered from Mound A levels II–VIII (A2). Caldwell thought he detected a hiatus of occupation between A1 and A2 because the lower deposit contained grit-tempered handled jars but lacked Fort Walton Incised and Lamar Plain. The presence of handled jars in A2 indicates an affiliation no later than the Singer phase. A radiocarbon sample (Beta-2270) of wood charcoal from Mound A (Scarry 1984:Table 2) probably dates the A2 component: two-sigma cal A.D. 1240–1400, with an intercept of A.D. 1290 (Table 4.1). Mound A excavation stopped at 2.13 m below the final summit, leaving the remaining 4.57 m above the base of the mound unexamined.

Like Mound A, the final use of the Mound B summit (B1) was also in the Stewart phase. Beneath B1, the B2 assemblage does not appear to differ substantially from B1 except for the absence of Rood Incised, which might be attributed to sample size. Excavations in Mound B did not penetrate to the mound base. Excavations in the smaller Mounds D and F did reach the mound bases, and identified one occupation level in each mound. No decorated pottery was recovered from either mound. The grit-tempered, handled

Table A.1. Provenience of Ceramic Types, Mound A, 9SW1.

CERAMIC TYPES	A1N	A1E	A1S	A1W	A1C	TOTAL A1
Fort Walton Incised	17	51	77	90	14	249
Lamar Comp. Stamp.	61	90	143	286	13	593
Lamar Plain	8	23	15	35	11	92
Bold Incised	3	7	8	29	4	51
Columbia Incised	1	2	9	3	1	16
Rood Incised	2	9	13	13	1	38
Cool Branch Incised	1	3	1	2	0	7
Fine Incised	0	1	1	7	0	9
Check Stamped	0	1	5	8	0	14
Nunnally Incised	1	0	0	0	0	1
Total Decorated	94	187	272	473	44	1070
Shell Plain	*	*	*	*	*	148
Grit/Sand Plain	*	*	*	*	*	5052
Total Plain	*	*	*	*	*	5200
Total Sherds	*	*	*	*	*	6270

jar sherds collected from the surface of Mounds E and H suggest a date no later than the Singer phase.

The initial history of mound construction at Rood's Landing is unresolved. The small pottery sample from premound D has a high frequency of shell-tempered ware, which meets our criterion for placement in the Rood I phase (A.D. 1100–1200). Mound construction during the Rood I phase, however, is undocumented at the site, yet cannot be discounted because excavation units did not penetrate the lower levels of several mounds. This is important because we wish to know if Rood's Landing became a multiple-mound center and the dominant regional power at an early date. There has been no additional excavation at Rood's Landing since Caldwell's investigation. The two moats are undated. Thus the nature of initial Mississippian occupation at Rood's Landing and the site's early role in regional prehistory remains unknown.

Caldwell (1955, 1958) proposed that his "Earlier" and "Middle" period ceramics at Rood's Landing were the product of the "Mississippian Culture," and represented a cultural discontinuity with antecedent indigenous traditions in Georgia. He interpreted the Earlier and Middle periods as a continuous occupation at the site. He noted that the use of shell temper was confined to the Earlier period and suggested this component was the product of a population movement from the west or north. The Middle period represented a ceramic style continuum with the Earlier period, with the exception that grit temper replaced shell temper, thus Middle period peoples were

Table A.2. Provenience of Ceramic Modes, Mound A, 9SW1.

CERAMIC MODES	A1N	A1E	A1S	A1W	A1C	TOTAL
Stamped motif						
Bull's Eye	0	2	5	7	1	15
Figure 9	0	1	0	4	1	6
Figure 9 with dot	0	2	9	0	0	11
Cross-in-circle	2	2	0	5	1	10
Cross-in-circle (dots)	3	0	0	1	0	4
Linked Circles	0	0	1	4	0	5
Total Stamped	5	7	15	21	3	51
Arcade motif						
Eyelash	1	2	0	1	0	4
Unembellished	0	1	1	1	0	3
Total Arcades	1	3	1	2	0	7
Rim						
Plain Appliqué	0	2	3	1	1	7
Notched Appliqué	2	10	8	11	4	35
Pinched Appliqué	6	11	4	20	6	47
Scalloped Appliqué	0	0	0	3	0	3
Pinched Below Lip	12	21	30	37	9	109
Lip Notched	9	20	16	19	13	77
Lip Ticked	9	27	46	36	2	120
Noded	3	7	9	11	6	36
Folded Pinched	2	0	5	3	0	10
Bulge Collar	0	1	0	2	0	3
Castellations	0	1	0	2	1	4
Horizontal Incised	0	1	3	3	1	8
Total Rims	43	101	124	148	43	459
Vessel						
Simple Jar	9	23	23	32	19	106
Handled Jar	3	11	9	7	0	30
Open Bowl	0	9	8	7	2	26
Rounded Bowl	0	2	2	7	1	12
Carinated Bowl	3	14	11	16	0	44
Bottle/Beaker	1	0	2	0	0	3
Flaring-Rim Bowl	1	2	6	7	1	17
Miniature Jar	0	0	0	1	0	1
Total Vessels	17	61	61	77	23	239
Handle						
Plain Strap	3	4	3	3	0	13
Plain Loop	0	0	2	1	0	3
Top Node	0	1	0	1	0	2
Double Top Node	0	3	2	1	0	6

Continued on the next page

Table A.2. *Continued*

CERAMIC MODES	A1N	A1E	A1S	A1W	A1C	TOTAL
Top Double Ridge	0	1	0	0	0	1
Top Tri-Ridge	0	2	0	0	0	2
Horizontal Lug	1	5	2	6	0	14
Vertical Lug	0	5	7	7	0	19
Effigy Tail	0	0	1	1	0	2
Effigy Head	0	1	0	3	0	4
Total Handles	4	22	17	23	0	66

Table A.3. Provenience of Ceramic Types, Various Mounds, 9SW1.

CERAMIC TYPES	A2	B1	B2	PD	E	F	G	H	TOTAL
Grit/Sand Temper									
Fort Walton Incised	0	8	4	0	0	0	0	2	14
Lamar Complicated Stamped	1	10	1	0	0	0	0	0	12
Lamar Plain	0	5	7	0	0	0	0	0	12
Bold Incised	0	1	5	0	0	0	0	1	7
Columbia Incised	1	0	1	0	0	0	0	1	3
Rood Incised	0	4	0	0	0	0	0	0	4
Cool Branch Incised	0	1	1	0	0	0	0	1	3
Fine Incised	0	0	0	0	0	0	1	0	1
Check Stamped	0	1	0	0	0	0	0	0	1
Nunnally Incised	0	2	1	0	1	0	0	0	4
Grit/Sand Plain	96	392	121	23	77	91	34	160	994
Shell Temper									
Moundville Incised	1	0	0	3	0	0	0	0	4
Shell Plain	3	18	2	37	0	5	0	5	70
Total Plain	99	410	123	60	77	96	34	165	1064
Total Decorated	3	32	20	3	1	0	1	5	65
Total Sherds	102	442	143	63	78	96	35	170	1129

most likely the "descendants of the original invaders" (Caldwell 1955:44). The "Later" period ceramic assemblages, however, were derived from the Fort Walton and Lamar ceramic traditions. Citing the discontinuity of ceramic vessel form and decoration, Caldwell proposed that the Later period represented a radical cultural and temporal break with the Earlier and Middle period occupation at Rood's Landing. Our research generally supports Caldwell's chronological and cultural interpretation in broad outline.

Table A.4. Provenience of Ceramic Modes, Various Mounds, 9SW1.

CERAMIC MODES	A2	B1	B2	PD	E	F	G	H	TOTAL
Stamped motif									
Cross-in-Circle	0	1	0	0	0	0	0	0	1
Total Stamped	0	1	0	0	0	0	0	0	1
Arcade motif									
Eyelash	0	0	0	3	0	0	0	0	3
Punctated	0	0	1	0	0	0	0	0	1
Unembellished	1	1	0	0	0	0	0	0	2
Total Arcades	1	3	1	3	0	0	0	0	8
Rim									
Plain Appliqué	0	0	1	0	0	0	0	0	1
Notched Appliqué	0	3	4	0	0	0	0	2	9
Pinched Appliqué	0	2	2	0	1	0	0	0	5
Pinched Below Lip	0	3	2	0	0	0	0	1	6
Lip Notched	2	1	5	0	1	0	1	1	11
Lip Ticked	0	6	2	0	0	0	0	1	9
Noded	1	3	3	0	0	1	0	1	9
Pinched Folded	0	1	0	0	0	0	0	0	1
Total Rims	3	19	19	0	2	1	1	6	51
Vessel									
Simple Jar	0	3	4	0	0	0	0	0	7
Handled Jar	5	7	3	3	1	0	0	1	20
Open Bowl	0	0	2	0	1	0	0	2	5
Rounded Bowl	0	0	1	0	0	0	0	0	1
Carinated Bowl	0	2	2	0	0	0	0	0	4
Bottle/Beaker	0	2	1	0	1	0	0	0	4
Flaring-Rim Bowl	0	1	0	0	0	0	0	0	1
Total Vessels	5	15	13	3	3	0	0	3	42
Handle									
Plain Strap	2	1	0	3	0	0	0	0	6
Plain Loop	2	2	0	0	0	0	0	0	4
Top Node	0	1	0	0	0	0	0	0	1
Double Top Node	0	1	1	0	0	0	0	0	2
Top Tri-Ridge	0	1	1	0	0	0	0	0	2
Vertical Lug	0	0	0	0	1	0	0	0	1
Effigy Tail	0	0	1	0	0	0	0	0	1
Total Handles	4	6	3	3	1	0	0	0	17

Table A.5. Provenience of Miscellaneous Artifacts, 9SW1.

	A1 No./ Material	B1-2 No./ Mat.	E No./ Mat.	F No./ Mat.	H No./ Mat.
FLAKED STONE					
Stemless Triang. PP/K	3/LC	0	0	0	0
Misc. Stemmed PP/K	1/LC	0	0	0	0
Debitage	P/LC	P/LC	0	P/LC	0
GROUND STONE					
Worked Chunks	2/H, 2/L, 2/PW	1/H	0	0	0
Celt Fragment/Flake	6/G	0	1/G	1/G	0
Discoidal	1/Q	0	0	0	0
Discoidal Preform	1/S	0	0	0	1/G
Mortar/Anvil	3/H, 1/L	0	0	0	0
Hammer Stone	1/Q	0	0	0	1/Q
OTHER ARTIFACTS					
Disk	11/C	4/C	0	0	0
Smoking Pipe	5/C	4/C	0	0	0
Bead	1/C	0	0	0	0
Fired Daub	P/C	P/C	0	P/C	0
Red Ocher Pigment	P	0	0	0	0
Cut Marine Shell	15g	0	0	00	0
Fossil Shark Teeth	4	1	0	0	0
Pottery Phallus	1/C	0	0	0	0
RAW MATERIAL					
Hematite	P	0	0	0	0
Limonite	P	0	0	0	0
Marl	P	0	0	0	0
Petrified Wood	P	0	0	0	0
Unidentified Bone	P	P	0	0	0
Unidentified Botanical	P	P	0	0	0
Unidentified Shell	P	0	0	0	0

KEY: projectile point/knife (PP/K), local chert (LC), limonite (L), hematite/ferruginous sandstone (H), quartzite (Q), greenstone (G), petrified wood (PW), sandstone (S), ceramic (C), present but not quantified (P), grams (g).

In his 1955 report, Caldwell observed that the ceramic sequence at Rood's Landing did not agree with the sequence at the Lake Jackson site, as interpreted by John Griffin (1950). The principal difference was that the zone-punctated type Fort Walton Incised was associated with arcade-decorated, handled Mississippian jars in the earliest levels at Lake Jackson, whereas at Rood's Landing, Fort Walton Incised was largely confined to the Later period. The implication that Fort Walton Incised appeared as a major type in the lower Chattahoochee River valley at a time later than at sites to the south was not given sufficient attention by some archaeologists (i.e., Belovich et al. 1982; Scarry 1984, 1990), who erroneously placed components like Caldwell's Earlier and Middle periods into an overextended Fort Walton culture, and thus failed to perceive the divergent history that produced the regional Mississippian phases (Blitz and Lorenz 2002).

Excavations at the Singer-Moye Site (9SW2)

The Singer-Moye site setting is unique among the mound centers in this study in two respects. First, the site is not on the river. Instead, the mounds are on the north side of Pataula Creek, in an upland setting of the Red Hills physiographic zone, some 27 km in a direct line from the Chattahoochee River, or about 45 km from the creek's confluence with the river. The interfluvial location lacks the floodplain resources that some researchers claim as the defining criterion of "Mississippian subsistence-settlement systems" (Smith 1978:480). Apparently, subsistence concerns were not the primary influence on the choice of site location, but we have no direct evidence to suggest why the site is located in this unusual setting.

A second unusual characteristic of the Singer-Moye site setting is that the mounds were not built on level land. Because the land slopes downward from north to south toward the creek, the ground elevation of the mound complex drops nearly 15 m from the northern site edge at Mounds E and D to the southern end of the site at Mound G. A peculiar result of the sloping terrain is that the level summits of the platform mounds appear to observers on the ground surface to be higher on the south sides than on the north sides. For example, Mound D, which has a level summit, is less than a meter high on the north side, but 3 m high on the south side.

Archaeologists did not investigate the Singer-Moye site until the late 1950s, when Joseph Mahan of the Columbus Museum of Arts and Crafts and Harold A. Huscher of the Smithsonian Institution visited the site to secure surface collections. Beginning in 1967, portions of the Singer-Moye site were donated to the Columbus Museum by landowners. In 1983, the last remaining portion of the 13-ha archaeological preserve was acquired by the museum. Only brief published summaries are available for some research (Knight 1979; Schnell 1968, 1998a; Schnell and Wright 1993:18–20; Schnell et al. 1981:238–240), so we present the results of the mound excavations below, drawn from unpublished overviews, notes, and photographs produced by Frank T. Schnell, Margaret C. Russell, and Donald Gordy at the Columbus Museum, and analysis of all excavated artifacts by Russell and the authors. With the exception of extensive trenching between Mounds C and E, and limited horizontal exposure of the premound surface beneath Mound H, nonmound areas of the site have not been sampled.

N300

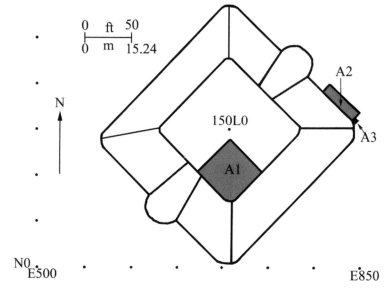

A.4. Plan of Mound A, 9SW2.

Mound A Excavations

Mound A is a steep-sided, flat-topped, pyramidal mound with ramps that extend out from the northeast and southwest mound flanks. The preeminent mound at Singer-Moye, the Mound A summit is 11 m above the current ground surface at the northern corner, and approximately 13 m above the current ground surface at the southern corner, the difference in heights due to the slope of the ground surface as described above. Excavations were placed on the mound summit and along the northeastern mound base (Figure A.4). Excavations conducted in 1970–1972 were focused on the southern quarter of summit of Mound A, where a low, rounded mound of clay was clearly visible. This low mound proved to be a clay cap 1 m thick that covered the remains of a burned wattle-and-daub building (Structure A1). Structure A1 was a square building with a floor surface area of 144 m^2, eight large roof support posts, and walls of single-set post construction. Structure A1 walls had the same alignment as the sides of Mound A, with corners oriented to the approximate cardinal directions. The structure entrance, protected by a small projecting screen or wall, was at the northern corner. Masses of white daub plaster were recovered from the Structure A1 excavation unit, but apparently only the entranceway wall was daubed. Like the structures on Rood's Landing Mound A, Singer-Moye Structure A1 lacked a prepared fire basin and, instead, had a central burned area on the floor. Charred roof timbers and thatching were found on the floor where they fell when the building burned. A wood charcoal sample (UGa-357) from one of these timbers (Noakes and Brandau 1974:34) produced a radiocarbon date of two-sigma cal A.D. 1290–1440 with an intercept of A.D. 1410 (Table 4.1).

On the Structure A1 floor were two copper fragments, weighing only a few grams, no doubt portions of larger ornaments of an undetermined form. Sherds of a polychrome human effigy bottle, depicting a modeled human head, were found 1 m east of the central hearth area. Also associated with Structure A1 were mica sheets (< 5 g), three ground stone discoidals, two greenstone celt fragments, two pottery disks, and 14 smoking pipe fragments. Animal bone and broken pottery suggest that food was consumed in the building. Several small, shallow pit features produced botanical remains. No complete analysis of the faunal and botanical sample is available. We interpret Structure A1 as an elite residence.

In 1970, a 15.24-x-3 m (50-x-10 ft.) excavation unit (A2) was placed at the base of the northeastern side of Mound A near its eastern corner. The long axis of the trench was laid out parallel to the mound base. Excavations penetrated to 45 cm below surface and a large quantity of potsherds and animal bone were recovered. This material is interpreted as a talus slope of midden and other debris cast down from the summit, for it contained the same white clay daub encountered in the Structure A1 excavation. The A2 ceramic assemblage is generally similar to the A1 ceramic assemblage, suggesting the deposits are close in age, although A2 contained Fort Walton Incised and A1 did not.

Little was learned about the earlier history of Mound A because the A2 unit did not penetrate very far into the mound flank. It was suspected that sheet erosion had deposited soil along the northeastern and northwestern mound base. In 1989, a smaller but deeper test (A3) was dug near the eastern corner of the current mound base in order to determine the elevation of the original base. A series of humus levels buried repeatedly by water-laid deposits bore witness to multiple erosion events. Presumably, the sources of these erosion deposits were the sides of Mound A and the open "plaza" areas to the north, which were plowed in the recent past. It was discovered that the original ground surface was 1.7 m below the present ground surface, and therefore the true average height of Mound A is greater than the dimensions cited above.

Mound C Excavations

Mound C is a rectangular platform mound situated on the edge of a gully. The east side of the mound, which faces the open "plaza" area, is elevated

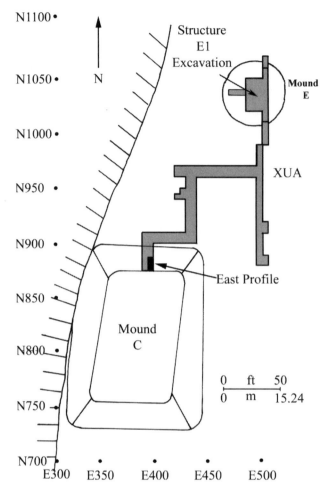

A.5. Plan of Mound C, XUA trench, and Mound E, 9SW2.

3 m above the ground surface. The west side of the mound is elevated 4.9 m above the gully floor. The Mound C summit measures 32.9 m north to south and 26.8 m east to west. A north-south trench, 10.6-x-3.0 m long, was placed perpendicular to the north side of Mound C. The Mound C trench was one segment of a large contiguous excavation unit (XUA) that linked Mound C and Mound E (Figure A.5). The XUA trench cut the flank of Mound C from the edge of the northern base to the edge of the northern summit, a distance of 7.6 m. Figure A.6 illustrates the strata A-F exposed in the 3-meter-high east profile of Mound C at N885–870/E400. Built upon a premound occupation surface (A), the initial white clay mound (B) was a

A.6. East profile of Mound C, 9SW2, 1968.

flat-topped platform covered by red clay-and-sand mound fills (C) and another white clay construction episode (D). Mound stage D was an apronlike
horizontal extension of the mound. At least one clay-and-sand stage (E, and
a possible additional stage, F) completed the construction sequence. Wood
charcoal from premound stratum A, associated with shell-tempered Moundville Incised potsherds, and produced a radiocarbon date (Beta-153709) of
two-sigma cal A.D. 1170–1300 with an intercept of A.D. 1270 (Table 4.1).

In comparison to the other mound excavations at Singer-Moye, the
Mound C trench produced a low density of sherds relative to the volume of
the excavated deposit, a relatively high proportion of shell-tempered pottery,
and a disproportionate representation of sherds from fine-ware bottles and
beakers (Nunnally Incised, n = 33). This concentration of serving fine wares
may be from a single-event deposit similar to that found at Cemochechobee

Mound A Feature 3 (Schnell et al. 1981:69–70), in which fancy beakers were buried in rites associated with the addition of a new mound construction stage. The exact depositional context of the Mound C sherds, however, is unclear due to the lack of horizontal exposure. Besides potsherds, the only other materials present were one sherd disk, one smoking pipe fragment, and a small quantity of unidentified animal bone, most of which was confined to the premound stratum. The absence of daub and other indications of structures are notable, although the Mound C trench was not carried forward into the mound to the extent required to reveal summit surfaces. So other than the high visibility of decorated bottles/beakers in the sample, we can say little about how Mound C was used by the site's inhabitants.

Mound D Excavations

Mound D, a rectangular platform approximately 85 m east to west and 60 m north to south, marks the northern boundary of the mound precinct. Mound D produced the most puzzling architectural remains at the site. It rises less than a meter on the north side, but due to the sloping terrain, the summit is 3 m above the current ground level on the south side. A low slope of earth that projects outward from the southwest mound flank toward Mound E may be a ramp. A 1.5-x-6.0 m (5-x-20 ft.) trench (D1) was cut into the west flank of Mound D in 1967 (Figure A.7). Beneath the shallow plow zone and slope wash, the excavators encountered a natural soil horizon, not mound fill, which revealed that Mound D is a natural terrace formation modified by cutting and filling to create a rectangular platform.

More extensive excavations in 1969 exposed part of the Mound D summit. In this unit (D2), an area of 1,402 m² was taken down to just beneath the plow zone, a depth of 30 cm below the summit surface. A few scattered post molds were noted but no pattern was discernable. The most distinctive features were a series of six large fire basins set at 6 m intervals in a straight east-west line spanning the long axis of the Mound D summit. The features are probably too close together to be inside separate structures and too far apart to be inside one large structure (which would require a building 36 m in length). So it would appear that roofs did not cover these fire basins. A considerable amount of broken pottery was deposited on the Mound D summit, together with one small triangular arrow point, two greenstone celt fragments, two sandstone discoidals, four pottery disks, two clay smoking pipe fragments, fired daub, and red ocher pigment.

Mound E Excavations

Mound E is a low, dome-shaped mound about 90 cm high and 14 m in diameter. Excavation in 1968 and again in 2002 revealed that the dome of earth covered the remains of an earth-embanked structure or "earth lodge"

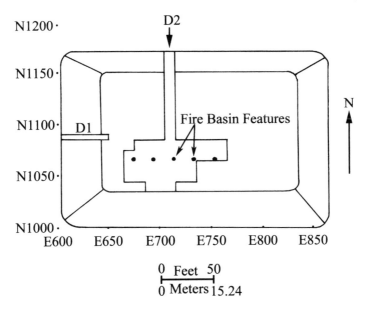

A.7. Plan of Mound D, 9SW2.

(Structure E1). The Mound E excavation unit was one segment of a continuous excavation unit (XUA) that linked Mound D and Mound E (Figure A.5). Structure E1 was an 8-x-7.5 m wattle-and-daub building with a red clay floor (Figure A.8). Structure E1 was built on level ground, over a premound surface that exhibited some midden development, but little of this premound stratum was excavated. Over the premound surface, a layer of hard red clay, 3–4 cm thick, was laid down as a floor. Around the perimeter of the red clay floor, walls were constructed of single-set posts and plastered with white clay daub. Next, a berm of red clay was piled against the exterior walls to a height of 70–80 cm. Four interior post molds indicate roof supports, but it is not known if soil covered the roof, as is the case with the earth lodge of Plains Indian traditions. A 50 cm gap in the western wall is probably the entranceway.

At the time of abandonment, Structure E1 was not burned. Instead, the wall posts were removed to dismantle the building. Hollow cavities were left where some of the posts had stood, and these cavities were sealed off when unfired white wall daub collapsed over them. At several places, white wall daub was found where it fell into the building interior, superimposed over the red clay floor. After the wall posts were pulled up, earth fill was piled into the interior above the floor up to the level of the surrounding berm, which resulted in the remarkable preservation of standing structure walls as

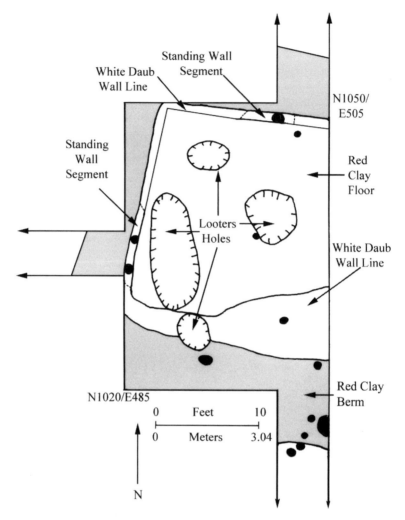

A.8. Plan of Mound E features, 9SW2.

much as 70 cm high. Molds of the wall posts were present in the white daub of the standing wall. This final covering of dismantled Structure E1 created Mound E; thereafter, this structure was abandoned and never used again.

Only artifacts from the 1968 Mound E excavation were examined (the 2002 excavation sample remains unanalyzed). Twelve decorated ceramics were present, including Cool Branch Incised, Fort Walton Incised, Columbia Incised, and five eroded complicated stamped sherds. The only nonvessel artifacts were two smoking pipes of clay. A charcoal sample (UGa-356) from a pit in the floor of Structure E1 produced a radiocarbon date (Noakes and Brandau 1974:34) of two-sigma cal A.D. 1210–1420, with an intercept of A.D. 1290. In addition to unidentified wood charcoal, Structure E1 contained charred maize. There are few clues as to the purpose or function of Structure E1.

Mound H Excavations

Excavations at Mound H uncovered the most complex sequence of strata and features at the Singer-Moye site. Located east of Mound A, Mound H rises little more than 1 m above the surrounding terrain. Mound H was found when undergrowth was cleared from the area in the early 1990s. To determine if Mound H was a cultural feature, nine 1.5-x-1.5 m (5-x-5 ft.) test units were placed on the elevated area. At a depth of 1.2 m below surface, the burned remains of a building were found, and the presence of decorated bottle sherds and mica sheet fragments suggested special-purpose or elite activities. When investigations terminated in 2001, the remains of several buildings, a palisade wall segment, and numerous premound features had been uncovered. We can provide only an overview of these complex investigations here. Below, we discuss the major features in chronological order, beginning with the oldest remains encountered on the premound surface and ending with the final activities that formed Mound H.

Premound Features and Palisade Figure A.9 is a plan view of the oldest features discovered in the Mound H excavations at 1.7–2.1 m below datum: post molds, wall trenches, and midden on the premound surface, and a palisade line that originates above the premound surface and intrudes into it. Premound features were exposed in two deep excavations, an east-to-west 1.52-x-13.71 m (5-x-45 ft.) section (N65–70/E870–915) and a north-to-south 1.52-x-4.57 m (5-x-15 ft.) section (N45–60/E885–890). A premound midden, 38–40 cm thick, had accumulated on top of the preoccupation ground surface. Wall trenches and post molds originated in this midden level and intruded into the underlying preoccupation ground surface. Nine wall trench segments were recorded but none were fully exposed. Two wall trench segments associated with a burned floor seemed to be from the same structure (Structure 1H, Feature 2). Abundant artifacts, thick midden, and numerous post molds indicate a very intense occupation. A wood charcoal sample (Beta-153710) from Feature 10, an ash-filled hearth on the premound surface, produced a radiocarbon date of two-sigma cal A.D. 680–980, with an intercept of A.D. 790, which we consider too early to be an accurate age for the premound ceramic assemblage (Table 4.1).

A very substantial wall trench (Feature 7) proved to be a palisade wall. The palisade postdates the premound features, for it originated above the

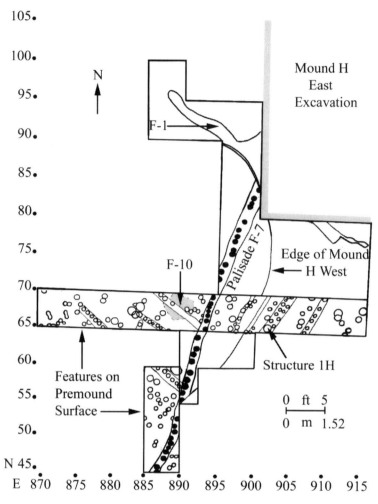

A.9. Plan of Mound H west features, 9SW2.

premound level and intruded into it. Post holes were present in the palisade wall trench. The palisade wall had not burned but, instead, the posts had been removed, and soil deposited over them. The palisade posts left holes in a clay soil so compact that the hollow cavities did not fill in the subsequent centuries. The palisade was traced in a straight line for 20 m without any sign of termination. The palisade wall does not parallel the general north-south orientation of the site as might be expected if it were designed to aid in the defense of the entire mound group. It does, however, run northeast to southwest, which is parallel to the southeastern side of Mound A. We suspect that the palisade was constructed for the purpose of enclosing Mound A, either as a screen to shield it from public view or as a defensive wall to defend it from attack.

Mound H West and Feature 1 After the palisade wall was dismantled, a complex series of events ensued in the Mound H area. Multiple soil layers were deposited over the premound midden and palisade remnant. It was obvious that some of these strata were composed of fill dirt mined from elsewhere on the site, and then dumped over the Mound H area. We interpret these strata as at least two episodes of mound construction that built up a low rounded area designated Mound H West. Only a small portion of Mound H West was exposed horizontally, but a curving edge of the mound flank can be seen in plan view in Figure A.9. Apparently, Mound H West was created by successive occupation surfaces and mound fill zones, but the situation is very complex, and it is impossible to decipher all of the construction activities that formed Mound H West without additional excavation.

At the exposed eastern edge of Mound H West was a low area filled with midden and soil, Feature 1. Feature 1 is distinct from Mound H West and postdates the premound midden. Feature 1 apparently formed during or after Mound H West was established. A large linear mass of clay, an architectural feature of unknown function, also abuts the edge of Mound H West. Features 1 and the clay feature filled in the low space between Mound H West and another concentration of architectural features, Mound H East.

Mound H East, Structure 2H, and Structure 3H Mound H East is that part of Mound H just 1.5 m east to northeast of the edge of Mound H West, the palisade wall, and Feature 1. Here, the remains of two large wattle-and-daub buildings were unearthed (Figure A.10). It is probable that Mound H East formed through successive deposits of earthen fill in the same manner as Mound H West. Both areas are at the same elevation. The early construction history of Mound H East remains obscure, however, because excavations were not as deep as those that penetrated the premound surface at Mound H West.

Structure 2H is the remains of a 9-x-9 m building with single-set post walls (Figure A.10). The hard-packed floor of Structure 2H was discovered 1.2 m below datum, just above the level of the premound midden encountered in Mound H West. On the interior floor were four large post molds, 60–70 cm in diameter, where roof support posts once stood. Each of these post molds had adjoining "slide trenches" (indicated by dotted lines in Figure A.10) dug either to ease the heavy posts into position or to remove them. A projecting entranceway or vestibule, constructed with two parallel wall trenches, was placed at the southwestern corner. A line of post molds, per-

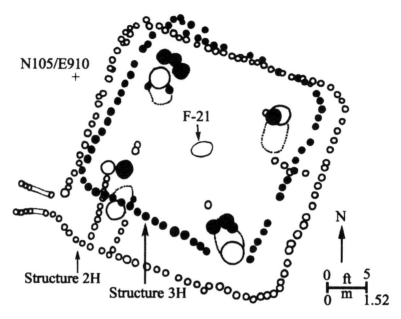

N105/E910
+

F-21

Structure 2H

Structure 3H

N

0 ft 5

0 m 1.52

A.10. Plan of Structures 2H and 3H, Mound H east, 9SW2.

pendicular to the interior wall just inside the entranceway, indicates a wall was erected to further screen off the interior room from the vestibule. The northeast-southwest alignment of the Structure 2H walls roughly parallels the palisade line (and the southwest side of Mound A). Structure 2H post-dates the palisade, however, because the vestibule wall trenches intrude down into the palisade wall trench.

Two important features are associated with Structure 2H. On the central floor was a circular burned area (Feature 21), 90 cm in diameter, composed of hard-baked clay, ash, and charcoal. Feature 21 was not a prepared fire basin, but a hearth placed directly on the floor. A wood charcoal sample (Beta-15049) from Feature 21 produced a radiocarbon date of two-sigma cal A.D. 1260–1310, with an intercept of A.D. 1290 (Table 4.1). A large "ash pile" (Feature 13), composed of ash, small artifacts, and charred organic remains was deposited at the northern corner of Structure 2H. A large quantity of the Feature 13 contents were sieved and floated to retrieve ecofacts, but these remains have yet to be analyzed.

Apparently, Structure 2H was dismantled by removing wall posts because several Structure 2H wall posts were preserved as hollow cavities partially filled or sealed by the rapid deposition of a stiff, unfired white clay. Because the deposit followed the wall alignments, we think the white clay is wall daub. Upon removal of the posts, a thin earth fill was dumped over the old floor, and a new building, Structure 3H, was erected superimposed over the razed foundation of Structure 2H. Structure 3H conformed to the wall alignments of the earlier building, but it was smaller, 7.6-x-7.6 m, and built of single-set posts with interior roof supports. Like the earlier building, Structure 3H was also dismantled upon abandonment, then covered with a layer of earth fill. When viewed in profile, the redeposited fill surrounding Structures 2H and 3H appears to be embanked against the building as an earthen berm. Due to excavation boundaries, it is difficult to differentiate between the various forms of mound building and the intentional covering of structure remains, but the "burial" of Structure 3H terminated the use of Mound H East.

The sequence of construction at Mound H can now be summarized. Occupation began on the premound ground surface with midden deposits, the erection of wall-trench structures, and various other signs of intense habitation. Next, a palisade transected the area. Later, the palisade was dismantled, followed by a series of construction and fill episodes that created the elevated surfaces of Mound H West and Mound H East. Two superimposed single-set post buildings were erected at Mound H East. Each was dismantled and buried after use. We interpret the Mound H East buildings as elite domiciles. Not enough of the Mound H West surface was exposed to determine the nature of buildings placed there, but it appears that Mound H West and East were once separate, low mounds that were later joined into a continuous edifice by dumping fill into the space between them. Feature 1 is the result of this mound-building fill.

Artifact Provenience and Chronology

We analyzed all of the excavated materials at the Singer-Moye site and placed the individual artifact lots into larger sets to create provenience groups (Tables A.6–A.9). The provenience groups are consistent with stratigraphic relationships and feature associations, and obviate some of the problems posed by comparing lots with low artifact counts. These provenience groups are summarized as follows:

A1. This provenience group is from the excavation unit on the summit of Mound A, including Structure A1 (unit field and catalog designation: XUD; grid coordinates: N100–140/L10–30, R10).

A2. This provenience group is from the excavation unit at the base of the northeastern side of Mound A (unit field and catalog designation: XUE; grid coordinates: SE10–60/R10–20, L10). It consists of midden dumped from the mound summit.

C1. This provenience group is from the upper levels of Mound C (unit field and catalog designation: XUA; grid coordinates: N910–875/E390–400).

C2. This provenience group is from the lower levels of Mound C (same unit and grid coordinates as C1).

D2. This provenience group is from the Mound D summit excavation (unit field and catalog designation: XUB; grid coordinates: N1035–1175/E665–775).

E. This provenience group is from the excavation of Mound E, including Structure E1 (unit field and catalog designation: XUA; grid coordinates: N1013–1050/E485–505). It includes lots from the floor and features of Structure E1 and the redeposited fill added above the floor at the time of abandonment.

H1. This provenience group is from the redeposited fill added above the floor of Structure 3H (1.2–1.4 m below datum) at Mound H East (grid coordinates: N105–110/E930–935).

H2. This provenience group is from the floor and features of superimposed Structures 2H and 3H (1.4–1.5 m depth below datum) at Mound H East, including the Feature 13 ash pile (same grid coordinates as H1 and H2).

H3. This provenience group is Feature 1, a zone of redeposited fill at Mound H (grid coordinates: N70–80/E900–915).

HP1. This provenience group consists of lots from all post molds, wall trenches, and other features encountered in the premound midden at Mound H (grid coordinates: N65–70/E870–915; N45–60/E885–895). The Feature 7 palisade is included (grid coordinates: N45–105/E885–905).

HP2. This provenience group is from the premound midden at Mound H (same grid coordinates as HP1).

Based on a subsample of the total excavated ceramics from the Singer-Moye site, Knight (1979) identified major trends in ceramic change through time: shell temper declined and grit temper increased; arcade-decorated handled jars decreased; and Lamar Complicated Stamped appeared late in the sequence. Our seriation largely confirms Knight's sequence. In part, this is because we used the same provenience groups, but instead of a subsample, we analyzed all available ceramics, and included additional materials from the Mound H excavations. These data, together with three additional radiocarbon dates, permit us to subdivide the ceramic sequence at Singer-Moye into three time spans of occupation.

The earliest Mississippian component at the site is represented by the small sample from the premound and lower levels of Mound C (C2). This assem-

Table A.6. Provenience of Ceramic Types, Various Mounds, 9SW2.

CERAMIC TYPES	C1	C2	A1	A2	E	D2
Grit/Sand Temper						
Cool Branch Incised	0	2	1	1	1	1
Lamar Complicated Stamped	0	0	10	12	0	2
Lamar Plain	0	0	28	34	3	21
Fort Walton Incised	0	0	0	32	2	10
Complicated Stamped	0	0	1	22	5	1
Columbia Incised	1	0	7	8	1	6
Bold Incised	0	0	0	0	0	2
Fine Incised	1	0	0	1	1	0
Nunnally Incised	33	0	12	2	0	0
Red Filmed	0	0	9	16	1	1
Painted	0	0	3	2	0	0
Combed	0	0	0	8	0	0
Grit/Sand Plain	208	26	1240	1534	382	865
Shell Temper						
Moundville Incised	5	1	0	0	0	0
Red Filmed	0	2	0	0	0	0
Shell Plain	123	50	36	14	14	7
Total Plain	331	76	1276	1548	396	872
Total Decorated	40	5	71	138	14	44
Total Sherds	371	81	1347	1686	410	916

blage represents a time when shell temper occurred in a relatively high frequency (66 percent) compared to grit temper, and Moundville Incised and Cool Branch Incised were the predominate decorated types. The frequency of shell-tempered pottery in the upper portion of Mound C (C1) decreases somewhat in comparison to C2 but it is still relatively high (37 percent), so C2 also falls early in the Singer-Moye sequence. The latest Mississippian component is the terminal occupation of Mound A summit (A1), the associated dump at the base of Mound A (A2), and the Mound D summit (D2). In these late assemblages, shell temper declined from the earlier high frequencies to less than 3 percent and shell-tempered Moundville Incised was no longer used. Arcade-decorated handled jars were still present in the form of grit-tempered Cool Branch Incised, but in low frequencies, replaced in popularity by the carinated bowls of Fort Walton Incised and the simple jars of Lamar Complicated Stamped.

Ceramic samples from Mound E (E), the Mound H premound, and the various episodes of Mound H use exhibit frequencies of ceramic types and modes that span a middle interval between the early and late periods. In this

Table A.7. Provenience of Ceramic Types, Mound H, 9SW2.

CERAMIC TYPES	H1-2	H3	TOTAL H	HP1	HP2	TOTAL HP
Grit/Sand Temper						
Cool Branch Incised	11	5	16	7	12	19
Columbia Incised	5	11	16	1	6	7
Complicated Stamped	8	9	17	5	9	14
Lamar Plain	5	6	11	2	9	11
Nunnally Incised	3	9	12	1	7	8
Fort Walton Incised	1	0	1	0	0	0
Red Filmed	1	1	2	0	0	0
Fine Incised	0	0	0	0	1	1
Grit/Sand Plain	2988	3313	6301	738	1138	1876
Shell Temper						
Moundville Incised	2	2	4	3	9	12
Red Filmed	0	1	1	0	0	0
Interior Incised	0	3	3	0	0	0
Shell Plain	231	91	322	138	103	241
Total Plain	3219	3404	6623	876	1241	2117
Total Decorated	36	47	83	19	53	72
Total Sherds	3255	3451	6706	895	1294	2189

middle period, shell temper ranged from 5–11 percent and Moundville Incised declined in frequency relative to Cool Branch Incised. Columbia Incised and Lamar Plain (appliqué rims) became common. Lamar Complicated Stamped was absent and Fort Walton Incised was rare. Also in the middle and late period assemblages are miscellaneous complicated stamped sherds. Some of these sherds are eroded, but others exhibit the fine-to-medium stamping and occasional motif sufficient to type them as Etowah Complicated Stamped and Savannah Complicated Stamped. Either local copies or imports, these complicated stamped vessels indicate some form of interaction between the people of Singer-Moye and populations to the north or east where the paddle-stamped ceramic tradition was predominant.

Excavations at Cemochechobee (9CY62)

Unlike excavation results at other regional mound centers, the Cemochechobee excavation report is readily available, and it is an exemplary job of archaeological reporting. Given our newly expanded database for regional mound sites, however, it is important that we reconsider the Cemochechobee

Table A.8. Provenience of Ceramic Modes, Various Mounds, 9SW2.

CERAMIC MODES	C1	C2	A1	A2	E	D2	H1	H2	H3	HP1	HP2
Arcade Motif											
Eyelash	1	1	1	1	0	1	*	*	2	5	8
Punctated	3	1	0	0	0	0	*	*	1	1	3
Unembellished	1	1	0	0	1	0	*	*	4	4	10
Rim											
Plain Appliqué	0	0	6	2	0	2	0	0	0	0	0
Notched Appliqué	0	0	4	15	3	12	3	2	6	2	9
Pinched Appliqué	0	0	18	16	0	7	0	0	0	0	0
Scallop Appliqué	0	0	0	1	0	0	0	0	0	0	0
Pinched Below Lip	0	0	10	26	4	11	0	0	0	0	0
Lip Notched	2	0	11	37	4	19	13	21	19	8	14
Lip Ticked	0	0	2	8	4	7	1	2	0	0	0
Noded	0	0	17	65	6	8	3	1	5	3	2
Horizontal Incised	0	0	0	3	0	1	11	22	8	0	7
Bulge Collar	2	0	0	1	0	0	5	1	8	0	6
Castellations	0	0	0	1	0	1	0	0	2	0	0
Total Rims	4	0	68	175	21	68	36	49	48	13	38
Vessel											
Simple Jar	0	0	25	41	3	9	0	0	0	0	0
Handled Jar	8	4	8	27	13	15	32	10	39	16	15
Open Bowl	1	0	3	0	2	1	21	1	36	17	21
Rounded Bowl	0	0	5	9	0	0	1	0	20	1	0
Carinated Bowl	0	0	0	4	1	0	0	0	0	0	0
Bottle/Beaker	33	0	12	2	0	0	1	3	9	1	7

Continued on the next page

Table A.8. *Continued*

CERAMIC MODES	C1	C2	A1	A2	E	D2	H1	H2	H3	HP1	HP2
Flaring-Rim Bowl	0	0	7	9	1	6	3	1	11	1	6
Miniature Jar	0	1	0	0	0	0	0	0	0	0	0
Total Vessels	42	5	60	92	20	31	58	15	115	36	49
Handle											
Plain Strap	0	0	2	10	4	4	5	0	0	0	3
Plain Loop	0	0	2	9	1	1	2	4	3	0	2
Top Node	1	0	3	13	2	9	3	4	6	1	8
Double Node	0	0	1	9	2	5	3	1	2	0	3
Top Double Ridge	0	0	0	0	1	0	0	0	0	0	0
Top Tri-Ridge	2	1	1	0	0	1	1	0	2	0	2
Incised	0	0	0	0	0	0	0	4	4	1	0
Horizontal Lug	0	0	1	4	1	1	2	0	1	0	2
Vertical Lug	0	0	2	18	1	4	3	2	7	1	1
Effigy Tail	1	0	0	0	0	1	0	0	1	0	1
Effigy Head	0	0	1	3	0	1	0	3	0	0	1
Total Handles	4	1	13	66	12	28	19	18	26	3	23

Table A.9. Provenience of Miscellaneous Artifacts, 9SW2.

	A1 No./Material	A2 No./Mat.	C No./Mat.	E No./Mat.	D2 No./Mat.	H No./Mat.	HP No./Mat.
FLAKED STONE							
Stemless Triang. PP/K	0	0	0	0	1/LC	0	1/LC
Debitage						P/LC P/Q	P/LC
GROUND STONE							
Worked Chunks	0	20g/L 30g/H	0	0	0	4/LM 3/L 3/H	3/LM 1/H
Celt Fragment/Flake	2/G	0	0	0	2/G	1/G	2/G
Discoidal	1/S, 2/G	1/Q, 1/S	0	0	1/S	2/S, M	2/S
Discoidal Preform	0	0	0	0	1/S	0	0
Mortar/Anvil	0	0	0	0	0	1/S	1/S
OTHER ARTIFACTS							
Disk	2/C	4/C	1/C	0	4/C	4/C	1/C
Smoking Pipe	14/C	4/C	1/C	3/C	2/C	0	2/C
Fired Daub	0	0	0	0	P/C	0	P/C
Unfired White Daub	P/C	P/C	0	0	0	P/C	P/C
Red Ocher Pigment	0	0	0	0	5g/H	10g/H	0
Yellow Ocher Pigment	0	0	0	0	0	5g/L	0
Ornament Fragments	2/CP	0	0	0	0	0	0
Cut Turtle Shell	0	0	0	0	0	1	1
Cut Marine Shell	0	0	0	0	0	1	1
Marine Shell Bead	0	0	0	0	0	1	0

Continued on the next page

Table A.9. *Continued*

	A1 No./ Material	A2 No./ Mat.	C No./ Mat.	E No./ Mat.	D2 No./ Mat.	H No./ Mat.	HP No./ Mat.
RAW MATERIAL							
Mica Sheet Fragments	< 5g	0	0	0	0	< 10g	< 5g
Hematite	P	0	0	0	0	P	P
Limonite	P	0	0	0	0	P	P
Unidentified Bone	P	P	P	0	0	P	P
Unidentified Botanical	P	0	0	P	0	P	P
Unidentified Shell	0	0	0	0	0	P	P

KEY: projectile point/knife (PP/K), local chert (LC), limonite (L), limestone (LM), hematite/ferruginous sandstone (H), sandstone (S), quartzite (Q), greenstone (G), copper (CP), marl (M), ceramic (C), present but not quantified (P), grams (g).

excavations in order to accomplish two goals. First, we place the site within the revised cultural sequence, based on seriation of ceramic samples from stratigraphic mound contexts. Second, the numerous radiocarbon samples from the excavations are the basis for much of the absolute chronology for the Mississippi period in the region. We reanalyzed these dates to produce a more accurate age for the site.

Eighteen radiocarbon dates spanning more than five centuries led the excavators to assign the Cemochechobee site to the Rood phase, A.D. 900–1400. Given what we now know about other lower Chattahoochee River valley mound sites, this occupation span is too early and too long. An occupation span estimate that is more consistent with ceramic assemblages and radiocarbon dates from the other mound centers would fall somewhere A.D. 1150–1250, within what we call the Rood II phase, a refinement and subdivision of the original Rood phase concept.

In the review of mound strata, ceramic samples, and calibrated radiocarbon dates presented below, 17 different occupation levels of Mounds A and B are sorted into provenience groups that represent three sequential subphases, Cemochechobee 1, 2, and 3. These subphases serve to subdivide the Rood II ceramic phase at the Cemochechobee site. Each subphase is defined by specific frequencies of ceramic types and ordered by stratigraphic superposition and radiocarbon assays. The earliest subphase, Cemochechobee 1, begins with a premound occupation beneath Mound A, continues with the initial construction of Mound A, stages AI–III, and includes the adjacent structures just north of Mound A on the premound B level. The middle subphase, Cemochechobee 2, includes the initial building of Mound B, stages BI–V. The final subphase, Cemochechobee 3, includes terminal Mound A stages AIV–V, Mound B stages BVI–X, and Mound C. The majority of the excavations took place on Mounds A and B, and most of the interpretation of the site's occupational history comes from these proveniences.

Mound Stratigraphy

Premound A and B A 10–40 cm thick, premound midden underlay both Mounds A and B. Premound A had several deep tombs. One of these burials contained the remains of an adult male interred with an elongated spatulate celt of polished greenstone (i.e., a "spud" celt). These long-stemmed greenstone celts are known throughout the Mississippian Southeast as symbols of authority (Pauketat 1983). The Cemochechobee celt is similar to two celts found in a similar premound context at the Cool Branch site, 24.5 km to the north. Another premound A burial had a headdress with sheet-copper arrow symbol badges similar to other such artifacts recovered at major centers such as Moundville, Etowah, and Lake Jackson (Brain and Phillips 1996:372–373), and minor centers such as Lubbub Creek (Blitz 1993:102).

Premound B was at first used for public rituals and then later for elite domiciles and nonmortuary ceremonial buildings (temples or meeting houses).

Mounds A and B Premound A was covered by Mound A. The mortuary functions of premound A continued with Mound A, although only premound A contained a mortuary or charnel house structure (Structure 2), and only two mound stages on Mound A were actually associated with human burials. The other three Mound A stages were interpreted as ritually purifying clay mantles, some with ritually "killed" vessel concentrations, but no burials or structures. Premound B remained uncovered for a period of use after construction of Mound A. The first three mound-building stages of Mound A predate any mound construction on Mound B. The premound B midden grades into the same stratigraphic level as AII, the second stage of Mound A. Even though Mound A was built in five stages, a review of the profile map reveals that BI fill overlies AIII fill, but is itself overlain by AIV fill. Thus Mound A witnessed a hiatus of construction activities. Mound A was abandoned after the Mound BVI stage, but before the Mound BVII stage of construction. Mound B stages contained the remains of elite domiciles or public buildings.

Mound C Mound C, located 5 m north of Mound B, was built in two stages sometime after abandonment of Mound A. Perhaps Mound C continued some of the same functions of Mound A, but the limited excavations of Mound C produced few clues about mound-related activities. Because the fill of Mound C closely resembled that of stage BVII, the last mound stage on Mound B associated with mound summit structures, the excavators suggested that Mounds B and C were in use at the same time, very late in the Cemochechobee sequence (Schnell et al. 1981:146–147).

Relative Ceramic Chronology

To partition the massive Cemochechobee pottery sample into chronologically sensitive provenience groups, specific reclassification and resorting procedures were followed. In order to fit the samples into our seriation of regional mound centers, we reclassified some of the Cemochechobee ceramic types to conform to the pottery classification presented in Appendix C. Once this was done, changing frequencies of key ceramic types could be charted in the stratigraphic levels of the two major mounds over the length of the site occupation.

We excluded all premound B ceramics for the following reason. While the premound A zone was clearly the oldest occupation level at the site because it was sealed over after Mound A construction began, the premound zone beneath Mound B formed over a much longer period. Because Mound A was built first, all of the adjacent premound B zone remained exposed until after stage AIII and prior to stage BI. It was not until the substantial horizontal expansion of stage BVII that a number of premound B features were covered over. The premound B provenience is a mixed deposit that potentially incorporates artifacts from the earliest to the latest occupation (Schnell et al. 1981:201–202). Therefore, we excluded all premound B ceramics from further analysis. Over 65 percent of the entire ceramic assemblage of over 16,698 sherds from excavations of Mounds A and B come from this mixed deposit.

Because we found no significant difference in frequencies between primary and secondary contexts for the same ceramic type from the same mound-building stage, we felt justified in lumping primary and secondary deposits from the same mound-building stage in order to build a larger, more robust sample from each stratigraphic level (Table A.10). We include the counts of Nunnally Incised and Andrews Decorated, the fine-ware bottles and beakers, in Table A.10, but do not include them in our calculations of relative ceramic frequencies. These fine wares were smashed and deposited in activities related to the termination of certain mound stages, and then rapidly covered with the ritually purifying clay mantles. Because they make up as much as 25–50 percent of the entire assemblage in some stages, the special-purpose contexts of these fine wares skews the frequencies of Cool Branch Incised, Moundville Incised, Columbia Incised, and Lamar Plain, the utilitarian pottery types we use as chronological markers. At other regional mound sites, Nunnally Incised and Andrews Decorated make up less than 5 percent of the entire decorated assemblage, but when they do appear, the bottles and beakers seem to be restricted to mound-renewal contexts similar to the Cemochechobee situation.

As a result of this reclassification and resorting into provenience groups, we have a clearer picture of the relative ceramic chronology at Cemochechobee. The Cemochechobee pottery assemblages are used to define the Rood II phase, subdivided at the site into the Cemochechobee 1–3 subphases. The ceramic type composition and provenience of the subphases can now be summarized.

Cemochechobee 1 Subphase Pottery The provenience units are premound A, mound-building stages AI–III. Cool Branch Incised represents almost 80 percent of the entire decorated assemblage (after we exclude the special-purpose bottles and beakers from our calculations), and contains the highest frequency of Moundville Incised (7 percent) and shell-tempered plain wares (12 percent) of the three subphases compared. Columbia Incised is present. There is a very low percentage of Lamar Plain (2 percent) and no Fort Walton Incised.

Table A.10. Provenience of Ceramic Types, 9CY62.

CERAMIC TYPES	PMdA	AI/II	AIII	BI	BII	BIII	BIV	BV	BVI	AIV	AV	BVII	BVIII	BIX/X	PMdB
Grit/Sand Temper															
Cool Branch Incised	58	43	43	73	41	0	32	7	18	7	18	22	10	26	234
Nunnally Incised	15	38	17	84	22	0	13	2	10	3	29	47	18	4	103
Andrews Decorated	11	31	2	1	1	0	0	0	0	0	20	5	1	1	17
Fort Walton Incised	0	0	0	1	1	0	0	0	0	0	0	2	2	3	8
Columbia Incised	12	7	2	18	3	0	5	1	2	1	0	3	2	3	53
Point Washington Incised	2	1	1	6	4	0	4	1	2	0	0	1	0	1	27
Lamar Plain	1	2	0	6	3	0	5	1	0	1	3	1	6	6	9
All Appliqué Noded	0	0	1	0	0	0	0	0	0	0	0	0	0	0	1
Red Filmed	0	0	0	0	0	0	3	0	0	0	0	0	0	0	4
Grit Plain	718	1437	1167	2738	1414	24	1903	366	1260	605	575	2170	703	1726	9724
Shell Temper															
Moundville Incised	3	3	8	1	3	0	4	0	0	0	0	1	2	0	15
Shell Plain	124	205	116	37	37	0	41	23	124	73	116	182	44	44	632
Total Decorated	102	125	73	190	78	0	66	12	32	12	70	82	41	44	471
Total Plain	842	1642	1183	2775	1451	24	1944	389	1384	678	691	2352	747	1770	10356

Cemochechobee 2 Subphase Pottery The provenience units are from the early construction of Mound B, stages BI–V. There is a continuation of the dominance of Cool Branch Incised (69 percent), with a concomitant rise in Lamar Plain (from 2 to 7 percent) and Columbia Incised (from 11 to 12 percent). Fort Walton Incised appears for the first time, but in trace amounts (< 1 percent). The frequency of Moundville Incised drops from 7 to 4 percent, along with a drop in shell-tempered plain wares from 12 to 2 percent.

Cemochechobee 3 Subphase Pottery The third and final subphase of site occupation is composed of these provenience units, arranged from earliest to latest: mound stages BVI, AIV–V, BVII–X. Cool Branch Incised continues to dominate the decorated assemblage at 71 percent, followed by an increase in the frequency of Lamar Plain (from 7 to 12 percent). Columbia Incised, declines (from 12 to 7 percent) in this latest subphase, a trend that continues on into the succeeding Rood and Singer phases, when Columbia Incised declines to less than 5 percent of the decorated assemblage. Fort Walton Incised also increases from < 1 to 5 percent in this final subphase. Because no Lamar Complicated Stamped ceramics were recovered from the entire site, this last period of mound construction must pre-date the Singer phase (A.D. 1400–1450), when Lamar Complicated Stamped first appears in the lower Chattahoochee River valley.

Rood II phase ceramics do not match Rood I phase pottery because Columbia Incised and Lamar Plain are present, and frequencies of Moundville Incised and shell-tempered plain wares are much lower. Also, frequencies of Cool Branch Incised are much higher in the Rood II phase than that found in Rood III phase assemblages (A.D. 1300–1400). The Rood II phase ceramics also differ from Singer phase ceramics because Fort Walton Incised and Lamar Plain do not increase in frequency until the latter portion of the site occupation in Cemochechobee 3. By no means do these later types dominate the Cemochechobee 3 assemblages as they do in the Singer phase components at the Gary's Fish Pond site and the later stages of occupation at the Singer-Moye multiple-mound center, both sites with radiocarbon dates ranging from A.D. 1350 to A.D. 1450.

Radiocarbon Chronology

In his analysis of radiocarbon dates from the Cemochechobee site, Knight (1981b) used the radiocarbon midpoints for each dated sample to arrive at a mound chronology (Long and Rippeteau 1974). He rejected seven of the 18 samples because they had radiocarbon midpoint dates that were either too early or too late to agree with the stratigraphic sequence from Mounds A and B. He concluded that the 11 acceptable dates yielded a date range from A.D. 930 to A.D. 1285, with an estimated total duration of site occupation of A.D. 900 to A.D. 1350. Since Knight's work, reporting the results of dated samples across a two-sigma range of standard deviation has become the procedure recommended by radiocarbon laboratories. The radiocarbon midpoint is not the best estimate for the radiocarbon age if the deviation on either side of that midpoint is ignored. A midpoint is merely a value that falls at the halfway point in the possible range of years calculated (with a 95 percent degree of confidence) for any given sample. It is somewhere within this range of years that provides the best estimate for the sample's date. Of course, a wide range of years is a much less precise estimate for the age of a sample (i.e., the sample is not dated to an exact year as it was using the midpoint), but it is more accurate.

For this reason we applied the current radiocarbon calibration curve (Stuiver et al. 1998) to all 18 of the Cemochechobee dated samples and calculated the two-sigma probability that each sample date falls within a particular span of time. Of the 18 samples, four rather than seven can be discarded because their estimated dating ranges do not correspond to their stratigraphic position at the site. These rejected samples are too early (ranging from A.D. 600 to A.D. 900) or too late (post-A.D. 1550) to correspond to site components. The remaining 14 dated samples (Table 4.1) were compared to the mound strata and ceramic samples.

Cemochechobee 1 Subphase Dates The earliest date of cal A.D. 784–1156 comes from the premound A burial with the elongated spatulate celt. Another radiocarbon sample from a premound A wall trench feature was dated cal A.D. 981–1210. Two more radiocarbon samples were dated for the Structure 7 and Circular Structures complex located on premound B and thought to be contemporaneous with the early construction stages of Mound A (AI–III). Even though the premound B dates had a cumulative estimated dating range from cal A.D. 1163 to A.D. 1482, these presumably contemporaneous samples showed an overlapping range from cal A.D. 1163 to A.D. 1385. The earlier part of this estimated dating range overlaps with the premound A wall trench date. Two samples from the early stages of Mound A (AI–II) produced two-sigma calibrated dates that range from A.D. 985 to A.D. 1219, with a similar 50 to 60–year overlap (A.D. 1160–1220) with the samples from the premound precinct. The overlapping radiocarbon dating ranges attest to the probability that Structure 7 and the Circular Structures Complex of the premound B zone were in use at the same time as Mound A stages AI–III. Thus radiocarbon dating of six samples point to an initial site occupation associated with the Cemochechobee 1 subphase A.D. 1150–1220.

Cemochechobee 2 Subphase Dates Five radiocarbon dates for the Cemochechobee 2 subphase come from early stages of Mound B (BI, BII, and BIV).

These two-sigma calibrated dates ranged from A.D. 893 to A.D. 1296, with an overlap between four of these dates (from BI and BIV) of A.D. 1159–1262, the best-estimate time range for the early stages of Mound B. If the earlier Cemochechobee 1 subphase dates to A.D. 1150–1220, then the Cemochechobee 2 subphase probably could not begin until sometime after A.D. 1200, thus providing an estimate of A.D. 1200–1250 for the Cemochechobee 2 subphase.

Cemochechobee 3 Subphase Dates The final occupation of the mounds, associated with the Cemochechobee 3 ceramic samples, is documented with three calibrated radiocarbon dates from mound stage BVI Structure 1, with a cumulative estimated dating range of A.D. 1164 to A.D. 1451. Because all three dates came from the same structure, we assume the three samples are contemporaneous, so the overlapping range of A.D. 1164 to A.D. 1303 provides a better dating estimate. We can compress the Cemochechobee 3 subphase date range further by maintaining stratigraphic order with the dating ranges from the previous Cemochechobee 2 subphase samples; thus we estimate the likely contemporaneousness of these samples falls A.D. 1250–1300. The latest stages of Mound A (AIV–V) and Mound B (BVII–X) either was not sampled for radiocarbon or has dates that do not agree with their stratigraphic location in the mound. We conclude that the abandonment of Mounds A, B, and C would have occurred prior to A.D. 1300.

The site began as a single-mound center, and only two mounds were used at any one time. The radiocarbon dates fall into three stratigraphic groupings with the following ranges: Cemochechobee 1 subphase (A.D. 1150–1220), Cemochechobee 2 subphase (A.D. 1220–1250), and Cemochechobee 3 subphase (A.D. 1250–1300). The entire Cemochechobee occupation sequence may span no more than 100 years. This new site chronology is only one-quarter of the time span proposed by the excavators. The shortened time span may explain why so little ceramic assemblage variation existed from the earliest to the latest occupation levels. Also, the refined chronology presented in our study does not support the chronological reassessment of Cemochechobee put forth by Brain and Phillips (1996:185–187), who place the occupation at least 150 years later.

Appendix B
The Single-Mound-Center Excavations

In this appendix we present detailed overviews of all archaeological investigations at the single-mound sites in the lower Chattahoochee River region that date A.D. 1100–1650, including previously unpublished excavation results. The overviews supplement the site synopses in Chapter 3. Our intent is to provide information on the provenience and context of the mound artifact samples and associated radiocarbon dates used to construct the regional chronology presented in Chapter 4.

Excavations at the Abercrombie Site (1RU61)

C. B. Moore (1907:449–450) found the mound at Abercrombie to be 4.2 m (14 ft.) high and 25.9-x-28.9 m (85-x-95 ft.) at the base. Moore remarked on the density of surface debris around the mound and concentrated his efforts there, but was disappointed to find only a protohistoric-period component. Next to dig at the site, Brandon (1909:Figure 39) illustrated three vessels from the mound; two are jars with wide, flat handles, and one jar with incision below the rim. These jars are similar to protohistoric-period pottery in eastern Tennessee. Another artifact from the mound, a shell mask gorget (Brandon 1909:Figure 40), appears to be either the Chickamauga or McBee style in the Brain and Phillips (1996) classification. Distribution of these mask gorgets concentrate in eastern Tennessee. Unfortunately, Brandon's illustration is too poor for precise identification, and we could learn nothing more about the gorget. Both the jar and gorget styles are most likely a post-A.D. 1550 development attributable to the historically known influx of Muskogee speakers into the valley from the north.

In 1947, Wesley R. Hurt (1975) of the University of Alabama recovered artifacts from a 3.0-x-1.5 m (10-x-5 ft.) trench excavated to the depth of 30 cm (1 ft.) into the mound. He also placed seven test units in the off-mound habitation area. University of Alabama archaeologists returned in 1962, and again excavated in the off-mound habitation area (Kurjack 1975). Seriation of both mound and off-mound ceramic samples by 15-cm (.5-ft.) levels showed that from lower to upper deposits, grit-tempered pottery decreased as shell-tempered pottery increased, the relative frequency of burnished pottery increased, and that Lamar Complicated Stamped and Fort Walton Incised were minority types compared to burnished pottery (Kurjack 1975:Table 25, Figure 63). Abercrombie became the type site for an Abercrombie phase defined by these ceramic assemblage characteristics and estimated to date A.D. 1550–1650 based on associated trade material from the off-mound area (Knight 1994a, b; Schnell 1970).

In 1967, Frank T. Schnell of the Columbus Museum of Arts and Crafts conducted the most extensive investigation of the mound. He mapped an oval-shaped mound 60 m in diameter and 1.8 m high. These dimensions indicate that the mound had been flattened and spread, with a loss of at least half the original height between 1907 and 1967. Schnell's main excavation unit was a 3.0-x-24.3 m (10-x-80 ft.) trench (XUA), oriented east to west (N480–490/W400–480), which began some distance off-mound and extended into the mound center (Figure 3.9). Schnell excavated in 15-cm (.5-ft) levels. We used Schnell's profile drawings, field photographs, cataloged artifact proveniences, and notes to identify the major mound-building stages.

A 15.2 m section of the XUA trench, revealing a profile from the mound center to the mound edge, is illustrated in Figure B.1. The mound sequence began with occupation layer H laid down on premound surface I. Stratum H is either a thin initial mound stage or an intense premound occupation, but strata C and B are definite mound stages. Strata D, E, and F are additional mound-building episodes originally superimposed over H, C, and D, but later truncated by the plow zone, A. D and E are undisturbed remnant stages because Burial 2 (G) is intact. Stratum F, the remnant final mound stage, was also truncated by later mound destruction. We combined unit and level lots into eight provenience groups in an attempt to isolate components. The provenience groups are XUA–Mound Edge, Mound 3–upper levels (M3U), Burial 2 (B2), excavation units B, C, and D (XUB-D), Mound 3–lower levels (M3L), mixed Mound 3 and Mound 2 (M3/M2), Mound 2 (M2), and Mound 1 (M1). These provenience groups are arranged in order from the western end of XUA trench east to the mound center.

The XUA–Mound Edge (N480/W440–480) provenience group is composed of four 3-x-3 m (10-x-10 ft.) units in the western portion of XUA

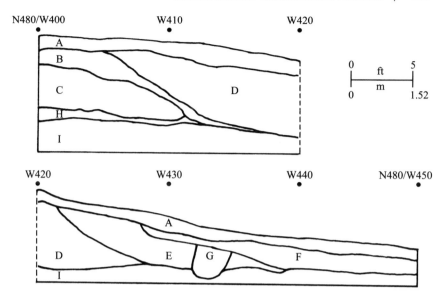

B.1. South profile XUA, Abercrombie mound.

Trench. XUA–Mound Edge units appear to be off-mound, mound edge, or mound redeposit (strata A, F, I), so we grouped all lots into four 15-cm levels; artifacts from these levels are inventoried in Table B.1. We detect at least two components here: Abercrombie phase ceramics characterized by burnished shell-tempered or grit-tempered ware mixed with an older Averett phase component.

Artifacts from the mound are quantified in Tables B.2–4. Mound 3–upper levels (M3U) are portions of the trench from 0 to 76 cm below surface in N480–490/W430–440. M3U sampled the plow zone (stratum A), and a layer of "blue mottled clay midden" and "disturbed black humic clay" (stratum F). M3U has only a trace of the burnished shell-tempered ware present in XUA–Mound Edge. Mound 3–lower levels (M3L) ranged from .76 to 1.2 m below surface (N480–490/W430–440). M3L is an Averett mound-building episode of "blue and tan basket loaded clay" (stratum E). B2 (G) is a burial pit intrusive into M3L, apparently originating from M3U (Burial 1 was assigned to isolated bone fragments from the B2 feature). B2 contained the poorly preserved remains of at least one adult.

M3/M2 is a mix of Mound 3 and Mound 2. This provenience group resulted from digging the arbitrary levels from 0 to 1.6 m below surface in the sloping mound strata in N480–490/W420–430 (strata A, F, E, D, I). Mound 2 is another construction stage identified by Schnell as "tan and blue basket loaded clay." M2 includes lots from unit N480–490/W410–420,

Table B.1. Provenience of XUA-Mound Edge Ceramics, 1RU61.

CERAMIC TYPES	0–15 cm	15–30 cm	30–45 cm	45–75 cm	TOTAL
Grit/Sand Temper					
Lamar Complicated Stamped	6	24	15	16	61
Complicated Stamped	4	1	1	1	7
Rood Incised	7	5	23	28	63
Lamar Plain	3	2	4	1	10
Bold Incised	1	2	3	0	6
Fine Incised	1	0	3	2	6
Fort Walton Incised	0	0	2	0	2
Averett Plain	0	0	3	1	4
Interior Incised	1	1	1	1	4
Engraved	0	3	0	2	5
Roughened	0	4	1	3	8
Red Filmed	0	0	1	7	8
Check Stamped	0	0	0	1	1
Burnished Grit/Sand Plain	34	98	66	86	284
Unburnished Grit/Sand Plain	142	169	213	269	793
Total Grit/Sand Plain	176	267	279	355	1077
Shell Temper					
Burnished Incised	0	2	0	0	2
Incised	0	4	0	0	4
Burnished Shell Plain	1	21	10	12	44

CERAMIC TYPES	0–15 cm	15–30 cm	30–45 cm	45–75 cm	TOTAL
Unburnished Shell Plain	6	45	41	15	107
Total Shell Plain	7	66	51	27	151
Total Plain	183	333	330	382	1228
Total Decorated	23	48	57	63	191
Total Sherds	206	381	387	445	1419
CERAMIC MODES					
Simple Jar	1	3	1	0	5
Open Bowl	2	2	1	0	5
Rounded Bowl	0	1	1	2	4
Flaring-Rim Bowl	1	1	0	1	3
Notched Appliqué	3	0	2	1	6
Pinched Appliqué	0	2	2	0	4
Lip Notched	1	1	0	1	3
Pinched Folded	0	0	0	3	3
Pinched Below Lip	0	0	0	1	1
Horizontal Lug	0	1	0	0	1

Table B.2. Provenience of Ceramic Types, 1RU61.

CERAMIC TYPES	M3U	B2	XUB-D	M3L	M3/M2	M2	M2/M1	M1
Grit/Sand Temper								
Averett Plain	0	1	10	17	6	18	10	12
Lamar Comp. Stamped	11	7	0	0	1	0	0	0
Complicated Stamped	0	3	11	1	5	5	11	13
Bold Incised	2	0	0	0	1	0	0	0
Fort Walton Incised	1	0	0	0	0	0	1	0
Lamar Plain	1	0	0	0	1	0	0	0
Interior Incised	1	0	0	0	0	0	0	0
Engraved	1	0	0	0	0	0	0	0
Roughened	0	1	2	0	3	9	4	10
Red Filmed	0	0	2	0	0	0	2	2
Check Stamped	0	2	0	0	4	1	0	0
Cool Branch Incised	0	0	0	0	1	0	0	0
Burnished Grit/Sand Plain	5	2	13	0	1	0	1	7
Unburnished Grit/Sand Plain	122	269	619	135	434	554	222	695
Total Grit/Sand Plain	127	271	632	135	435	554	223	702
Shell Temper								
Incised	1	0	0	0	0	0	0	0
Burnished Shell Plain	0	0	1	0	0	0	0	0
Unburnished Shell Plain	4	1	3	0	5	0	2	0
Total Shell Plain	4	1	4	0	5	0	2	0
Total Plain	131	272	636	135	440	554	225	702
Total Decorated	18	14	25	18	22	33	28	37
Total Sherds	149	286	661	153	462	587	253	739

Table B.3. Provenience of Ceramic Modes, 1RU61.

CERAMIC MODES	M3U	B2	M3L	XUB -D	M3/ M2	M2	M2/ M1	M1
Vessel								
Simple Jar	0	3	12	17	8	18	10	12
Handled Jar	0	0	0	1	1	0	0	0
Open Bowl	1	0	0	1	1	0	2	5
Rounded Bowl	1	5	3	0	2	1	4	1
Flaring-Rim Bowl	1	0	0	0	0	0	0	0
Bottle	0	0	0	0	0	0	1	0
Total Vessels	3	8	15	19	12	19	17	18
Rim								
Notched Appliqué	1	0	0	0	1	0	0	0
Lip Notched	1	1	0	0	0	0	0	0
Pinched Folded	3	0	0	0	0	0	0	0
Pinched Below Lip	3	0	0	0	0	0	0	0
Total Rims	8	1	0	0	1	0	0	0
Stamped Motifs								
Figure 9 with dot	1	0	0	0	0	0	0	0
2 Bar Circle	0	3	0	2	0	0	0	2
3 Bar Circle	0	0	0	0	0	0	0	2
Ladder Base Diamond	0	0	0	0	1	0	0	0
Bull's Eye	0	0	0	0	1	0	0	0
2 Bar Diamond	0	0	0	0	0	1	2	5
2 Bar Cross Diamond	0	0	0	0	0	1	1	0
2 Bar Cross Diamond A	0	0	0	0	0	0	0	2
3 Bar 3 Cross Diamond	0	0	0	0	0	0	0	1
2 Bar Diamond A	0	0	0	0	0	0	2	1
1 Bar Cross Diamond	0	0	0	0	0	0	0	1
Total Stamped Motifs	1	3	0	2	2	2	5	14

0 to 2.1 m below surface, a trench segment from N481/W436 at 1.3 m below surface, and an "ash lens" at 1.5 m below surface (N489/W421.5) (strata A, D, B). To judge from the ceramic content, M2 is an Averett phase mound stage. M2/M1 is a mix of M2 and the upper portion of M1, composed of "brown clayey sand with charcoal flecks." M2/M1 consists of lots from N480–490/410–400, at 0 to 1 m below surface (a mix of strata A, B, and D).

M1, from 1.2 to 2.2 m below surface in N480–490/W400–410, represents the initial mound construction stages or mound core. M1 had clay-sand strata that represent construction stages (strata B, C, H), but it was not possible to assign artifacts to individual strata. M1 was constructed during

Table B.4. Provenience of Miscellaneous Artifacts, 1RU61.

	M3 No./ Material	B2 No./ Mat.	M3/M2 No./Mat.	M2 No./ Mat.	M1 No./ Mat.
FLAKED STONE					
Stemless Triang. PP/K	0	0	0	0	1/LC
Debitage	0	0	0	0	P/Q
GROUND STONE	0	0	0	0	0
Grinding Slab Fragment	0	0	3/GR	0	0
Worked Chunks	0	1/G	5g/H	1g/PW	2/G
Celt Fragment	0	0	0	1/G	0
OTHER ARTIFACTS					
Disk Ornament	0	0	0	1/M	0
Beaver Incisor Chisel	0	0	0	6	0
Bead, Cylindrical	0	0	0	1/C	0
Red Ocher Pigment	0	0	0	5g/H	0
Disk	1/C				
Smoking Pipe	0	1	0	1/C	0
Fired Daub	P/C	P/C	0	0	0
ECOFACT					
Unidentified Bone	0	P	0	P	P
Unidentified Shell	0	P	0	P	P

KEY: projectile point/knife (PP/K), local chert (LC), white quartzite (Q), greenstone (G), hematite/ferruginous sandstone (H), petrifled wood (PW), unident. metal (M), unidentified hard gray stone (GR), ceramic (C), present but not quantified (P), weight in grams (g).

the Averett phase. Finally, XUB-E consists of four 1.5-x-1.5 m (5-x-5 ft.) units placed in the mound center. The XUB-E units penetrated no deeper than 76 cm below surface, and contain a mix of the earliest Averett phase component and the later component with burnished pottery.

There are few indications of mound activities apart from the food consumption that left ecofacts and potsherds. Due to limited horizontal excavation, the nature of mound buildings is unknown, but fired daub implies the presence of architecture associated with M3. Minor quantities of red ocher pigment, grinding slab fragments, and faceted hematite chunks are residues of pigment production and use in M2/M3. Burial 2 leaves no doubt that the mound was the scene of at least one funeral, but we cannot conclude that mortuary activities were the primary mound function.

Mound Chronology

The construction history of Abercrombie mound began in the Averett phase (A.D. 900–1300) when two or three mound-building strata (M1) were laid down. A radiocarbon sample from M1 produced an intercept of cal A.D. 1270, with a two-sigma range of cal A.D. 1170–1320 (Beta-157589) (Table 4.1). Next was M2, also Averett phase, which includes a thick mound stage. M3L followed, possibly another stage because Schnell drew a division line between M2 and M3L, but the physical description of the two strata is similar. Abercrombie M1, M2, and possibly M3L are examples of Averett-phase mound building. The form and function of the Averett mound is not clear, but the presence of multiple strata suggests the multiple episodes of construction typical of platform mounds. The radiocarbon date and trace quantities of Cool Branch Incised suggest that the mound was constructed after A.D. 1100, most likely between A.D. 1200 and A.D. 1300.

Finally, there is M3U, which clearly overlies M3L. M3U stratum F is interpreted as the remnant final mound stage, put down after the Averett phase. The distressingly small M3U ceramic sample (n = 149) lacks Averett pottery, contains burnished grit-tempered pottery, but lacks the burnished shell-tempered pottery used to mark the onset of the Abercrombie phase. On this basis alone, we would assign M3U stratum F to the preceding Stewart phase (A.D. 1550–1600), when burnished grit-tempered pottery first becomes important in regional assemblages. However, burnished grit-tempered pottery continued into the succeeding Abercrombie phase, and Hurt's 1947 mound unit ceramic sample, which is larger than the M3U ceramic sample, includes the addition of burnished shell-tempered pottery. From these observations, we conclude that an Abercrombie phase component is associated with the final mound stage F. Evidently, there was a 300-year hiatus in mound use between the Averett phase M3L episode (stratum E) and the final Abercrombie phase M3U mound-building episode.

We interpret the XUA–Mound Edge as mixed deposit that includes material re-deposited by the plow from the upper portion of the mound. The Averett component is present, but XUA-Mound Edge differs from the M3U assemblage by the addition of Rood Incised, shell-tempered burnished pottery, and two sherds of Abercrombie Incised, a difference we attribute to the vagaries of sampling. As was the case with the mound deposits, the Abercrombie component is present in the off-mound deposit, superimposed over the Averett component.

Some archaeologists see problems with the identification and use of the Abercrombie phase as a cultural-historical unit. Braley (1998:9–11) suggests that the Abercrombie phase is not a valid phase, but a mixture of pottery from late Stewart phase components and Blackmon phase (A.D. 1650–1715) components. He attributes this mixing to a reoccupation of Stewart phase sites by Blackmon phase peoples, immigrants from the north who brought shell tempered pottery and Guntersville style arrow points. If so, that would extend the Stewart phase time span another fifty years, and place the arrival of the Muskogees from the north in the mid-seventeenth century. Alternatively, perhaps the Stewart phase is the product of indigenous Hitchiti speakers and the Blackmon phase is the result of an immigrant Muskogee-indigenous Hitchiti cultural exchange or fusion of ceramic attributes (Worth 2000:274). This alternative scenario treats the Abercrombie phase as a valid cultural-historical unit that spans the time of initial Muskogean settlement; it may represent the earliest products of this proposed immigrant-indigenous fusion. The cultural affiliations of these phase populations are central to the issue of Creek ethnogenesis. Can these assemblages be assigned to an ethnic group? Does the immigrant-indigenous fusion of pottery styles signal the initial formation of the multiethnic Creek Confederacy?

Given the potential mixing of components at Abercrombie, we are not in a position to resolve the issues raised by Braley's critique of the Abercrombie problem. Until additional evidence is forthcoming, however, we will treat the Abercrombie phase as a valid cultural-historical unit. We are confident that the ceramics recovered by Hurt and Schnell place the upper portion of the mound in the Abercrombie phase, which we estimate to date A.D. 1600–1650. Certainly, the off-mound habitation area has components that date from the late sixteenth through seventeenth centuries; some glass and silver beads from village burials date to ca. A.D. 1590 (Knight and Mistovitch 1984:225). A perforated broad-bit spatulate celt (Brandon 1909:Figure 42) from the off-mound cemetery is the "late form" that dates from A.D. 1500 into the 1600s (Brain and Phillips 1996:140). A Thirty Acre Field–style embossed copper artifact from the off-mound habitation area at Abercrombie dates to A.D. 1565–1600 (Smith 1987:101).

Note on Curation

All excavation records and artifacts are at the Columbus Museum, Columbus, Georgia.

Excavations at the Kyle Site (9ME3)

We examined artifacts from the Kyle mound stored at the Smithsonian Institution's Museum of the American Indian Museum Support Center in Suitland, Maryland. An antiquarian, F. W. Miller, dug the artifacts from the mound about a century ago. Peter Brandon (1909) claims that Miller found 16,000 beads in a single mound burial! Most were shell beads, but Brandon tells us that "white and yellow quartz, and several dozens of amethyst" beads were recovered. That no glass beads are mentioned suggests a pre-A.D. 1600 age for this extraordinary burial because glass beads largely replaced shell beads after 1600 (Smith 1987:47). Brandon says little about the mound pottery, but mentions that three "hoe-shaped implements" were found.

Brandon refers to perforated broad-bit spatulate celts. Brain and Phillips (1996:379) cite illustrations of these Kyle mound celts (Moorehead 1910: Figure 373), identify them as the "intermediate form," and estimate an age of A.D. 1450–1550. Marvin Smith (1987:101) assigns a wider temporal span to this celt type, from A.D. 1350 into the 1600s.

One of the perforated spatulate celts mentioned by Brandon is present. Both shell and glass beads are in the collection, but time constraints precluded a more detailed analysis. Instead, we classified eight whole vessels from the mound. Like the other artifacts from the Kyle mound, there is no contextual information about the pots. Assuming the pots were in primary context, which is likely for whole vessels, they provide relative date estimates for mound use. Two intervals of mound use can be identified: an initial Averett phase (A.D. 900–1300) occupation and a protohistoric Abercrombie component (A.D. 1600–1650). The earlier Averett component is represented by a single Averett Plain simple jar. Vessels that belong to the later protohistoric component include two burnished, shell-tempered jars (one with vestigial handles and the other a simple jar without handles), an Abercrombie Incised jar, and an unusual carinated bowl with a complicated-stamped body and bold incision on a tall, collarlike rim. Two plain jars with horizontal lug handles, and a plain simple bowl, all grit tempered, may also belong to the protohistoric component. Admittedly, these eight pots are a rather slim basis for dating the mound. Still, we know Averett Plain dates no later than A.D. 1300, and the burnished, shell-tempered vessels appear with the Abercrombie phase about A.D. 1600.

As previously mentioned, the Abercrombie phase spans a critical interval between the archaeologically known societies of the region and the historic-period peoples known as the Lower Creeks. The Kyle mound is surrounded by a nearly continuous distribution of Lower Creek sites. Worth (2000: 274), citing Hawkins (1980:310, 327), noted that the Kyle mound is in the general locale where the Creeks told Hawkins that the Kasihtas, coming from the west, first "crossed the river" and "took possession of the country" from "a race of people with flat heads in possession of the mounds in the Cussetuh fields." Worth suggests the site is in the general location of this first Kasihta town.

If the Creek story has historical reality, does the Abercrombie phase component at the Kyle mound represent the immigrant Kasihtas? How can we attribute the Averett component to the indigenous "race of people with flat heads" (a reference to the practice of cranial deformation) mentioned in the Kasihta migration story if there is a 300-year hiatus between the earlier Averett component and the later Abercrombie component? In an alternative scenario more accommodating to the chronological estimate, perhaps the indigenous flat-headed people left the Abercrombie phase remains at the mound and the Kasihtas produced the post-A.D. 1650 components, dominated by brushed and red-filmed pottery, present in the fields that surround the mound.

Such are the puzzles one confronts in attempts to reconcile archaeology with oral tradition. Even so, the Kasihta story is in agreement with archaeological interpretations in at least one important way: reoccupation of earlier mounds by later cultural groups is clearly revealed at several sites.

Note on Curation

Miller's collection from the Kyle mound is in the Smithsonian Institution Museum of the American Indian Museum Support Center in Suitland, Maryland.

Excavations at the Shorter Site (1BR15)

The Shorter site is Moore's (1907:448) "Mound Near Upper Francis Landing"; it was 30.4 m in diameter and 3.9 m high in 1906. In 1947, Hurt assigned the mound a site number (1BR2), made a surface collection, but did not excavate. During his 1958 RBS survey, Harold A. Huscher (1959a: 85–86) mapped the mound, dug two shallow 3-x-3 m (10-x-10 ft.) units, and put the site on the A1 priority list for future excavation. Also, it should be noted that Hurt's site descriptions of the Shorter mound and the nearby Lampley mound (1BR14) were switched with each other when an edited version of his report was published 28 years later (Hurt 1975:57).

As revealed in DeJarnette's excavation, the Shorter primary and secondary mounds were sequential, flat-topped stages built during the Mandeville phase (A.D. 1–300) (Knight and Mistovich 1984:219). The Late Mississippi period tertiary mound was composed of sand and clay piled no more than 1.5 m high, and so heavily eroded that "little remained of the once flat top" (Kurjack 1975:97). No Mississippian features were found on the tertiary mound stage. Due to the contrast in soils, the excavators easily traced the contact point between the clay secondary and sandy tertiary stages (Kurjack 1975:97). Likewise, the ceramic sample from the stratified mound stages shows a clear separation between the Middle Woodland component in the primary and secondary mounds, and the Late Mississippian component in the tertiary mound (Kurjack 1975:Table 17, 18). Although the excavators recognized the two components, and noted, "No Fort Walton–Lamar types were present below the tertiary mound," they nevertheless concluded, "The present interpretation is that the three mound stages of 1BR15X1 were built during the Fort Walton–Lamar occupation." That the excavators chose to ignore the implications of their own data attests to the power of the then-current position that there were no pre-Mississippian flat-topped mounds, dogma that did not wane until the 1980s (see Knight 1990b:166–172).

Turning to the issue of a phase affiliation for the tertiary mound ceramic assemblage (Table B.5), we find an absence of arcade-decorated handled jars, the presence of Lamar Plain (notched and pinched rim modes), a trace amount of shell-tempered sherds, and the predominance of Fort Walton Incised (57 percent of the total decorated pottery) over Lamar Complicated Stamped (22 percent of the total decorated pottery). The assemblage is post-Singer phase due to the absence of arcade-incised handled jars. Based on these observations, we place the final mound stage in the Bull Creek phase (A.D. 1450–1550).

Note on Curation

All records and artifacts of the University of Alabama investigations are stored at Moundville Archaeological Park, Alabama.

Excavations at the Lampley Site (1BR14)

Most of the relevant information on this mound is presented in Chapter 3, so only a few comments are necessary. C. B. Moore (1907:448) provides the first record of the site, his "Mound above Eufaula, Barbour County, Ala." Moore found that half of the red clay structure had been swept away by floodwaters. Moore's workers discovered nothing to interest him, and he concluded that the mound was "domiciliary."

Wesley R. Hurt arrived at Lampley in 1947, but details of his investigation are lacking. In the state site file, he recorded the mound dimensions; converted from English to metric scale, the mound was 2.1 m high, 7.6 m wide, and 33.5 m long at the base, and 2.4-x-15.2 m at the summit. Hurt (1975:Table 10) assigned the site to his "Ceramic Complex F, Fort Walton–Lamar." As mentioned above, Hurt's description of the Lampley site was erroneously attributed to the Shorter site in the 1975 edited version of his report. Even more unfortunate, it is not clear if Hurt's pottery sample came from the mound or the adjacent habitation area. Therefore, Huscher's excavation, as limited as it was, constitutes the only confirmed ceramic samples from the mound. Pottery from Huscher's 1961 mound surface collection and 1962 mound test units are combined in Table B.6.

Handled jars are absent from both the Hurt and Huscher samples, so the occupation postdates the Singer phase. The predominance of Fort Walton Incised and the absence of the pottery type Rood Incised suggest that mound use did not extend into the Stewart phase. Thus the Lampley mound

Table B.5. Tertiary Mound Ceramics, 1BR15.

CERAMIC TYPES

Grit/Sand Temper

Fort Walton Incised	36
Lamar Complicated Stamped	14
Lamar Plain	8
Fine Incised	2
Residual Incised	3
Grit/Sand Plain	271

Shell Temper

Shell Plain	6
Total Plain	277
Total Decorated	63
Total Sherds	340

CERAMIC MODES

Pinched Below Lip	3
Plain Appliqué	1
Notched Appliqué	3
Pinched Appliqué	4
Lip Ticked	2
Total Rims	13

assemblage is very similar to the Bull Creek component at the Shorter site only 2.4 km away. Like the Shorter assemblage, we estimate the Lampley mound was constructed in the Bull Creek phase.

Note on Curation

All records and artifacts are stored at the Smithsonian Institution's Museum Support Center in Suitland, Maryland.

Excavation of Gary's Fish Pond Site (9QU1)

Prior to inundation by Walter F. George Lake, the mound stood 1.9 km east of the river at the upland edge of the floodplain. Because the site was not readily observable from the river, perhaps this settlement location was chosen with defense as an important consideration. The mound received minor test excavations by C. B. Moore in 1906. Moore (1907:448) described the "Mound near Georgetown, Quitman County, Georgia" as circular, 30.4 m in diameter and 1.6 m high. Moore's effort did not yield many artifacts. He was unable to detect mound strata, concluded that the mound was domicili-

Table B.6. Mound Ceramics, 1BR14.

CERAMIC TYPES

Grit/Sand Temper

Fort Walton Incised	26
Lamar Complicated Stamped	13
Bold Incised	1
Lamar Plain	9
Fine Incised	6
Grit/Sand Plain	827

Shell Temper

Shell Plain	3
Total Plain	830
Total Decorated	55
Total Sherds	885

CERAMIC MODES

Lip Ticked	4
Lip Notched	3
Pinched Below Lip	2
Pinched Folded	4
Pinched Appliqué	5
Notched Appliqué	2
Plain Appliqué	1
Scalloped Appliqué	1
Total Rims	22

ary, and moved on to more productive sites. Therefore, Huscher's RBS investigation is the primary record for the mound.

Mound Excavations

Detailed field notes are lacking for the 1958–1962 RBS investigation. Our analysis of the RBS Gary's Fish Pond project relied on a few extant maps, numerous field photographs, and weekly summary reports written in Huscher's uninformative and digressive style. No detailed descriptions of mound stratigraphy or level-by-level excavation notes survive, and only two profile maps of the mound could be found at the Smithsonian Institution.

Before excavation, Huscher (1959a) described the bulldozer damage as "regular North-South cuts through the center of the mound leaving an undisturbed margin at the east and west sides." Huscher (1959a:69, 100) identified a "very extensive village site" (9QU3) extending "indefinitely southwest" from the mound, with surface pottery "predominately Fort Walton–Lamar."

In 1958, Huscher excavated a north-south 3.05-x-6.10 m (10-x-20 ft.) test trench on the eastern margin of the mound to obtain a ceramic sample of the mound fill. Fifty-five field lots were assigned for lithics and ceramics recovered from the surface and from trench excavations of the first 15 cm level below the surface, presumably in the plow zone. Based on his findings, Huscher placed the site on his A1 priority list. In the spring of 1960, Huscher began full-scale excavations of the entire mound. He laid out a .91-x-18.3 m (3-x-60 ft.) trench (X-3) on the eastern undisturbed mound margin oriented roughly north-to-south along the axis of the bulldozer cuts. Provenience in X-3 was recorded in 3 m (10 ft.) sections dug in 15 cm (.5 ft.) arbitrary levels and all material was screened through 9.7 mm (3/8 in.) screens. X-3 was taken down about 1.2 m below the 1960 ground surface, a level below the earliest mound.

An east-west trench (X-4) was laid out perpendicular to both the 1958 trench and X-3 in an effort to connect the two north-south trenches. X-4 was also recorded in 3 m sections dug in 15 cm arbitrary levels down 1.2 m into the premound level. In the lowest levels of X-4, Huscher identified a 30-centimeter-thick ashy midden with abundant artifacts at the premound-mound contact zone, and a premound pit (Feature 8) filled with charred chinquapin nuts (*Castanea*) located just below the midden layer. Profiles were drawn for X-3 and X-4, and it is from these two surviving maps that we have been able to interpret mound stratigraphy and assign excavated artifact collections to their appropriate mound levels. With these profiles, Huscher documented a partial clay mantle in the upper mound level superimposed over a lower ash-midden mound core containing Fort Walton and Lamar pottery types (Huscher 1961:3).

In December 1960, Huscher focused his attention on the undisturbed western mound margin and on the disturbed central mound. No profiles of these excavations survive. We reconstructed the western and central mound excavations using an incomplete plan map of the mound excavation, field photographs, and the weekly reports. The western half of the mound was stripped in 15 cm levels within a large block excavation, which was not assigned excavation unit numbers in the notes or on the plan map. This stripping operation revealed:

> the roots of a circular mound faced with clay, probably originally 200 feet in circumference at the base. A section trench cut through the west margin revealed the clay carefully built up at a steep angle, the actual base of the mound about four feet below the present surface in the area. A palisade of spaced, large-diameter posts followed the curve of this clay wall, just to the outside or just to the inside, but the posts did not seem actually set into the wall. The indications are of some sort

of clay-faced, circular, caracol-type mound. Additional bedding lines outside the circular periphery indicated a possibility that some sort of overlying rectangular mound had been built on the core of the original circular mound [Huscher 1961:4–5].

A 6-x-6 m (20-x-20 ft.) excavation block (X-1) was placed into the bull-dozed central portion of the mound. The first 15 cm level below the surface was not screened, but the next 15 cm levels were screened and excavated down to the premound levels. Thus it appears that the bulldozer removed the upper mound levels, and Huscher was only able to recover the lowest mound-building level. At the premound level, Huscher mapped many post molds, but no clear structure outlines could be discerned. Post molds were 8–16 cm in diameter and formed linear alignments, presumably segments of wall outlines of premound structures. Huscher found several "midden pock-ets" in X-1 early mound and premound levels with a high frequency of early Mississippian ceramics, which predate the Fort Walton–Lamar pottery types found in the upper mound levels.

The final excavation block mentioned by Huscher was laid out along the southeastern margin of the mound (X-8). This block removed a 12.2-x-21.3 m (40-x-70 ft.) mound section, excavated as 28 separate 3-x-3 m grid units. Each unit was excavated down below the premound-mound contact level and features were mapped and artifacts collected for each 15 cm arbitrary level. About 25 percent of the units had post molds but no pattern was identified. No wall trench features were found at X-8 or anywhere on the site. One human burial (Feature 16) was recovered within an oval pit from the pre-mound level. Huscher described the burial as being partly flexed, lying head to the east, facing south with no grave goods (although the extant Smith-sonian collections produced a single perforated clay bead that was found near the right ear of the skull). The burial pit contained a single Cool Branch Incised sherd with the eyelash arcade motif, clearly associated with the pre-mound occupation at the site.

Several small pits filled with charred corncobs (i.e., "smudge pits") were discovered from just outside the margins of one of the rectangular mound stages exposed in X-8. Huscher identified the level of origin for the corncob features as the upper mound surface just prior to the addition of the final mound cap. Although no profile maps exist for X-8, the X-4 profile (located 15.2 m northeast of the excavated area of X-8 in question) seems to confirm the stratigraphic position of the corncob features.

The stripping operation uncovered the dimensions of three mound stages, which Huscher defined by mapping the horizontal limits of the yellow clay mound mantles. In the case of the so-called caracol mound, the yellow clay was associated with a line of post molds that Huscher identified as a "palisade," although it is something more akin to a summit curtain or fence that commonly lined the perimeter of Mississippian mound precincts (Figure 3.14). The "caracol" mound margins are depicted on the excavation plan map as a 12.1-meter-diameter circle in the center of the mound, but it is better described as square with rounded corners. The other two clay mantles delimit 24.3-x-27.4 m square-to-rectangular platform margins. Although Huscher does not provide any interpretation of mound strata on his profile maps, a close reading of the profiles from X-3 and X-4 on the eastern margins of the mound show that Huscher's field identification of three mound construction stages was accurate. Artifacts other than potsherds found in the five stratigraphic levels are summarized in Table B.7.

Mound Chronology

Our "excavation" of the RBS documents and analysis of the artifact collections permits us to reconstruct the occupational history of Gary's Fish Pond mound. Beginning with the original ground surface, the sequence is composed of five stratigraphic levels: Premound Surface (Rood I and Rood II phases), Premound Midden (Rood III phase), and Mounds 1, 2, and 3 (Singer phase). Each of these stratigraphic levels is defined below.

Two stratified levels characterize the premound zone beneath the mound: the premound ground surface (Premound Surface), and the artifact-rich premound midden that overlies it (Premound Midden). Many post molds were present, but no structure patterns were identified in the premound zone. The Feature 16 single burial was also in the premound zone. The Feature 8 chinquapin pit originated at the premound ground surface level and seems to have been filled before the midden accumulated. Feature 8 contained ceramics suggestive of a Rood I phase occupation with shell-tempered plain sherds predominant (66 percent) over grit-tempered plain sherds (34 percent). The decorated types Moundville Incised and Cool Branch Incised were predominant in Feature 8 with a total absence of any Fort Walton–Lamar types. An AMS radiocarbon sample from the nuts in Feature 8 yielded an intercept of cal A.D. 1320/1340/1390, with a two-sigma range of cal A.D. 1290–1420 (Beta-154048) for the premound occupational period prior to midden accumulation (Table 4.1).

The first mound-building stage is designated as Mound 1 and corresponds to Huscher's "caracol" mound. A partition of wooden posts enclosed Mound 1. The X-3 profile reveals a yellow clay mantle located on the Mound 1 summit. The X-3 trench exposed 7.6 m of the edge of Mound 1. On either side of the mound edge, the profile reveals a horizontal construction stage, which added an apronlike extension onto the original Mound 1 without increasing its height. This horizontal stage, designated Mound 2, is visible in profiles of X-3 and X-4. Like Mound 1, Mound 2 also had a yellow

Table B.7. Provenience of Miscellaneous Artifacts, 9QU1.

	Pre Md No./Material	Pre-Md Midden No./Mat.	Md 1 No./Mat.	Md 2 No./Mat.	Md 3 No./Mat.	Total
GROUND STONE						
Abrader	1/Q(40g)	0	0	0	0	1
Hammer Stone	0	0	0	2/Q	0	2
Discoidal	1/S	0	0	0	2/Sc	3
Grinding Slab	0	0	1/H(150g)	1/H(2500g)	1	3
Hematite Chunks	345g	927g	480g	1960g	145g	3857g
Limonite Chunks	10g	0	900g	1255g	0	2165g
Sandstone Chunks	0	0	0	0	120g	120g
Pitted Stone	0	0	0	1/Q	1/Q	2
OTHER ARTIFACTS						
Cut Marine Shell	0	0	0	1(10g)	0	1
Fired Daub	T	T	T	539g	T	539g
Bead	1/C	0	0	0	0	1
Disk	1/C	5/C	21/C	12/C	23/C	62
Fired Lump/Paste	10g	0	30g	60g	0	100g
Red Ocher Pigment	0	0	6g/H	5g/H	0	11g
Smoking Pipe Fragment	0	1/C	1/C	3/C	1/C	6
RAW MATERIAL						
Ferruginous Stone	10g	156g	10g	2300g	8g	2484g
Limonite	0	30g	0	8g	65g	103g

KEY: hematite/ferruginous sandstone (H), quartzite (Q), sandstone (S), schist (Sc), ceramic (C), present but not quantified (P), trace quantities (T), gram (g).

clay mantle. The final mound construction stage visible in profile is designated Mound 3, and it served to increase both the horizontal and vertical dimensions of the mound all the way to the plow zone. A yellow clay mantle is also visible on the summit of portions of Mound 3. In the X-4 profile, the comparable datum level that Huscher gives for the corncob features corresponds to the contact zone between the two uppermost mound construction stages. The corncob features from X-8 originated just above the yellow clay mantle of Mound 2, marking the beginning of Mound 3 construction. Confident that we could date the upper mound, we submitted a carbon sample from one of the X-8 corncob features for an AMS radiocarbon assay; the intercept is cal A.D. 1450, with a two-sigma range of cal A.D. 1420–1520 (Beta-154047) (Table 4.1).

When we look at ceramic frequencies across the five designated stratigraphic levels, significant differences allow us to construct a seriation sequence that corresponds to other mound sites in the immediate region (Tables B.8–9). The shell-tempered decorated type, Moundville Incised, is (with a single exception probably attributable to redeposition) restricted to the Premound Surface, albeit in a very small percentage. The grit-tempered equivalent, Cool Branch Incised, predominates in the combined Premound Surface and Premound Midden levels with over 63 percent of the type from all five levels being found in these two lower levels. Also in these two early levels, Cool Branch Incised makes up 45 percent of the entire decorated premound assemblage. Grit-tempered plain wares (84 percent) dominate over shell-tempered ones (16 percent) in the Premound Surface level, but in the subsequent Premound Midden level, shell-tempered plain wares drop significantly from 16 percent to 4 percent of all plain wares. Thus the Premound Midden level dates to the Rood III phase (A.D. 1300–1400).

In Mound 1, Cool Branch Incised accounts for 10 percent of the decorated assemblage, with Lamar Plain (appliqué fillets, pinching, and noding below the lip) at 49 percent and Fort Walton Incised at 20 percent comprising the majority of the ceramic decoration. Columbia Incised, the shallow flaring-rim bowl form, increases to its highest frequency of any mound stage (11 percent of the decorated assemblage at that level). Lamar Complicated Stamped is present in trace quantities. Thus Mound 1 is Singer phase (A.D. 1350–1450).

In the Mound 2 sample, Cool Branch Incised declines to a trace; there is the first significant presence of Lamar Complicated Stamped (7 percent), a rise in Fort Walton Incised (28 percent), and the highest frequency of Lamar Plain (59 percent). Mound 2 is assigned to the Singer phase. The final mound-building stage, Mound 3, mirrors Mound 2 ceramic frequencies and is also assigned to the Singer phase. Aided by the ceramic seriation and the

Table B.8. Provenience of Ceramic Types, 9QU1.

CERAMIC TYPES	Pre-Md Surface	Pre-Md Midden	Mound 1	Mound 2	Mound 3	TOTAL
Grit/Sand Temper						
Cool Branch Incised	44	31	26	9	10	120
Columbia Incised	3	5	29	4	10	51
Nunnally Incised	4	4	3	1	2	14
Andrews Decorated	1	2	1	0	0	4
Complicated Stamped	0	9	7	0	0	16
Fort Walton Incised	2	17	51	99	156	325
Lamar Plain	4	12	74	127	178	395
Bold Incised	0	0	4	6	6	16
Fine Line Incised	1	3	5	3	4	16
Lamar Comp. Stamped	0	0	3	25	63	91
Red Filmed Interior	0	0	1	1	0	2
Check Stamped	0	0	0	0	2	2
Grit/Sand Plain	894	1286	3745	3471	5361	14757
Shell Temper						
Moundville Incised	2	0	1	0	0	3
Shell Plain	169	48	7	10	14	248
Total Plain	1063	1334	3752	3481	5375	15005
Total Decorated	61	83	205	275	431	1055
Total Sherds	1124	1417	3957	3756	5806	16060

Table B.9. Provenience of Ceramic Modes, 9QU1.

CERAMIC MODES	Pre-Md Surface	Pre-Md Midden	Mound 1	Mound 2	Mound 3	TOTAL
Arcade Motif						
Eyelash	25	12	12	7	6	62
Punctated	1	0	2	0	0	3
Unembellished	18	19	12	2	4	55
Total Arcades	44	31	26	9	10	120
Rim						
Plain Appliqué	1	3	11	11	38	64
Notched Appliqué	1	6	30	29	42	108
Pinched Appliqué	1	1	7	42	37	88
Scallop Appliqué	1	2	26	45	61	135
Pinched Below Lip	0	6	20	16	55	97
Pinched Folded	0	0	0	8	17	25
Lip Notched	10	20	49	27	57	163
Lip Ticked	0	6	24	55	61	146
Noded	4	13	30	64	95	206
Horizontal Incised	2	2	10	6	7	27
Bulge Collar	4	1	7	0	0	12
Castellations	0	0	3	2	4	9
Total Rims	24	60	217	305	474	1080

Vessel						
Simple Jar	4	9	28	15	20	76
Handled Jar	18	27	55	22	46	168
Open Bowl	8	11	17	22	24	82
Rounded Bowl	9	3	1	2	5	20
Carinated Bowl	0	2	6	16	15	39
Bottle/Beaker	5	6	2	0	2	15
Flaring-Rim Bowl	7	3	20	2	4	36
Miniature Jar	4	2	0	0	0	6
Total Vessels	55	63	129	79	116	442
Handle						
Plain Strap	4	12	24	11	25	76
Plain Loop	1	2	9	5	19	36
Top Node	9	2	15	4	9	39
Double Node	1	3	10	3	9	26
Top Tri-Ridge	8	6	10	1	3	28
Horizontal Lug	6	3	4	9	15	37
Vertical Lug	1	3	6	16	14	40
Effigy Tail	2	0	1	0	0	3
Effigy Head	0	0	1	2	3	6
Total Handles	32	31	80	51	97	291

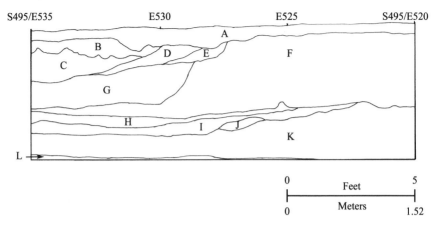

B.2. Profile of Cool Branch mound.

radiocarbon dates, we conclude that the Gary's Fish Pond mound was utilized for about 100 years.

Note on Curation

All records and artifacts are stored at the Smithsonian Institution's Museum Support Center in Suitland, Maryland.

Excavations at the Cool Branch Site (9QU5)

The Cool Branch site was excavated by Harold Huscher as an RBS project. Work began in 1960. Because the excavator's goal was to determine the mound's construction sequence, the X-1 trench, composed of 1.5-x-3 m (5-x-10 ft.) units, was dug in arbitrary 15 cm (0.5 ft.) levels to rapidly expose an 18.2-meter-long vertical profile. Deposits from all excavation units at the site were passed through 9.7 mm (3/8 in.) mesh. The most informative section of X-1 (Figure B.2), at the mound edge, suggests the following stratigraphic sequence from the oldest to most recent strata. A sterile sand subsoil (L) was underneath the premound soil development (K), which in turn was overlain by strata of midden and ash (J-H) deposited by premound activities. A thick layer of red clay (F) initiated mound construction. Clay-sand strata (G, E, D) were banked against the red clay mound, and possibly represent additional construction episodes, while clay-silt strata C and B appear to be slope-wash erosion events. Interpretation of the strata is ambiguous due to truncation by the plow (A), so the total number of mound stages and the final mound height cannot be confirmed.

Two concentric bands of clay-flecked silt, each about a meter wide, ringed the red clay mound perimeter. These bands were either remnant mound stages or slope-wash erosion deposits. While Huscher's mound excavation was hasty, it must be noted that the RBS effort was implemented as emergency salvage. Limited time and funds fostered an expedient "triage" attitude about site investigations, and Huscher was uncertain whether there would be any further work at the site.

Excavation resumed in 1961. The remains of two large wattle-and-daub buildings, paired together, were discovered on the premound surface. One premound structure, dubbed "Hematite House" (Feature 32 in Figure 3.15), was a 9.1-x-10.9 m rectangle of close-spaced, single-set posts with interior partitions (Figure 3.16). On the central floor of this structure, piled in an area 1 m in diameter, was a large quantity (4 kg) of hematite or ferruginous sandstone that Huscher (1971:8) referred to as "a ceremonial or figurative fire." Upon closer inspection, this material proved to be broken, abraded, and powdered fragments of a ferric stone representing all stages in the manufacture of red ocher pigment. Tabular slabs of sandstone were shaped and ground to serve as crude anvils or grinding slabs, and two heavy quartz cobbles were used as pounding implements. Both the sandstone slabs and the quartz hammer stones were found impregnated with red ocher. A small quantity of limonite was processed for yellow pigment.

Three meters south of Hematite House was a second structure, labeled "Spud House" by the excavators (Feature 33 in Figure 3.15). Spud House was a 9-x-9 m building of wall-trench construction (Figure 3.17). Three large features were found within Spud House. A shallow, basin-shaped hearth of fired clay, 1.4 m in diameter and filled with ash, was in the center of the building. A 4-x-2 m clay platform, raised about 40 cm above the structure floor, was found against the eastern wall. Huscher (1963:2) interpreted this platform feature as a "dais or altar." Positioned between the hearth and the platform was a 1-x-2 m rectangular pit, 1.5 m deep (Feature 47). At the bottom of this pit was a layer of poorly preserved human bone, and at each pit corner was a post mold. Due to poor condition, the bones were not removed from the field. Field notes list the presence of adult long bones and ribs in Feature 47, but it is unclear if more than one individual was present. Feature 47 also contained a ground greenstone blank, mica sheet fragments, and shell-tempered potsherds. Huscher (1963:2) identified Feature 47 as a "charnel pit" where "some kind of scaffold had been erected over the open pit." Ash from the hearth was found in the charnel pit fill.

The hearth, pit, and platform are an interrelated set of features used for rituals related to mortuary activities. Features and artifacts similar to those of Spud House were encountered in premound contexts at the Cemochechobee mound center, and while the feature arrangements are not identical, some of the same ceremonial elements are present. For example, the Spud

House charnel pit appears comparable to the "deep tomb burial" pit form in the Cemochechobee premound precinct, especially Burial 1 (XUB, Feature 24), which contained an elongated spatulate celt identical in form to the Cool Branch celts (Schnell et al. 1981:38–39, Plate 4.1). Cemochechobee Burial 1 was paired with a large, ash-filled, fired-clay hearth (XUB, Feature 17). This pairing of hearth and burial pit mirrors the pairing of a similar ash-filled hearth with the Spud House charnel pit. Unlike the Spud House example, however, the Cemochechobee tomb-and-hearth pairing was not adjacent to a clay platform, nor was it contained within a wall-trench structure (although a wall-trench structure was located nearby in the premound precinct).

Other artifacts in and around the Cool Branch premound buildings, in addition to a large potsherd sample, include stemless, triangular arrow points, mica sheet fragments, quartz crystals, an abraded cube of fossilized bone, a quartzite discoidal, a microdrill, pottery disks, fragments of ceramic smoking pipes, a clay bead, and fired-clay coils (the coils are evidence of pottery production nearby). Three Paleoindian–Early Archaic-period projectile points were recovered from the premound buildings: Beaver Lake, Kirk Corner Notched, and the base of an unidentified fluted point. No other artifacts of comparable age were found at the site, and their context suggests that these points may represent a case of prehistoric collecting by the Mississippian inhabitants. Flake debris was uncommon in mound and premound contexts. As these artifacts have a dubious cultural provenience, we have not quantified them. Stone and other nonpottery vessel artifacts from the mound and premound are tabulated in Table B.10.

Palisade Excavations

About 120 m north of the mound, Huscher's crew dug several 3-x-3 m (10-x-10 ft.) units and encountered rectangular wall-trench features. A bulldozer was employed to cut two long trenches east of the units and more wall-trench segments were discovered. At this point, Huscher submitted a progress report to Frank H. H. Roberts for use in the annual summary of RBS work for the year 1961, which stated his impression of the Cool Branch community plan. Roberts reproduced this portion of Huscher's report verbatim: "Rectangular, open-cornered houses, closely spaced but apparently not adjoining, were arranged in rows running NE-SW. Hearths appeared to be in the forecourt to the southeast, rather than within the houses. No clearly defined occupation floor could be identified, hence the associations are not certain" (Roberts 1962:14).

Huscher's interpretation proved to be premature, however, because further excavation determined that these features were not residential houses, but the bastions of a palisade. Huscher's mistaken identification of houses

Table B.10. Provenience of Miscellaneous Artifacts, 9QU5.

	Premound No./Material	Mound No./Material	Off-Mound No./Material
FLAKED STONE			
Stemless Triangular PP/K	3/LC	2/LC	2/LC
Triangular PP/K Preform	1/LC	0	0
Misc. Large Stemmed PP/K	9/LC, Q	0	P/LC, Q
Kirk Corner Notched PP/K	1/LC	0	0
Beaver Lake PP/K	1/LC	0	0
Unident. Fluted PP/K (basal end)	1/LC	0	0
Microdrill	1/LC	0	0
Debitage	P/LC, Q	P/LC	P/LC, Q
GROUND STONE			
Abrader	0	1/H	0
Hammer Stone	2/Q	0	0
Discoidal	1/Q	0	0
Elongated Spatulate Celt	2/G	0	0
Grinding Slab	4/H	1/H	2/H, G
Worked Chunks (red pigment)	580g/H ocher	0	0
Pitted Anvil/Mortar	1/H	0	2/H
OTHER ARTIFACTS			
Bead, Cylindrical	1/C	0	0
Disk	2/C	6/C	4/C
Disk, Perforated	0	1/C	0
Fired Coil/Paste (for pots)	1/C	0	1/C
Fired Daub/Hearth Fragments	P/C	P/C	0.5kg/C
Fossilized Bone, Abraded	1	0	0
Smoking Pipe	4/C	1/C	3/C
RAW MATERIAL/ECOFACT			
Quartz Crystal	2	0	0
Limonite	50g	0	0
Mica Sheet Fragments	25g	0	0
Ferruginous Stone	3.3kg/H	1.1kg/H	1.2kg/H
Unidentified Bone	P	P	P
Unidentified Botanical	P	P	P
Unidentified Shell	P	P	0

KEY: projectile point/knife (PP/K), local chert (LC), white quartzite (Q), hematite/ferruginous sandstone (H), greenstone (G), ceramic (C), present but not quantified (P), grams/kilograms (g/kg).

Table B.11. Provenience of Ceramic Types, 9QU5.

CERAMIC TYPES	Premound	Mound	Off-Mound	TOTAL
Shell Temper				
Moundville Incised	30	85	37	152
Complicated Stamped	0	1	0	1
Engraved	1	0	0	1
Interior Incised	0	1	0	1
Painted	1	7	0	8
Red Filmed	8	6	1	15
Shell Plain	547	1824	223	2594
Grit/Sand Temper				
Cool Branch Incised	5	11	19	35
Columbia Incised	0	4	3	7
Fort Walton Incised	0	4	55	59
Nunnally Incised	1	2	0	3
Engraved	0	2	0	2
Red Filmed	9	10	7	26
Grit/Sand Plain	604	910	1508	3022
Total Plain	1151	2734	1731	5616
Total Decorated	55	133	122	310
Total Sherds	1206	2867	1853	5926

in rows at Cool Branch has been repeated unwittingly in later summaries of the regional prehistory (Schnell et al. 1981:237). Once the palisade was identified, all efforts at Cool Branch were devoted to uncovering the palisade lines until excavations terminated in 1962. Huscher's single-minded focus on the palisade produced an impressive picture of the site's defenses, but at the cost of neglecting the rest of the site. Based on the presence of surface artifacts, the investigators identified the area between the mound and the surrounding palisade as a "village." With the exception of a test pit that uncovered the partial remains of a wall-trench structure, however, the presumed habitation area enclosed by the palisade was not excavated, so we know almost nothing about the form, density, or arrangement of house remains at the site. Artifacts from the palisade excavations are grouped together into an "off-mound" provenience and presented in Tables B.11–12.

Mound Chronology

Scattered features and midden produced by a late Middle Woodland occupation of the Cool Branch site (Mandeville and Kolomoki phases, ca. A.D. 1–500) were relatively minor compared to the Mississippian component. We mention the Middle Woodland occupation in passing only because it caused

Table B.12. Provenience of Ceramic Modes, 9QU5.

CERAMIC MODES	Premound	Mound	Off-Mound	TOTAL
Arcade Motif				
Eyelash	21	47	41	109
Punctated	8	19	11	38
Unembellished	6	30	4	40
Total Arcades	35	96	56	187
Vessel				
Handled Jar	47	141	70	258
Open Bowl	18	38	8	64
Rounded Bowl	0	1	0	1
Flaring-Rim Bowl	0	8	5	13
Carinated Bowl	0	1	1	2
Beaker/Bottle	1	5	3	9
Miniature Jar	0	2	2	4
Total Vessels	66	196	89	351
Handle				
Plain Strap	2	15	9	26
Top Tri-Ridge	5	1	7	13
Top Node	1	5	2	8
Horizontal Lug	1	0	3	4
Vertical Lug	1	1	1	3
Effigy Tail	1	7	9	17
Effigy Head	0	1	9	10
Total Handles	11	30	40	81
Rim				
Horizontal Incised	3	9	5	17

Huscher considerable confusion, for at the time of the excavations in the early 1960s, the Kolomoki phase was still thought by some southeastern archaeologists to be of Mississippian age. Portions of the premound and palisade excavations penetrated these earlier components. Huscher secured a radiocarbon date of A.D. 340 (SI-260) (Long and Mielke 1967:373) from the palisade trench with mixed Swift Creek and Mississippian ceramics that presumably dates the Kolomoki phase component (Table 4.1).

Several lines of evidence indicate that the premound buildings, the mound, and the fortifications date to the Rood I phase (A.D. 1100–1200). Rectangular premound building walls, the square sides of the mound, and the rectangular stockade walls all have the same orientation (i.e., the corners of these features are only a few degrees off the cardinal directions), which gives the impression of continuous architectural development. Ceramic assemblages from the mound area and from the palisade trenches are homogenous and attributable to the Rood I phase. Mound area ceramics can be sorted into two stratified provenience units: premound and mound (Tables B.11–B.12). Diagnostic types and modes reveal that the premound buildings date to the Rood I phase. From Feature 47, the premound charnel pit, Huscher obtained a radiocarbon date of A.D. 1290 ± 140 (SI-261) (Long and Mielke 1967:373). Scarry (1990:Table 26) presents three alternative tree-ring corrections for this sample, which provide midpoints of A.D. 1277, 1310, and 1275. We acquired an AMS radiocarbon date for a carbonized wood sample collected from Feature 47; the intercept is cal A.D. 1210, with a two-sigma range of cal A.D. 1040–1280 (Beta-130241) (Table 4.1).

Mound construction also dates to the Rood I phase. Compared to the premound ceramic sample, the mound ceramic sample shows few significant differences. One difference is that Columbia Incised ($n = 4$) and Fort Walton Incised ($n = 4$) make an initial appearance at the site, in the upper portion of the mound remnant. The trace quantities of Columbia Incised and the absence of Lamar Plain suggest abandonment of Cool Branch mound at the Rood I–Rood II phase transition. We submitted wood charcoal from Feature 6, an ash deposit associated with the red clay mound construction stage, for an AMS radiocarbon assay. The intercept is cal A.D. 1280, with a two-sigma range of cal A.D. 1210–1300 (Beta-130242) (Table 4.1). This dating range falls slightly later than our expectations derived from the relative ceramic chronology and the premound date, although it is consistent with the stratigraphic position of the sample. This dating range and the trace quantities of Columbia Incised raise the possibility that the Rood I phase at Cool Branch may have overlapped in time with the initiation of the Rood II ceramic phase elsewhere in the region.

The four Fort Walton Incised sherds from the upper mound deposit may postdate mound construction. Most of the Fort Walton Incised pottery at Cool Branch was found in association with a house feature well away from the mound. The single-post structure was found superimposed over the eastern palisade line, and therefore postdates construction of the palisade in the Rood I phase. The restricted distribution of Fort Walton Incised at Cool Branch suggests that this component represents a spatially limited occupation established after the Rood I phase inhabitants abandoned the site. It is possible that the four Fort Walton Incised sherds at the mound are attributable to this late component.

Note on Curation

All records and artifacts are stored at the Smithsonian Institution's Museum Support Center in Suitland, Maryland.

Table B.13. Ceramics from the Final Stage, Mound A, 9CY1.

CERAMIC TYPES	
Shell Temper	
Moundville Incised	32
Red Filmed	3
Interior Incised	3
Shell Plain	413
Grit/Sand Temper	
Cool Branch Incised	9
Fort Walton Incised	3
Red Filmed	1
Grit/Sand Plain	596
Total Plain	1009
Total Decorated	51
Total Sherds	1060
CERAMIC MODES	
Bulge Collar	11
Vessels	
Handled Jar	55
Open Bowl	27
Flaring-Rim Bowl	3
Carinated Bowl	2
Total Vessels	87
Handles	
Plain Strap	6
Top Node	3
Top Tri-Ridge	1
Total Handles	10
Arcade Motif	
Punctated	17
Unembellished	25
Total Arcades	42

Excavations at the Mandeville Site (9CY1)

The ceramic sample from the final Mississippian mound stage of Mandeville Mound A is presented in Table B.13. The chronologically salient characteristic is the high relative frequency of shell-tempered, handled jars with incised arcade decoration, attributable to the Rood I phase (A.D. 1100–1200). In addition to the accidental inclusion of Middle Woodland ceramics, there were a few sherds of later provenience in the final mound stage that we excluded from Table B.13, but should mention here. Nine Chattahoochee Brushed sherds are from "a brief stop" in the early historic period that "has nothing to do with the mound construction" (Kellar et al. 1961:37). Likewise, pottery identified as Mercier Check Stamped (n = 15) and two rims with appliqué fillets, one on a complicated stamped sherd, suggests a minor post-A.D. 1200 presence. Again, the excavators concluded that the sherds "probably represent another postmound group who stopped briefly at the site" (Kellar et al. 1961:37). Most likely, the three Fort Walton Incised sherds in Table B.13 also belong to this latter group, or conceivably, may indicate exchange with Early Fort Walton period groups to the south.

Note on Curation

All records and artifacts are stored at the Georgia Museum of Natural History, University of Georgia, in Athens.

Excavations at the Omussee Creek Site (1HO27/101)

Moore (1907:444–446) put several "trial-holes" into the summit of the "Mound Below Columbia, Ala" and met with "negative results." At the time of his visit, the riverbank had cut into the mound. Moore measured a long-axis length of 42 m (138 ft.) northwest to southeast, a maximum width of 26.8 m (88 ft.), and a height of 2.6 m (8.5 ft.) above the level field away from the river. David L. DeJarnette was next on the scene in 1931; he recorded the mound on early state site forms but apparently collected no artifacts. Hurt's 1947 investigation was limited to two 1.5-x-1.5 m (5-x-5 ft.) test units in the habitation area (1HO3) south of the mound (1HO1). On this basis, he identified the site as "Fort Walton–Lamar" (Hurt 1975:Table 10). When Huscher arrived 11 years later, he found Hurt's site locations to be inaccurate, so he assigned the site another number, 1HO27 (later, the State of Alabama changed the site number to 1HO101). Referring to the mound variously as the Crawford Mound and the Seaborn Mound, Huscher (1959b:10) described it as "half of a platform mound cut away on the long diagonal by the Chattahoochee River." On the side of the mound eroded by the river, Huscher (1959b:11) observed "several alternating layers of black soil and red clay, and at least one layer of rock, show on the exposed cut face (north) of the mound, seemingly indicating periodic rebuilding or renewal."

In 1959, following the standard RBS procedure, Neuman established a grid of 1.5-x-1.5 m (5-x-5 ft.) units and excavated in 15 cm (.5 ft) arbitrary levels. Neuman's investigation was extensive and well documented; the stratigraphic profiles, photographs, and abundant artifacts reveal much about mound construction and use. Although the RBS never funded production of an excavation report, Neuman published a brief description of the mound construction sequence:

> The east wall or profile of the excavation trench revealed that we were digging into a composite structure built in four stages. The primary mound was resting directly upon the sandy alluvium of a natural levee. Although the sub-mound stratum was clean, and appeared undisturbed in the area we exposed, I am not prepared to say whether or not it had been purposely cleaned. The fill of the primary mound was composed of a dark sand and village midden containing an enormous quantity of clam shells. The fill was covered with a bright reddish-orange clay mantle or finish. The primary mound was a truncated structure with noticeably ridged summit edges" [Neuman 1961: 75–76].

The second and third mounds were essentially of the same composition and shape as the first. They were built just high enough to cover the underlying structure, but were somewhat longer and broader in their dimensions. The summit edges of the third mound had been eroded away and on the fourth there remained no indications of the clay mantle on the top or along the sides; these too had presumably been destroyed by weathering (Neuman 1961:75–76). The major construction stages are readily apparent in the east profile, redrawn from Neuman's section (Figure B.3), and in the east profile photo (Figure 3.23).

Three aspects of mound construction require further comment. First, as Neuman indicates, the Mound 2 and 3 stages were horizontal building episodes that added apronlike extensions to Mound 1 with only minor increases in mound height. Construction of the Mound 4 stage deviated from this pattern by nearly doubling the final mound height. Horizontal stage additions are not uncommon in the construction of Mississippian mounds; similar horizontal stages were added to Mandeville Mound A, Gary's Fish Pond mound, Cemochechobee Mound B and possibly Singer-Moye Mound H. Second, Neuman did not encounter the stratum of limestone mentioned by Huscher; apparently the rock layer did not extend to the southern or western mound edge. A rock layer was also observed in the Purcell's Landing mound. Third, note the "ridged summit edges" on the primary and secondary mounds visible in Figures B.3 and 3.23. These features are similar to the clay "rampart" or "parapet" that framed the final summit of Mound A at Rood's Landing (Caldwell 1955:27). Caldwell found a line of post molds on the interior side of the clay rampart. At Omussee Creek, a large post mold

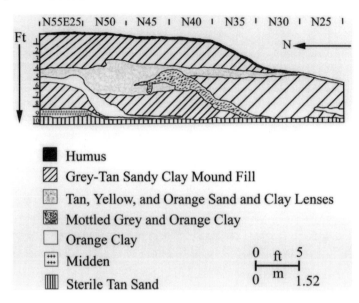

Humus

Grey-Tan Sandy Clay Mound Fill

Tan, Yellow, and Orange Sand and Clay Lenses

Mottled Grey and Orange Clay

Orange Clay

Midden

Sterile Tan Sand

B.3. East profile of Omussee Creek mound (redrawn from Neuman 1961).

is clearly visible just to the interior side of the secondary mound rampart in the profile figures. So it is likely that the Omussee Creek clay ramparts were backed by a wall of upright posts constructed around the mound summit perimeter, as was the case at Rood's Landing Mound A. Gary's Fish Pond mound also had a wall erected around the mound perimeter.

On the premound surface beneath Mound 1, a circular pit .9 m (3 ft.) in diameter (Feature 1) contained mussel shell, animal bone, potsherds, and charred corncobs. Additional charred cobs were recovered from one of five soil stains (Feature 2) exposed on the premound surface under the Mound 3 stage. Hugh Cutler of the Missouri Botanical Garden identified the maize from Features 1 and 2 as "northern flints" (Neuman 1961:80). No other features or botanical remains were recorded at the site. Animal bone and mussel shells were bagged by level. At the Smithsonian Institution we found a list of faunal remains identified by an anonymous analyst, but most ecofacts are now absent from the RBS collections.

Artifact and ecofact densities were highly variable in the deposits, with the highest concentration at mound edges. The possibility that some mound materials may have been dredged up from the adjacent borrow pit cannot be ruled out, of course, but the presence of large vessel fragments and restorable vessels suggests that most artifacts and midden were generated by mound-related activities. A review of artifacts other than potsherds from the mound (Table B.14) reveals something about these activities. A few post molds and

Table B.14. Provenience of Miscellaneous Artifacts, 1HO27.

	Premound No./Material	Mound 1 No./Mat.	Mound 3 No./Mat.	Mound 4 No./Mat.	Mixed No./Mat.
FLAKED STONE					
Stemless Triang. PP/K	0	0	1/LC	0	0
Misc. Stemmed PP/K	0	1/LC	3/LC	1/LC	4/LC
Preform PP/K	0	0	2/LC	0	0
Microdrill	0	0	1/Q	0	0
Debitage	P/LC	P/LC	P/LC	P/LC	P/LC
GROUND STONE					
Abrader	1/L	3/S	4/S	0	1/S
Celt Fragment	0	1/G	0	0	0
Hammer Stone	1/Q	0	1/Q	0	2/Q
Discoidal	0	0	1/L	0	0
Grinding Slab	1/H	1/H	2/H, L	0	1/H
Worked Chunks	3/L, 30g/H	2/H	3/H, L	1/H	0
Mortar/Anvil	0	1/S	2/S	0	1/S
Pebble, Polished	0	1/Q	1/Q	1/Q	0
OTHER ARTIFACTS					
Bone Awl	0	2	0	0	0
Cut Antler Tine	0	1	0	0	0
Cut Fossil Shell	0	0	1	0	0
Cut Marine Shell	1	2	1	0	0
Fired Daub	0	0	1/C	0	0
Disk	1/C	1/C	8/C	3/C	2/C
Drilled Turtle Shell	0	1	0	0	6/C

Continued on the next page

Table B.14. *Continued*

	Premound No./Material	Mound 1 No./Mat.	Mound 3 No./Mat.	Mound 4 No./Mat.	Mixed No./Mat.
Fired Lump/Paste	0	0	1/C	1/C	3/C
Red Ocher Pigment	0	5g/H	0	0	0
Smoking Pipe	1/C	2/C	1/C	0	0
RAW MATERIAL					
Bone	P	P	P	P	P
Botanical	P	0	0	0	0
Shell	P	0	0	0	0
Human Metacarpal	1	0	0	0	0
Limestone	0	0	1/20g	0	0

KEY: projectile point/knife (PP/K), local cert (LC), white quartzite (Q), hematite/ferruginous sandstone (H), limestone (L), sandstone (S), greenstone (G), ceramic (C), present but not quantified (P), gram (g).

Table B.15. Provenience of Ceramic Types, 1HO27.

CERAMIC TYPES	PreMd	Md 1	Md 3	Md 4	Mixed	TOTAL
Shell Temper						
Moundville Incised	0	3	0	0	0	3
Zone Punctated	0	1	0	0	0	1
Bold Incised	0	0	1	0	0	1
Shell Plain	104	114	16	12	17	263
Grit/Sand Temper						
Fort Walton Incised	0	4	88	60	13	165
Cool Branch Incised	1	18	3	0	4	26
Columbia Incised	0	11	4	0	2	17
Lamar Plain	0	6	15	6	11	38
Nunnally Incised	1	9	1	0	2	13
Fine Incised	0	5	0	2	1	8
Bold Incised	0	1	5	4	1	11
Complicated Stamped	0	0	0	1	0	1
Cord Marked	0	0	0	1	0	1
Engraved	0	0	0	0	1	1
Interior Incised	0	0	0	3	2	5
Painted	1	0	0	0	0	1
Red Filmed	0	1	1	0	1	3
Check Stamped	0	0	2	0	0	2
Grit/Sand Plain	145	225	601	596	339	1906
Other Temper						
Grog Plain	0	6	2	9	0	17
Limestone Plain	1	2	0	6	1	10
Total Plain	250	347	619	623	357	2196
Total Decorated	3	59	120	77	38	297
Total Sherds	253	406	739	700	395	2493

fragments of daub suggest the presence of buildings on mound summits, but no structure patterns were detected.

Mound Chronology

Mound ceramic data were grouped by associated mound stage; pottery that could not be assigned to a stage was placed in a "mixed" category (Tables B.15–16). Mound stage 2 potsherds were excluded due to the small quantity (n = 36) and lack of phase diagnostics. Based on changes in the relative frequency of ceramic types and modes in stratigraphic order, we can derive a chronology of mound construction at the Omussee Creek site. The pre-mound deposits were generated at a time when the frequency of shell temper

Table B.16. Provenience of Ceramic Modes, 1HO27.

CERAMIC MODES	Pre-Md	Mound 1	Mound 3	Mound 4	TOTAL
Arcade Motif					
Eyelash	0	1	0	0	1
Punctated	0	3	1	0	4
Unembellished	1	17	2	0	20
Total Arcades	1	21	3	0	25
Rim					
Plain Appliqué	0	0	1	1	2
Notched Appliqué	0	6	10	3	19
Pinched Appliqué	0	0	3	0	3
Ticked Appliqué	0	0	1	2	3
Pinched Below Lip	0	0	39	30	69
Lip Ticked	0	1	41	17	59
Lip Notched	14	41	58	32	145
Noded	0	6	26	7	39
Bulge Collar	2	1	0	0	3
Horizontal Incision	1	4	9	2	16
Total Rims	17	59	188	94	358
Vessel					
Simple Jar	6	12	53	8	79
Handled Jar	20	56	45	6	127
Open Bowl	8	15	31	8	62
Rounded Bowl	0	1	0	1	2
Carinated Bowl	0	3	6	11	20
Flaring-Rim Bowl	1	14	1	6	22
Beaker	0	2	0	1	3
Bottle	1	6	3	2	12
Miniature Jar	0	2	0	1	3
Ladle	1	0	0	0	1
Total Vessels	37	111	139	44	331
Handle					
Plain Strap	6	2	14	1	23
Plain Loop	4	6	3	8	21
Top Node	8	16	6	3	33
Top Tri-Ridge	0	3	0	0	3
Top and Mid Node	1	11	0	0	12
Double Top Node	0	11	5	1	17
Top Double Ridge	0	1	4	0	5
Horizontal Lug	0	1	6	1	8
Vertical Lug	1	21	16	7	45
Effigy Head	0	0	3	1	4
Total Handles	20	72	57	22	171

was relatively high (42 percent of total plain ware) and handled jars were a major utilitarian vessel form. There is no substantial presence of Wakulla phase pottery. Although radiocarbon samples were collected from this and other proveniences during excavation, no assays were run, and the samples are missing from the Smithsonian collections. In an attempt to date the beginning of mound construction, we submitted mussel shell from the pre-mound level Feature 1, Pit 1. We received an AMS date of two-sigma cal A.D. 20–240 (Beta-154046) for the shell, which falls in the Middle Woodland period, although no such component was evident from the recovered artifacts (Table 4.1).

In the Mound 1 assemblage, the frequency of shell temper declines, Cool Branch Incised and Columbia Incised are the most popular decorated types, and Fort Walton Incised and Lamar Plain appears. There is a stylistic and temporal hiatus between Mounds 1 and 3, possibly spanned by the inadequately sampled Mound 2. In the Mound 3 and 4 samples, Fort Walton Incised becomes the dominant type. Handled jars with arcade decoration and shell temper fall to trace amounts or disappear altogether. The absence of Lamar Complicated Stamped (one eroded complicated stamped sherd in Mound 4) implies that Omussee Creek peoples either did not have access to this pottery type, or more likely, abandoned the mound prior to its appearance in the Southern zone.

Note on Curation

All records and artifacts are stored at the Smithsonian Institution's Museum Support Center in Suitland, Maryland.

Appendix C
Pottery Classification

Our method of pottery classification was chosen to accomplish two research goals. First, we needed to date each excavated mound and arrange the sample of mounds into a chronological order. Seriation of the abundant pottery found in the mounds provided the means to accomplish this goal. Second, we wanted to detect evidence for the regional and inter-regional cultural interactions of the peoples who used the mounds. Our measure of these interactions was the patterns revealed in the spatial distribution of pottery styles. Thus the pottery classification effort was focused on identifying pottery attributes that changed through time and across space. Previous researchers recognized some of these time-and-space-sensitive pottery attributes. We have erected our chronological framework on the foundation laid by these archaeologists (Caldwell 1955; Chase 1963a, 1963b; Hurt 1975; Jenkins 1978; Ledbetter 1997a, b; McMichael and Kellar 1960; Schnell 1998b; Schnell et al. 1981; Schnell and Wright 1993).

The pottery sample classified in this appendix consists of 52,578 sherds from nine mound centers in the lower Chattahoochee River valley. The archaeological sites are Abercrombie, Cool Branch, Gary's Fish Pond, Lampley, Mandeville, Omussee Creek, Rood's Landing, Shorter, and Singer-Moye. Although we incorporated the Cemochechobee ceramic sample in our ceramic seriation, we exclude the Cemochechobee pottery from this appendix because these data are published elsewhere (Schnell et al. 1981). The size and scope of the prehistoric and protohistoric period pottery sample, unprecedented in the region's archaeological research, allowed us to construct a relative ceramic chronology, identify spatial variation in pottery styles, and measure the political and social forces of regional integration for the A.D. 1100–1650 interval.

The pottery classification is composed of three basic units of analysis: composition, form, and decoration. Composition refers to the physical properties of the ceramic paste. Form is vessel shape. Decoration refers to techniques of vessel surface treatment. Attributes that define these units may be observed together in various combinations on pots, of course, but we found it useful to analyze them as independent units. We did this because efforts to create comprehensive, catchall ceramic types that subsume too many attributes may obscure the attribute variation we wish to identify and understand. Although the lower Chattahoochee peoples used whole pots, our practical unit of observation is the potsherd, where one finds the associated attributes separated into pieces. Thus the analyst's task is to identify attributes of composition, form, and decoration on sherds and then "reassemble" them in ways that identify the association and variation of attribute clusters most suited to address the specific goals of the analysis. When attributes of composition, form, and decoration are analyzed separately, the pottery classification retains its utility for future researchers who may wish to use these data to address other goals.

In addition to examining attributes of composition, form, and decoration as discrete units of analysis, we also needed synthetic units of analysis: named or generic decorated ceramic types. In our classification system, a ceramic type is an analytical unit defined by specific combinations of composition, form, and decoration attributes. Decorated ceramic types have proven useful for developing relative ceramic chronologies, and seven of the decorated ceramic types described in this classification are used as chronological markers in the seriation presented in Chapter 4. Furthermore, the spatial distributions of shared ceramic types reveal inter-connections between sites and regions. Also, we utilized the concept of ceramic mode, an analytical unit distributed across ceramic types, such as decorative motif, rim decoration, or handle form.

Our method allowed all potsherds to be incorporated into the analysis, but not all sherds provided equal information on composition, form, and decoration. The composition attribute, temper, is identifiable for each sherd. In all assemblages, the vast majority of potsherds are undecorated. When present, decorative technique is usually identifiable on all sherds, but not all sherds are sufficiently large enough to reveal the decorative motif, nor can all sherds be assigned to a vessel form or a named ceramic type. Rim decoration modes are only visible on rim sherds. Vessel form is the unit of analysis most dependent on factors not always present for each sherd; overall sherd size and the area of the vessel from which the sherd was derived (especially rim sherds) are critical to correct form identification. Moreover, certain vessel forms are easier to identify as sherds than other forms. For these reasons, the recorded frequencies for composition, form, and decoration units of analyses in a provenience sample are not expected to be the same. Thus decorated ceramic type and mode totals are always a much smaller fraction of the total number of sherds analyzed. Descriptive terms of vessel morphology are those of Shepard (1980).

Temper

The material composition of the ceramic paste is an important unit of analysis because it may be observed on every potsherd. We found temper to be the most useful composition attribute because it exhibits temporal and spatial variation. We recognize four temper attributes based on the kind of aplastic particles added to the ceramic paste. These temper attributes, defined below, encompass previously defined named ceramic types sometimes used by archaeologists in the research area to classify undecorated pottery (type names enclosed in parentheses). Temper variation is quantified by tabulation in the artifact tables for each site.

Shell Temper

This category includes all pottery with crushed shell added to the ceramic paste (Mississippi Plain). In the lower Chattahoochee River region, shell temper often appears in ceramic pastes that also contain sand, but the presence of shell temper in any amount is the diagnostic attribute. The total number of shell-tempered plain sherds in the sample is 4,719.

Grit/Sand Temper

This category includes all pottery with sand grains or crushed rock particles (grit) added to the ceramic paste as the only tempering agent (Lake Jackson Plain, Ingram Plain, Nunnally Plain). For the goals of this study, it served no useful analytical purpose to attempt to separate thousands of plain sherds into types that partition the continuum from fine sand to grit, a labor that entails considerable subjective decision making. The total number of grit/sand-tempered plain sherds in the sample is 44,005.

Limestone Temper

This category includes all pottery with limestone particles added to the ceramic paste (Lake Jackson Plain). Only a handful of limestone-tempered potsherds were recovered, all from one site, Omussee Creek ($n = 10$ of 2,493 potsherds). Limestone temper in this region and time period is a localized phenomenon restricted to the southern portion of the valley where limestone is available. We interpret the Omussee Creek sherds as products of exchange or some other form of interaction with communities living farther south, such as occupants of the Waddell's Mill Pond site, a Fort Walton mound center in northern Florida where limestone temper occurs in high frequency (Scarry 1984:378).

Grog Temper

This category includes all pottery with crushed potsherds added to the ceramic paste (Lake Jackson Plain). Grog temper occurs in high frequency in Fort Walton ceramic assemblages in the Apalachicola River valley and at sites such as Lake Jackson (Scarry 1984:451). In the lower Chattahoochee River valley, grog temper is present on Mississippian sites at Cemochechobee (n = 80 of 15,896 sherds in primary context, Schnell et al. 1981:Table 4.20) and Omussee Creek (n = 17 of 2,493 potsherds), the two southernmost mound centers. The rare presence of grog temper at these sites suggests interaction with Fort Walton populations farther south.

Vessel Forms and Associated Named Decorated Types

All vessel forms are identified from potsherds or partially complete vessels. If examples of whole vessels are known, the provenience is noted below. The basic vessel forms are jars, bowls, beakers, and bottles (Figure C.1). We subdivided the basic forms into subcategories based on distinctive shape variations. The basic forms, their subcategories, and the associated decorated types are discussed below. Numbers in parentheses represent the quantity of sherds that can be assigned to a vessel form based on the shape of each sherd. Vessel forms are also quantified by tabulation in artifact tables for each site. Vessel form is a ceramic mode potentially distributed across ceramic types. Because specific vessel forms tend to be decorated in specific ways, however, some named decorated types are associated with only one or two vessel form subcategories. Named decorated types were identified on the basis of a specific temper and decorative technique, or a combination of decoration and vessel form. Named decorated types are quantified by tabulation in the artifact tables for each site, and seven decorated ceramic types are quantified by seriation in Chapter 4. We present the vessel form and ceramic type classification in the following order: basic form category, form subcategory, and the named ceramic types that occur in these forms.

Jars

Jars are vessels that are usually taller than they are wide and have orifices that are smaller than the maximum vessel diameter. The subcategory jar forms are simple jar, handled jar, and miniature jar.

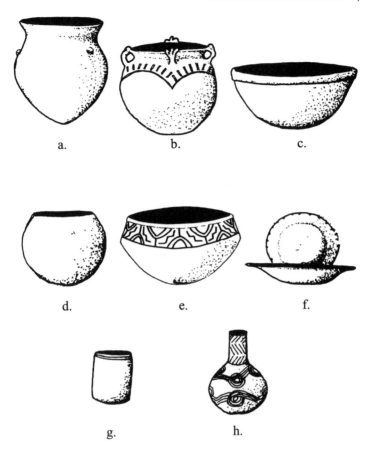

C.1. Common vessel forms: (a) simple jar, (b) handled jar, (c) open bowl, (d) rounded bowl, (e) carinated bowl, (f) shallow flaring-rim bowl, (g) beaker, (h) bottle.

Simple Jar (n = 431) This jar has a constricted neck, everted rim, and no handles (Figure C.1a). In our sample, simple jars are associated with the Lamar (South Appalachian Mississippian) ceramic tradition and the Averett ceramic complex. Lamar simple jars typically have appliqué strips, pinching, or small nodes that decorate the rim. Averett simple jars lack these rim modes (see Averett Plain, below). Jar bodies range from globular to elongate; at least some jars are taller than they are wide. Because the shape of simple jars overlaps with the shape of handled jars, sorting efforts relied heavily on the presence or absence of rim and handle modes. The simple jar is identical to the "everted-rim jar" identified at the Bull Creek site by Ledbetter (1997a).

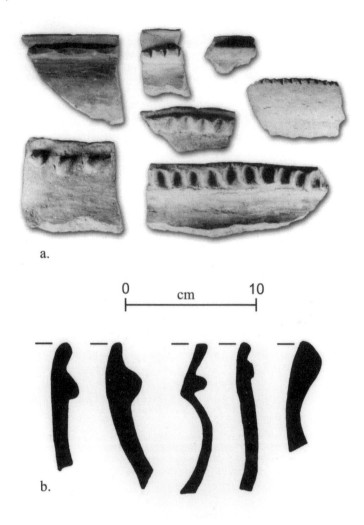

C.2. Lamar Plain: (a) rim sherds, (b) rim profiles, not to scale.

Simple jars have a utilitarian cooking and storage function (Hally 1986). Whole or nearly complete simple jars were found at Abercrombie, Bull Creek (Ledbetter 1997a:Figure 148), Kyle, and Rood's Landing.

Lamar Plain (n = 647, Figure C.2) This grit/sand-tempered ceramic type has a plain surface except for a horizontal appliqué fillet or strip of clay, plain or decorated, placed at the rim (Caldwell 1953). Surfaces are usually unburnished. Lamar Plain's diagnostic attributes are the rim modes recognizable only on rim sherds. Rim modes referred to as pinched-folded and pinched below lip (see below) are included in this type. At least some of these rim modes are also found on another ceramic type used in this study, Lamar Complicated Stamped. Even though the defining characteristic of Lamar Plain is a rim mode that may be found on other ceramic types, we chose to continue to use Lamar Plain as a decorated type because it has long been established in the regional literature, provides a useful summary device for these diagnostic rim modes on plain ware, and facilitates comparison to preexisting data sets.

Lamar Complicated Stamped (n = 827, Figure C.3) This is a grit/sand-tempered ceramic type stamped with a carved paddle (Jennings and Fairbanks 1939). The stamped designs are usually curvilinear, rather poorly executed, and often exhibit overstamping. Rims may have the same modifications as those present on Lamar Plain.

Averett Plain (n = 78, Figure C.4) This is a grit/sand-tempered ceramic type of the simple jar form, but it differs from the types above in specific ways. Averett Plain lacks the rim decoration of Lamar Plain. Typically, the jar has a flaring rim that tapers to a thin, flattened lip, often with a narrow, shallow groove at the apex of the lip. The other diagnostic attribute is the presence of several large nodes (at least four) on the vessel body below the neck. Nodes are the only decoration. Some jars have a slightly pointed or conical base. Chase's (1959) definition of Averett Plain included rounded bowls, but we limit the type definition to the simple jar form because the distinctive jar rims and body nodes are the only diagnostics of Averett ceramic assemblages.

Handled Jar (n = 847) This jar has a globular body, a constricted neck, a collarlike rim, and handles (Figure C.1b). Rims vary from straight to flared. The handled jar is the regional expression of the "standard Mississippian jar" (Steponaitis 1983) produced by Middle Mississippi tradition variants or archaeological cultures distributed from the Ohio–Mississippi River confluence area to peninsular Florida. This jar form has a utilitarian cooking and storage function (Blitz 1993). Whole or nearly complete handled jars were found at Cemochechobee (Schnell et al. 1981:Plates 2.7, 4.3–4.4), Cool Branch, Singer-Moye, Gary's Fish Pond, Omussee Creek, and Purcell's Landing (Figure 3.20c).

In the Cemochechobee report, all handled jars were classified as Lake Jackson Decorated and all associated decorative techniques were given variety names (Schnell et al. 1981). Thus all handled jars with arcade motifs were designated *var. Cool Branch;* handled jars with horizontal-line rim decoration

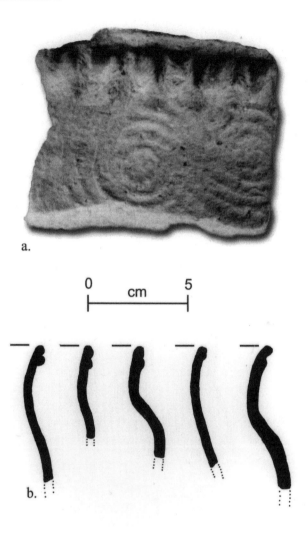

C.3. Lamar Complicated Stamped: (a) rim sherd, (b) rim profiles, not to scale.

were designated *var. Lake Jackson "A"*; and plain handled jars were classified as *var. Lake Jackson "B."* We did not adopt this classification because Lake Jackson Decorated type-varieties are too general for our purposes and obscure important attribute variation, such as temper, which has chronological and spatial significance.

Cool Branch Incised (n = 242, Figure C.5) Incised or punctated arch-shaped semicircles, which we refer to as arcade motifs, were placed end-to-end to

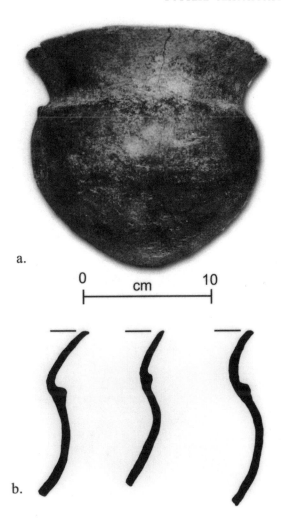

a.

b.

C.4. Averett Plain: (a) typical vessel (Chase 1963a:Figure 2, no scale, reprinted by permission of the Alabama Archaeological Society), (b) rim profiles.

encircle the upper portion of the exterior vessel surface. Surfaces are unburnished. In less than 5 percent of the sample, the vessel body is pushed out from the interior and/or arcades cut deeply into the vessel to create a lobed appearance. This ceramic type is the grit/sand-tempered equivalent of Moundville Incised (Sears 1967).

Moundville Incised (n = 209, Figure C.6) Incised or punctated arcades were placed end-to-end to encircle the upper portion of the vessel (Steponaitis

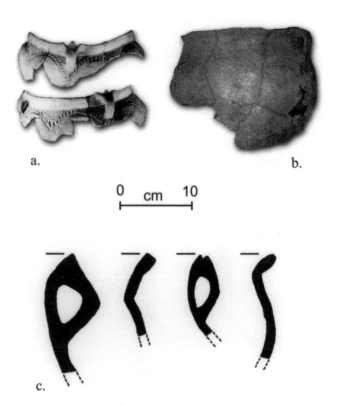

C.5. Cool Branch Incised: (a) rim sherds, (b) lobed vessel, (c) rim profiles, not to scale.

1983). Surfaces are unburnished. This ceramic type is the shell-tempered equivalent of Cool Branch Incised. As is the case with Cool Branch Incised, the lobed vessel body is a low frequency characteristic. The majority of examples in our sample have some grit/sand in the paste, but all contain shell temper.

Miniature Jar (n = 15) These jars with an orifice diameter of less than 8 centimeters are "pinch pots" constructed from uncoiled clay. Several examples have incised arcades (i.e., Cool Branch Incised) but most are plain. It is not known if miniature jars had a specific function. It has been suggested that they are the products of children learning through imitation (Knight 1978). Whole miniature jars were found at several sites including Cool Branch and Cemochechobee.

C.6. Moundville Incised: (a) rim sherds, (b) rim profiles, not to scale.

Bowls

Bowls are vessels with an orifice diameter roughly equal to or only slightly smaller than the maximum vessel diameter. Bowls are usually wider than they are tall. The subcategories, defined by the degree of orifice restriction or variation in rim form, are open bowl, rounded bowl, carinated bowl, and shallow flaring-rim bowl. Open and rounded bowls may be further modified by lugs and effigy rim adornos. These kinds of bowl appendages are classified as handle modes (see handle modes, below).

Open Bowl (n = 384) This bowl has an unrestricted orifice that is also the maximum vessel diameter (Figure C.1c). The majority of bowl shapes in this subcategory are hemispheres, i.e., "simple bowls," but also included are bowls with slightly outslanting rims, i.e., "outslanting bowls" (cf. Steponaitis 1983: Figure 67). While the chronological or functional significance of the outslanting bowl is not apparent, it might be informative to place it into a distinct subcategory within the open bowl form in future analyses. Open bowls have a noncooking food preparation and serving function (Blitz 1993; Hally 1986). Open bowls may have rim decoration modes. Handle modes such as effigy heads, effigy tails, and lugs are sometimes present. Whole or nearly complete open bowls were found at Cemochechobee (Schnell et al. 1981: Plates 4.14–4.15), Cool Branch, Gary's Fish Pond, and Singer-Moye.

Rounded Bowl (n = 93) This bowl has an incurving rim that creates a restricted orifice slightly smaller than the maximum vessel diameter (Figure C.1d). The bowl body is rounded. Rounded bowls may have rim decoration modes. This bowl has a noncooking food preparation and serving function (Hally 1986). Whole or nearly complete rounded bowls were found at Bull Creek (Ledbetter 1997a:Figure 152).

Lamar Plain This ceramic type, defined above under simple jars, also occurs as open and rounded bowls.

Lamar Complicated Stamped This ceramic type, defined above under simple jars, also occurs as open and rounded bowls.

Point Washington Incised See Fine Incised and Horizontal Incised below.

Carinated Bowl (n = 116) This bowl has a distinct shoulder or corner point at the maximum vessel diameter and a slightly restricted orifice (Figure C.1e). Whole or nearly complete vessels were found at Bull Creek (Ledbetter 1997a:Figure 40), Rood's Landing, and Omussee Creek.

Fort Walton Incised (n = 926, Figure C.7) This is a grit/sand-tempered ceramic type with punctations zoned by incisions or incisions placed on punctated backgrounds (Willey 1949). The decoration is usually placed on the upper portion of the vessel between the corner point and the rim. Design motifs are quite variable, including scrolls, rectilinear step figures, and other curvilinear and rectilinear elements. Scarry (1984) has defined 10 varieties

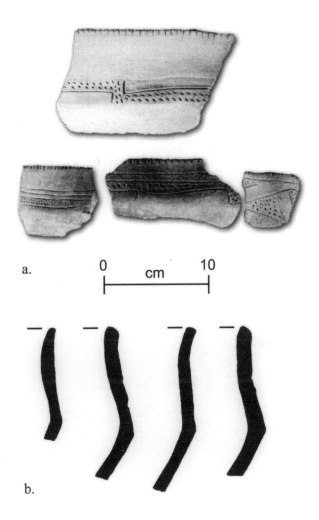

C.7. Fort Walton Incised: (a) rim sherds, (b) rim profiles, not to scale.

of Fort Walton Incised based on different design elements. We found Scarry's varieties impossible to sort as potsherds, and the supposed chronological significance of the varieties has not been demonstrated with published excavation data.

Rood Incised (*n* = 105, Figure C.8) This is a grit/sand-tempered ceramic type with medium-to-bold incising on a burnished surface. Decoration is placed on the upper portion of the vessel. Motifs are scrolls or rectilinear step figures, but some representational figures, such as hands and bones, also

C.8. Rood Incised (redrawn from Broyles 1963, no scale).

occur. Rood Incised is superficially similar to pottery defined elsewhere in Georgia as Lamar Bold Incised (Jennings and Fairbanks 1939), but it varies from that type in that it is fired in a reducing atmosphere and has a plain folded rim (Schnell 1998b). Rood Incised bears a close stylistic and morphological resemblance to protohistoric pottery in central Alabama (cf. Walthall 1980:262, bottom two rows of pots in figure). Caldwell (1955) first described this ceramic type based on examples recovered at Rood's Landing Mound A, in Stewart phase contexts. However, the popularity of Rood Incised apparently increased through time, because it is found in higher frequencies in later Abercrombie phase contexts at the Abercrombie site.

Shallow Flaring-Rim Bowl (n = 141) This shallow, platelike bowl form is shallower than open bowls (Figure C.1f). The rims are wide, flaring, and usually decorated with interior incising.

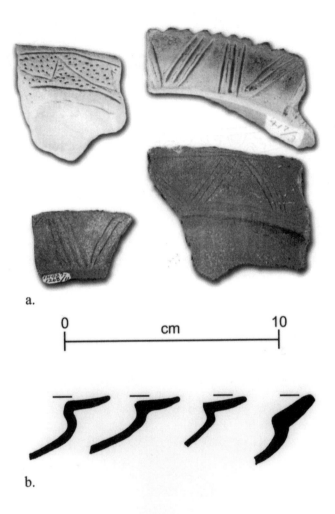

C.9. Columbia Incised: (a) rim sherds, (b) rim profiles, not to scale.

Columbia Incised (n = 140, Figure C.9) This grit/sand-tempered ceramic type has a vessel form like a modern "soup plate," with incisions on the interior of flaring rims (Schnell et al. 1981:173–175). Most designs are rectilinear. This decorated type is the regional interpretation of a widespread pottery style: a shallow, flaring-rim bowl associated with the Middle Mississippi tradition of shell-tempered, platelike vessels (i.e., O'Byam Incised *var. O'Byam*, Phillips 1970:144; Carthage Incised *var. Moon Lake*, Steponaitis 1983:310), an observation made some time ago (Schnell et al. 1981:235).

It is now known that O'Byam Incised and Carthage Incised *var. Moon Lake* do not appear in the initial Mississippian phase in their respective regional sequences (Knight et al. 1999:Figure 2; Wesler 2001:92;) and this is also true of the cognate type, Columbia Incised, in the study region. The timing of the initial appearance of O'Byam Incised on the lower Ohio River at ca. A.D. 1175 (Wesler 2001:92–96, 107), Carthage Incised *var. Moon Lake* in western Alabama later at ca. A.D. 1200 (Knight et al. 1999:Figure 7), and Columbia Incised even later at ca. A.D. 1250 make a plausible case for a north-to-south dissemination of this distinctive pottery style.

Beakers/Bottles (*n* = 115)

Beakers are small cylindrical vessels with unrestricted orifices, vertical to slightly rounded sides, and flat bases (Figure C.1g). Beakers are taller than they are wide. Bottles have spherical bodies resting on slightly flattened bases, and the neck is a narrow cylinder with a very small orifice (Figure C.1h). Beakers and bottles are described together here because they are often found in association and because they are sometimes difficult to separate when sorting sherds (see Nunnally Incised below). This sorting difficulty resulted in a combined beaker/bottle category in some of the artifact tables.

Bottles functioned to store and serve liquids; beakers functioned as drinking cups. Beakers and bottles are highly decorated, and have been found together in mass deposits in mound contexts (Schnell et al. 1981). The two forms are a set of fine-ware serving vessels that functioned together as objects of conspicuous display in special activity contexts that involved drinking (Sears 1967:69). Whole or nearly complete beakers and bottles were found at Cemochechobee (Schnell et al.1981:Plates 4.9–4.12).

Three subcategories of effigy bottles have been found as whole vessels at other regional sites but were not identified in the sherds examined for this analysis: negative-painted dog pots from the Bull Creek and Cemochechobee sites (Ledbetter 1997a:Figure 156; Schnell et al. 1981:Plate 2.10), a negative-painted hooded bottle in the form of a hunchback human from Cemochechobee (Schnell et al. 1981:Plate 2.11), and a negative-painted, hooded tripod bottle from the Purcell's Landing site (Figure 3.21a–b). A polychrome-painted ceramic human head was found at the Singer-Moye site (Figure 3.7), but the effigy vessel form was not identified (also see painted, below).

Andrews Decorated (n = 4) See Nunnally Incised below.

Nunnally Incised (n = 102) This sand-tempered type is defined as narrow-necked bottles incised with combinations of rectilinear and curvilinear designs (Schnell et al. 1981). Bottle necks have (1) multiple, horizontal lines incised in a band just below the rim, or (2) sets of opposed diagonal lines, or combinations of both designs; bottle bodies are incised with (3) multiple-line running scrolls, or (4) multiple horizontal lines. At least three different designs may be on the same bottle (Schnell et al. 1981:Figure 2.13, Plates 4.12–4.13). These same designs are also placed on beakers defined as Andrews Decorated (Schnell et al. 1981:Plates 4.9–4.11). This sharing of the same decorations on two different vessel forms results in a situation in which neither bottles and beakers, nor the decorated types defined for them, Nunnally Incised and Andrews Decorated, can be consistently sorted unless sherds are sufficiently large enough to unambiguously identify vessel form (which is often impossible). This is an unsatisfactory situation, but as the two types were already established, we used them for the sake of comparability with the massive Cemochechobee sample. As discussed above, for the purposes of this analysis, the sorting problem is not very critical because bottles and beakers represent a set of serving vessels that are functionally related and often associated in the same behavioral and temporal contexts.

Fort Walton Incised Three bottle sherds from the Cool Branch mound are zoned punctated and thus match our type criterion for Fort Walton Incised. However, a few zone-punctated bottles and beakers were recovered at Cemochechobee, and the investigators commented on the stylistic similarities to Safety Harbor Incised, a ceramic type concentrated in peninsular Florida (Schnell et al. 1981:166). Since this similarity is unlikely to be idiosyncratic decoration, the Cool Branch site sherds suggest similar connections; the fragmented designs are petal-shaped loops filled with punctations (cf. Sears 1967:Figure 9.1).

Ladle ($n = 1$)

A miniature, undecorated, grit/sand-tempered ladle was found at Omussee Creek. It is unique in this cultural context and the only recovered example of this vessel form.

Generic Ceramic Types

The artifact tables for each site include tabulations of descriptive or generic ceramic types defined by decoration. We chose to classify sherds into generic types when it was unclear if the sherd fit an established named type, the sherd was too small for further description, or when a possibly applicable named ceramic type served no clear analytical purpose and might even obscure variation in the stylistic or morphological attributes we wished to emphasize. Because we lack adequate vessel form data for most of these sherds, the generic types are separated here from the vessel forms discussed above.

Because the generic types are self-explanatory, we discuss only those types that provide potential insights into the time-space framework or pose special classification problems. Sample totals for each generic type are provided below.

Complicated Stamped (n = 134)

These are sand-tempered ceramic types stamped with a carved paddle. We placed complicated stamped sherds into this generic category because they did not conform to Lamar Complicated Stamped; the paste is less gritty, the surfaces are smoother, and the stamped motifs are different from those of Lamar Complicated Stamped. These sherds could be typed as Etowah/ Savannah Complicated Stamped, and certainly that is the stylistic, morphological, and historical connection. Because the lower Chattahoochee River valley is largely peripheral to the South Appalachian carved-paddle ceramic tradition during the A.D 1150–1450 interval when these types are present, the small quantities at the Singer-Moye site probably represent imports from elsewhere in Georgia. The only shell-tempered complicated stamped sherd in the sample, from the Cool Branch mound, conforms to the type Hiwassee Island Complicated Stamped (Lewis and Kneberg 1946:104), no doubt an import from the north.

The association of complicated stamped sherds with the Averett component at the Abercrombie site, however, is a considerable proportion of the total ceramic sample, and so unlikely to represent the occasional import. The fact that similar complicated stamped pottery (usually typed Etowah Complicated Stamped) has been found in many Averett components (Chase 1963a; Ledbetter 1997b) suggests it is a locally made product of Averett assemblages. These associations reveal that Averett populations shared closer cultural affinities or had more intensive interactions with other indigenous societies, such as the Woodstock or Etowah cultures, than they did with the intrusive Middle Mississippian Cool Branch or Cemochechobee phase populations. Vessel form, identified for only a few sherds, is the simple jar.

Check Stamped (n = 27)

This ceramic type includes all sherds paddle-stamped with a pattern of checks. Most sherds have relatively large checks, conform to the type Mercier Check Stamped (Sears 1951), and appear in post-Rood phase contexts.

Bold Incised (n = 97)

This ceramic type includes all pottery incised with bold lines that could not be placed into one of the other types listed here. Much of this material would be typed as Lamar Bold Incised (Jennings and Fairbanks 1939) if found elsewhere in Georgia. In the excavation samples, Bold Incised is found associated with Lamar Complicated Stamped, reinforcing the probable cultural-historical origins for this type. Vessel forms are open and rounded bowls.

Fine Incised ($n = 52$)

This generic type is a catchall for all pottery incised with fine lines that could not be placed into one of the other types. Included here are sherds with multiple lines incised in scroll patterns. Fine Incised is a default category created when we abandoned our effort to type these sherds as Point Washington Incised (Willey 1949). Because the Cemochechobee investigators used Point Washington Incised, we retain that type in the Cemochechobee pottery tables. As others have pointed out (White 1998), Point Washington Incised, Andrews Decorated, Nunnally Incised, and Ocmulgee Fields Incised all may have multiple-incised, fine-line scrolls and so are not easily sorted as sherds unless additional criteria such as context or vessel form are available. Given these sorting difficulties and the discovery that Fine Incised was too uncommon and too persistent through time to be useful in the frequency seriation, this generic type proved to have little analytical utility for our research.

Shell-Tempered Burnished Incised ($n = 2$)

These sherds match the description of Abercrombie Incised (Kurjack 1975; Schnell 1998b:117–118), a ceramic type with a bold incised scroll motif that appears to be the shell-tempered equivalent of Rood Incised. These two sherds occur at the late end of the cultural sequence, apparently after Rood Incised was in use, in association with shell-tempered burnished plain pottery at the Abercrombie site. This Abercrombie phase component is guess dated to the seventeenth century, when the resurgence of the use of shell-tempered pottery in the region suggests the poorly documented but historically known immigration of Muskogean speakers and other peoples from the north (Smith 1989). Most of the Abercrombie phase component at the Abercrombie site is found in off-mound contexts, so it is poorly represented in our sample, which comes from the mound edge.

Painted ($n = 14$)

Eight shell-tempered painted sherds recovered at Cool Branch are negative black-on-buff depicting a spiral or concentric circle motif on a rounded vessel body. Although the vessel form could not be determined, Mississippian negative-painted pottery in this region is known only in the form of effigy vessels of the sort discussed above.

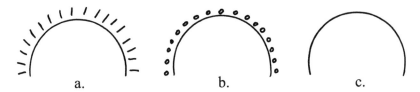

C.10. Arcade motifs: (a) eyelash, (b) punctated, (c) unembellished.

Red Filmed ($n = 70$)

Red filmed refers to all pottery covered with a film of red pigment. Red-filmed pottery is a minority surface treatment in Averett, Rood I, Rood II, and Rood III phase contexts. Although we classified red-filmed pottery as a generic type, we discovered a few red-filmed examples of Cool Branch Incised (see Schnell et al. 1981:Plate 2.7) and Moundville Incised. These red-filmed examples of named types are too infrequent and idiosyncratic to have any chronological utility, but they do demonstrate that (in retrospect) red filming is best classified as a mode distributed across ceramic types.

Ceramic Modes

In addition to composition and form, which we have already described, there are three important ceramic mode classes: decorative motifs, rim decorations, and handles. Our purpose in classifying ceramic modes was to search for significant time-space patterns with more discrete units of analysis than that afforded by the named decorated types. Despite this effort, few such patterns were identified, and we found that the named decorated types were better suited for this purpose. Nevertheless, the ceramic modes are quantified by tabulation in the artifact tables for each site, and sample totals of each mode are provided below.

Arcade Motifs (Figure C.10)

The incised semicircles or arcades of Cool Branch Incised and Moundville Incised handled jars show considerable variability in execution, but apparently have little chronological utility in the region (Schnell et al. 1981:214–216). Perhaps finer distinctions in arcade motifs, such as those illustrated by Schnell et al. (1981), might yet prove to have some spatial variability with useful social implications. But as is the case with most other ceramic modes, proliferation of mode classifications reduces meaningful sample size in any particular provenience unit. In light of these considerations, we reduced the arcade design variability to three general but distinctive motifs easily identified on small sherds.

Eyelash (n = 199, Figure C.10a) A series of incisions radiate above the arcades to create an "eyelash" motif. This arcade motif is equivalent to the motif on the well-known shell-tempered type-variety, Moundville Incised *var. Moundville* (Steponaitis 1983).

Punctated (n = 72, Figure C.10b) A series of punctations create an arcade above an incised arcade; less frequently, all arcades are punctated rather than incised. This arcade motif is equivalent to the motif on the well-known shell-tempered type-variety, Moundville Incised *var. Snows Bend* (Steponaitis 1983).

Unembellished (n = 166, Figure C.10c) The incised arcades are unembellished with any secondary design elements. This arcade motif is equivalent to the well-known shell-tempered type-variety, Moundville Incised *var. Carrollton* (Steponaitis 1983).

Complicated Stamped Motifs

These are the specific motifs paddle-stamped on Lamar Complicated Stamped and the generic complicated stamped type. Given the relatively small sample available to us, we need not describe each motif. Instead, the reader is referred to key references (Caldwell 1958; Wauchope 1966) for detailed discussions and illustrations of the motifs. The stamped motifs are Bull's Eye ($n = 16$), Cross-in-Circle ($n = 11$), Cross-in-Circle with dots ($n = 4$), Figure 9 ($n = 6$), Figure 9 with dot ($n = 12$), Ladder Base Diamond ($n = 1$), Linked Circles ($n = 5$), Two Bar Circle ($n = 2$), Three Bar Circle ($n = 2$), Two Bar Diamond ($n = 8$), Two Bar Diamond A ($n = 3$), One Bar Cross Diamond ($n = 1$), Two Bar Cross Diamond ($n = 2$), Two Bar Cross Diamond A ($n = 2$), and Three Bar Three Cross Diamond ($n = 1$).

Appliqué Rim Modes (Figure C.11)

This rim mode is a horizontal fillet or strip of clay placed just below the lip. When found on plain grit/sand-tempered pottery in the study area, this rim mode is diagnostic of Lamar Plain, a decorated ceramic type that we use for comparative purposes and describe above. We recognize several mode variations.

Plain (n = 86, Figure C.11a) The appliqué strip has no additional alteration.

Notched (n = 240, Figure C.11b) The appliqué strip was cut or indented with a tool to create large notches.

Pinched (n = 194, Figure C.11c) The appliqué strip was pinched with the fingers.

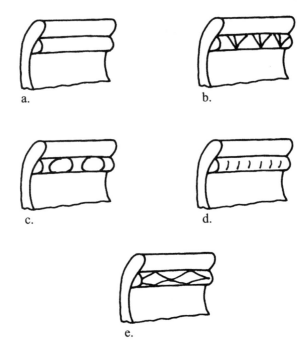

C.11. Appliqué rim modes: (a) plain, (b) notched, (c) pinched, (d) ticked, (e) scalloped.

Ticked (n = 3, Figure C.11d) Tiny notches or groves were cut into the appliqué strip.

Scalloped (n = 140, Figure C.11e) Long shallow scoops of clay were cut from the appliqué strip to create a scallop effect. For additional illustrations and discussion of appliqué rim modes in the region, see Ledbetter (1997a).

Miscellaneous Rim Modes (Figure C.12)

Noded (n = 400, Figure C.12a) Nodes are rounded conical projections of clay. The noded rim mode is a horizontal row of small nodes placed just below the lip; it is part of the same design concept as the various appliqué rim modes discussed above, and some noded rims appear to be modeled from an appliqué strip. This mode is sometimes referred to as a "beaded rim" (Steponaitis 1983). Noded rims have a wide time-space distribution in the American Southeast. A second, different use of nodes consists of large nodes widely spaced on simple jar bodies well below the rim. We recorded such nodes as the type Averett Plain, present in the Averett component at the

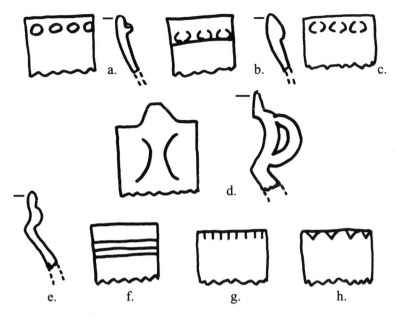

C.12. Miscellaneous rim modes: a–h identified in the text.

Abercrombie site. Nodes on handles are considered separately (see handles, below).

Pinched Folded (*n* = 36, Figure C.12b) This mode is a rim folded to the exterior and pinched along the bottom edge of the fold. A chronological trend toward increasing folded rim width has been used to order Lamar assemblages elsewhere in Georgia (Hally and Oertel 1977), where it seems to be a more popular rim mode than in the lower Chattahoochee region. Ledbetter (1997a:167) identified this rim mode at the Bull Creek site, but his effort to duplicate the chronological method of folded rim width resulted in a later chronological placement for the Bull Creek component than is indicated by other data. Because of the rather ambiguous results obtained from the Bull Creek sample, we made no rim fold measurements, so we are unable to cast further light on this issue.

Pinched Below Lip (*n* = 341, Figure C.12c) This rim mode consists of clay pinched with the fingers to create a horizontal row just below the lip. It clearly belongs to the same design concept as the appliqué rim modes, even though appliqué is absent, and we included this mode in the totals of Lamar Plain.

Castellations (n = 17, Figure C.12d) These are rim points or peaks that project above the rim, usually at handle attachment points.

Bulge Collar (n = 52, Figure C.12e) Found on handled jars, the collarlike rim bulges outward to create a convex profile (cf. Schnell et al. 1981:Figure 4.2d–f).

Horizontal Incised (n = 120, Figure C.12f) This rim mode consists of one or more lines incised parallel to the rim on the vessel exterior. It appears on handled jars and on open and rounded bowls. This rim decoration was described at the Lake Jackson site in Florida as Pinellas Incised B (Griffin 1950), and then later redefined as Lake Jackson Incised (Sears 1967) or Lake Jackson Decorated *var. Lake Jackson "A"* in the lower Chattahoochee region (Schnell et al. 1981). When found on bowls at the Cemochechobee site, it was typed as Point Washington Incised *var. Point Washington* (Schnell et al. 1981:165). When the horizontal incised rim mode is found farther west on shell-tempered pottery it is typed by many archaeologists as Mound Place Incised (Steponaitis 1983). Because horizontal incision is a rim mode, it may be found on several ceramic types with additional decorative motifs. We do not use the type-varieties defined on the basis of the horizontal incised rim mode in order to avoid the awkward situation of having multiple ceramic type names for different portions of a single pot! Not surprisingly, this rim mode has so far proven to have little chronological utility in the lower Chattahoochee River region.

Lip Ticked (n = 364, Figure C.12g) Tiny shallow notches or grooves are incised on the lip.

Lip Notched (n = 522, Figure C.12h) Large notches are cut into the lip.

Handle Modes

Handles are appendages added to the vessel. Following Hilgeman (2000), we recognize two basic forms: closed and open handles. Closed handles are attached to the vessel at two end points in a vertical position like the handle on a coffee cup; open handles are tablike projections or lugs attached to the vessel at one point only.

Closed Handle Modes Closed handles are found on handled jars. The majority of closed handles are placed where a point meets the lip, but a few examples are placed lower down on collarlike rims (Schnell et al. 1981:Plate 2.7). We recognize several closed handle mode variations.

Plain Loop (n = 24, Figure C.13a) This is an undecorated handle that is round in cross-section.

Plain Strap (n = 64, Figure C.13b) This is an undecorated handle that is flattened in cross-section.

Top Node (n = 50, Figure C.13c) A single node placed on the handle top.

Double Top Node (n = 77, Figure C.13d) Two nodes placed on the handle top.

Top and Middle Node (n = 12, Figure C.13e) One node placed on the handle top and one node placed on the middle of the handle.

Top Double Ridge (n = 8, Figure C.13f) Two keel-like modeled ridges are on the handle top.

Top Tri-Ridge (n = 58, Figure C.13g) Three keel-like modeled ridges on the handle top.

Incised (n = 9, Figure C.13h) Lines incised on the handle. Additional illustrations that match these closed handle mode variations are in Schnell et al. (1981:Plates 4.20–4.21).

Open Handle Modes

Horizontal Lugs (n = 76, Figure C.14a) are round, oval, or triangular tabs that project at a right angle or curve slightly downward from bowl rims at the lip. Horizontal lugs differ from rim castellations because they occur singly and do not project upward. Because we have reason to believe that incised horizontal lugs represent effigy tails (see below), only undecorated examples were placed in this rim mode.

Vertical Lugs (n = 147, Figure C.14b) are small vestigial handles placed on the exterior rim. Vertical lugs mimic closed handle forms, but they are collapsed and fused to the vessel body to create "pseudo handles" (cf. Schnell et al. 1981:Plate 4.19j, Plate 4.20y). Vertical lugs may represent a stylistic trend in which functional closed handles were gradually reduced through time in size and form to become decorative vestigial open handles. If so, there was a period of stylistic overlap: handled jar rims were found with vertical lugs alternating with closed handles around the rim.

Effigy Heads and Tails (n = 37, Figure C.15) are "rim riders," a widespread form of bowl appendage or adorno found in the Middle Mississippi ceramic

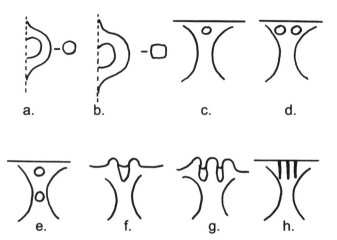

C.13. Closed handle modes: a–h identified in the text.

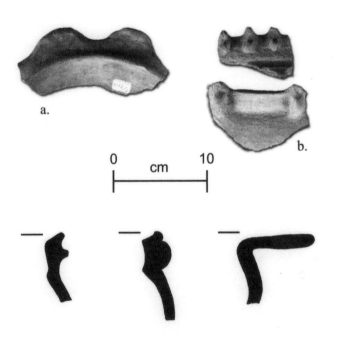

C.14. Open handle modes: (a) horizontal, (b) vertical.

a.

b.

c.

d.

0   cm   5

C.15. Effigy heads and tails: (a) popeyed bird, (b) raptor, (c) turkey, (d) effigy tail.

tradition. Oddly, given our large pottery sample, they are not particularly common. We classify them as open handle mode variations. Steponaitis (1983:74–75) describes bowls with these appendages as "lug-and-rim effigy bowls," with an effigy head and tail mounted on the bowl rim opposite each other. Many effigy heads in the sample are fragments that defy further classification. Five subcategories can be identified: human ($n = 1$), mammal ($n = 2$), bird ($n = 17$), frog ($n = 3$), and fish ($n = 2$). A crude human effigy head was recovered at Singer-Moye. Two nondescript "mammal" effigy heads were recovered at Cool Branch, one from the mound and one off-mound. Two "popeyed" bird heads, one off-mound at Cool Branch (Figure C.15a) and one from Singer-Moye Mound A duplicate a style more common in west-peninsular Florida dated to ca. A.D. 1400–1700 (Luer 1992). A pelican effigy head was recovered from Rood's Landing Mound A. Other bird effigy heads were crested duck, owl, raptor (Figure C.15b), and turkey (Figure C.15c). Frog effigy heads were found at Rood's Landing Mound A,

Gary's Fish Pond mound, and Omussee Creek mound stage four; all are crude, flat, luglike heads. Fish effigy heads occur at Rood's Landing Mound A and Omussee Creek mound stage three. We will not discuss the effigy tails ($n = 30$) in detail, but note that they are incised and/or modeled horizontal lugs; our examples suggest bird (Figure C.15d) and fish tails.

Appendix D
Seriation Methods

To identify mound pottery samples with a similar composition of decorated type frequencies and place them into ceramic phases in a statistically valid manner, we conducted cluster analyses of the 21 mound pottery samples analyzed in our frequency seriation of ceramic types (see Fox 1998; Kreisa 1998; Mainfort 1999). Cluster analysis is a set of multivariate statistical techniques used to group objects together based on their similarities. In a cluster analysis, mound provenience units that yield similar frequency percentages of the seven ceramic types are grouped into the same cluster. The resulting clusters generated by this technique show high within-cluster resemblance and low between-cluster similarity (Hair and Black 2000:147). Two basic forms of clustering, hierarchical and nonhierarchical, can be employed.

Cluster Analysis

In using the hierarchical method, the researcher has no predetermined number of clusters in mind to group the data. The hierarchical cluster technique begins by forming single-member clusters in which each site assemblage is uniquely a member of its own cluster. Then, in a step-wise manner, all single-member clusters are combined into larger and larger clusters until a single large cluster encompasses all of the cases. Similarities between clusters are measured in Euclidean distance between plotted points on a graph, and larger clusters are formed by the combination of smaller existing clusters. This technique can be summarized visually as a dendrogram forming a tree-like graph with the twigs and branches of the tree forming the smallest clusters with the greatest resemblance to each other, and the larger branches and trunk of the tree forming fewer groups with a greater range of distance between assemblages. Often this technique is used first to identify and quantify clusters in the data set.

The second type of cluster analysis, nonhierarchical or K-means cluster analysis, requires the researcher to specify how may clusters are to be generated. The analysis then proceeds to group the total number of cases into the specified number of clusters based on the goodness of fit determined by ceramic type frequency similarity. Analysis of variance (ANOVA) tests are run for each given cluster solution to determine the strength of the statistical fit for each cluster solution requested. Researchers must use their judgment to determine which cluster solution best fits the data set. To find the best cluster solution, three checks are applied to the statistical clusters results (Hair and Black 2000:180–185).

First, a check is made to ensure that cluster sizes are roughly equal with no small clusters suggestive of outliers that might not be representative of the larger population. Outliers are deleted from the analysis and the analysis is performed again. Once the cluster analysis produces clusters of roughly equal size, a second check is made for the cluster solution with the highest statistical significance of all the variable means compared in the ANOVA statistic. In some cluster solutions, the goodness of fit for some variables is not as strong as other cluster solutions. The final check is called the stopping rule.

One kind of stopping rule involves a comparison of the similarity of measured distance between cases within a cluster, with a stress scale ranging from 0 (indicating a perfect fit) to 1 (indicating the worst fit). When fewer clusters are requested to group the entire data set, more dissimilar data sets are combined to form larger clusters, thus producing higher stress values between cases within a given cluster. When the stress values markedly increase from those values in the preceding higher number cluster solution, then that higher number cluster solution before the increase is judged to be the best cluster solution (Hair and Black 2000:184). We employed all of the aforementioned methods of cluster analysis on the 21 stratified mound proveniences in the frequency seriation to further organize the data into statistically valid groupings of similar ceramic assemblages or ceramic phases. In order to avoid unrepresentative sample sizes for each sample mound, only the 21 proveniences with 50 or more decorated potsherds were used in the analysis.

Results of the Hierarchical Cluster Analysis

We used the statistical program SYSTAT (Wilkinson et al. 1992) to generate a dendrogram of cluster patterns (Figure D.1). The dendrogram revealed

CERAMIC ASSEMBLAGES (Letter symbols denoted in text and on MDS graph)

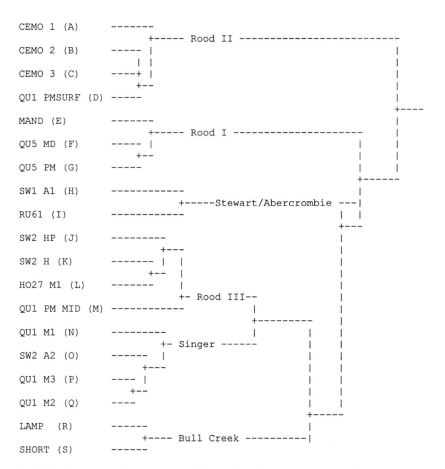

D.1. Dendrogram of ceramic assemblages from lower Chattahoochee River mound centers.

that the 21 proveniences formed six subcluster groupings based on similarities of ceramic frequency percentages of the seven decorated types. Overall, the dendrogram produced two large clusters with smaller nested subclusters. The first large cluster contains a subcluster of Early Mississippi period Rood I phase components from the Cool Branch and Mandeville mounds. A second related subcluster consisted of Rood II phase assemblages from all three ceramic subphases of the Cemochechobee occupation and from the premound surface at Gary's Fish Pond mound. The remaining larger cluster was composed of four smaller subclusters of Rood III, Singer,

Bull Creek, and Stewart phase assemblages. The Rood III subcluster contained proveniences from the premound midden overlying the premound surface at Gary's Fish Pond and the premound and mound levels of Singer-Moye Mound H. Because the Rood III phase assemblage is superimposed over the Rood II assemblage at Gary's Fish Pond, we are confident in placing the Rood III phase later in time than the Rood II phase.

The other related subcluster in this second large cluster grouping consisted of Singer phase dated assemblages from Mound levels 1, 2, and 3 at Gary's Fish Pond, and from the uppermost levels of Singer-Moye Mound A. A third related cluster came from the upper mound levels 3 and 4 at Omussee Creek, and from the Lampley and Shorter mound sites. Ceramics from this subcluster conform most closely, although not perfectly, with Bull Creek phase assemblages. The final subcluster is distantly related to the previous three, and comes from the latest dated mound assemblages of the Stewart phase from the Abercrombie mound site and from the upper levels of Rood's Landing Mound A.

Results of the K-Means Cluster Analysis

The Figure D.1 dendrogram revealed six clusters, but this result is not necessarily the only possible cluster solution that best fits the ceramic frequency patterns. A nonhierarchical K-means cluster analysis was run using a range of cluster solutions from eight to three clusters. When we ran the eight-cluster solution, we obtained a clustering similar to the dendrogram, with the exception that the Lampley and Shorter cluster was now distinct from the Omussee Creek mounds 3 and 4 cluster; and Rood's Landing Mound A and Abercrombie formed their own individual single-member clusters. When we reduced the number of clusters to seven, Rood's Landing and Abercrombie combined to form a single cluster. When we ran the six-cluster solution, we found that the Singer phase cluster identified in the dendrogram combined with the Lampley and Shorter cluster, leaving Omussee Creek mounds 3 and 4 as a separate distinct cluster. When we ran a five-cluster solution, we found that the two related Rood III phase clusters from the dendrogram were combined into a single eight-member cluster. The four-cluster solution caused the Omussee Creek mound levels 3 and 4 subclusters to combine with the larger Singer–Bull Creek cluster produced originally in the six-cluster solution. Finally, when we requested that the program reduce the data set to three clusters, the Cool Branch assemblages defined in the dendrogram combined with the two related Rood II and Rood III clusters formed in the five-cluster solution. This formed one super cluster of 11 proveniences, with Singer–Bull Creek and Rood's Landing–Abercrombie making up the remaining clusters.

We applied the three checks to determine which cluster solution best fit our data patterns. The eight-cluster solution and seven-cluster solution were ruled out because they failed to pass the small cluster outlier rule. While the six-cluster solution was suggested by the dendrogram, there were still two small two-member clusters among the six clusters. Results of F tests for analysis of variance produced very low probabilities ($p < .01$) that these assemblage groupings could occur by chance, but the five-cluster solution proved to have an even stronger statistical fit with p values $< .005$, despite the fact that there are still two small two-member clusters among the five clusters generated. The four-cluster solution yields only one small two-member cluster (Abercrombie–Rood's Landing) with p values of $< .003$. When the three-cluster solution is requested, two of the ceramic types for the compared assemblages have p values of $> .05$, suggesting that this grouping into three clusters is not statistically valid, and that the within-group members are not similar enough to form a statistically significant cluster pattern. We are left with three possible cluster solutions that hold statistical significance: the six-cluster solution, the five-cluster solution, and the four-cluster solution, so we must choose the best one.

The six-cluster solution has higher p values for significance than does the five-cluster solution, and it has two small two-member clusters, thus excluding it as a best fit solution because of the outlier rule. The five-cluster solution has smaller p values, but it also must be omitted as a possible choice due to the outlier rule. The four-cluster solution has the fewest small clusters and its p values are the smallest. When we perform the final check to determine whether the best cluster solution is four or five clusters, we find the two groups are almost identical with regard to measured distance within clusters. The mean squared error for the five-cluster solution is .0066125, while it is .0074125 for the four-cluster solution. Therefore, while the five-cluster solution shows the greatest similarities among its members within each cluster, the similarities among members of the four-cluster solution are nearly as strong, and it passes the criteria for the other two stopping rules, and must be deemed the best fit of the patterns of ceramic assemblage data.

Multidimensional Scaling Analysis

Multidimensional scaling (MDS) analysis measures the degree of similarity between groups. MDS assesses the strength of the correlation of measured Euclidean distances between clusters with regard to time-space relationships between the mound pottery samples. When MDS results are plotted on a graph, those ceramic assemblages that show high resemblance to one another are spatially located closer to one another and form their own cluster, while those assemblages located farther apart form different clusters. Thus, a two-dimensional graph that charts time on one axis and north-south geographical space on the other can provide an illustration of which mound site prove-niences are more closely related with regard to time-space dimensions.

Results of the MDS Analysis

MDS analysis of the 21 mound site provenience units produced a distinctive cluster pattern that showed a great deal of variability across geographic space (y-axis) and less variability across time (x-axis). The plotted cluster pattern conformed to the groupings achieved in the K-means cluster analysis with respect to our Rood I, Rood II, Rood III, and Singer phase clusters. The Bull Creek phase assemblages formed by the cluster of Omussee Creek mound levels 3 and 4, Lampley, and Shorter mounds did not form a tight cluster, but rather formed their own two-member clusters. Likewise, the Rood's Landing and Abercrombie sites formed their own single-member clusters. The stress value for this configuration was .072, indicating a good fit between the data and the configuration generated.

From the standpoint of ceramic assemblage similarity, the aforemen-tioned poorly clustered site proveniences were regarded as outliers, and a new MDS was run with the omission of these six provenience units of the Bull Creek and Stewart phase clusters. Because all six proveniences fall at the most recent part of the time scale, we removed the late ceramic type, Rood Incised, from the analysis since none of the remaining 14 site proveniences contained any Rood Incised. Based on this revision, the MDS results (Fig-ure D.2) revealed an even better fit of the plotted configuration with the data, as the stress value was .009. The resulting configuration reveals a time-space relationship between assemblages that fits our radiocarbon-dated esti-mates for mound site occupations.

In Figure D.2, the dimension of time is plotted on the x-axis with mound provenience samples chronologically ordered from the latest samples located on the left side of the graph and earlier provenience samples on the right side of the graph. We hypothesize that the y-axis is the dimension of geo-graphical space, with samples from the northernmost sites located toward the bottom of the graph and samples from the southernmost sites on the top. However, upon close examination, the plotted components on the graph as they relate to the similarity of MDS distance measures do not conform as well to the actual north-south locations of these mound sites in the valley as the chronological ordering of components on the x-axis.

For example, radiocarbon dates from the Rood I and Rood II phase clus-ters have overlapping time span estimates, but these two-phase clusters con-tain sites that are not in close geographic proximity to one another. Mande-

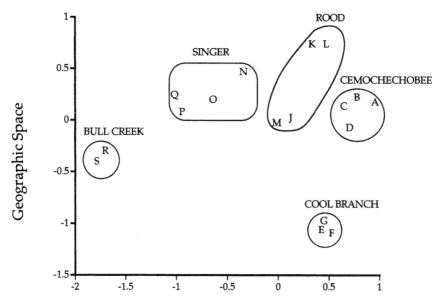

D.2. Multidimensional scaling (MDS) of ceramic phase clusters.

ville Mound A is part of the Rood I phase ceramic cluster, yet it is located 19 km from the Cool Branch site and only 6 km from the Cemochechobee site. If geographical space is an important determinant in grouping assemblage types, then the Mandeville assemblage (E) should be located higher on the y-axis closer to the Cemochechobee site cluster. As a further contrast, the Gary's Fish Pond premound surface (D) contains ceramics that cluster with the Rood II phase, yet it is located only 3 km from Cool Branch and 27 km from Cemochechobee.

Our MDS analyses help us detect the relevant temporal and spatial patterns in the ceramic data, but it is difficult to assign a temporal affiliation to the six outliers omitted from the second MDS analysis. We do know, however, that the unique combination of high frequencies of Fort Walton Incised with the virtual absence of Lamar Complicated Stamped in the Omussee Creek assemblages is strongly influenced by the location of this mound center in the Southern zone, nearest to the contemporary Fort Walton archaeological culture farther south where Fort Walton Incised is the dominant ceramic type. In contrast, the Lampley and Shorter sites have a significant percentage of Lamar Complicated Stamped ceramics, but a much lower percentage of Fort Walton Incised, due to the northern location closer to the Lamar archaeological culture in the Georgia piedmont. The

Abercrombie and Rood's Landing mound sites appear as their own single member clusters largely due to the fact that by this late period, three of the seven diagnostic ceramic types have disappeared from the archaeological record (i.e., Moundville Incised, Cool Branch Incised, and Columbia Incised). Therefore, the two protohistoric period sites share little of the ceramic styles associated with the other 19 mound site proveniences.

References Cited

Anderson, David G.
1994 *The Savannah River Chiefdoms.* University of Alabama Press, Tuscaloosa.
1997 The Role of Cahokia in the Evolution of Southeastern Mississippian Society. In *Cahokia, Domination and Ideology in the Mississippian World,* edited by Timothy R. Pauketat and Thomas E. Emerson, pp. 248–268. University of Nebraska Press, Lincoln.
1999 Examining Chiefdoms in the Southeast: An Application of Multiscalar Analysis. In *Great Towns and Regional Polities in the Prehistoric American Southwest and Southeast,* edited by Jill E. Neitzel, pp. 215–241. University of New Mexico Press, Albuquerque.

Anderson, David G., David W. Stahle, and Malcolm K. Cleaveland
1995 Paleoclimate and the Potential Food Reserves of Mississippian Societies: A Case Study from the Savannah River Valley. *American Antiquity* 60(2): 258–286.

Baden, William W.
1987 *A Dynamic Model of Stability and Change in Mississippian Agricultural Systems.* Ph.D. dissertation, University of Tennessee. University Microfilms, Ann Arbor.

Baker, Robert George
1962 The Recarving and Alteration of Maya Monuments. *American Antiquity* 27:281–302.

Balter, Michael
1993 New Look at Neolithic Sites Reveals Complex Societies. *Science* 262:179–180.

Bartram, William
1958 *The Travels of William Bartram, Naturalist's Edition,* edited by Francis Harper. Yale University Press, New Haven.
1995 *William Bartram on the Southeastern Indians,* edited and annotated by Gregory Waselkov and Kathryn E. Holland Braund. University of Nebraska Press, Lincoln.

Bauer, Brian S., and Charles Stanish
2001 *Ritual and Pilgrimage in the Ancient Andes: The Islands of the Sun and the Moon.* University of Texas Press, Austin.

Belovich, Stephanie J., David S. Brose, Russell M. Weisman, and Nancy M. White
1982 *Archaeological Survey at George W. Andrews Lake and Chattahoochee River.* Archaeological Report No. 7. Cleveland Museum of Natural History, Cleveland.

Bense, Judith A.
1994 *Archaeology of the Southeastern United States: Paleoindian to World War I.* Academic Press, San Diego.

Blanton, Richard E., Gary M. Feinman, Stephen A. Kowalewski, and Peter N. Peregrine
1996 A Dual-Processual Theory for the Evolution of Mesoamerican Civilization. *Current Anthropology* 37(1):1–14.

Blitz, John H.
1993 *Ancient Chiefdoms of the Tombigbee.* University of Alabama Press, Tuscaloosa.
1994 Mound Reoccupation and Co-Option of Sacred Authority. Paper presented at the 59th Annual Meeting of the Society for American Archaeology, Anaheim, California.
1999 Mississippian Chiefdoms and the Fission-Fusion Process. *American Antiquity* 64:577–592.

Blitz, John H., and Patrick Livingood
2004 Sociopolitical Implications of Mississippian Mound Volume. *American Antiquity* 69(2):291–301.

Blitz, John H., and Karl G. Lorenz
2002 The Early Mississippian Frontier in the Lower Chattahoochee–Apalachicola River Valley. *Southeastern Archaeology* 21(2):117–135.

Bradley, Richard
1993 *Altering the Earth.* Society of Antiquaries of Scotland, Edinburgh.
1998 Ruined Buildings, Ruined Stones: Enclosures, Tombs, and Natural Places in the Neolithic of Southwest England. *World Archaeology* 30(1):13–22.

Brain, Jeffery P.
1978 Late Prehistoric Settlement Patterning in the Yazoo Basin and Natchez Bluffs Regions of the Lower Mississippi Valley. In *Mississippian Settlement Patterns,* edited by Bruce D. Smith, pp. 331–368. Academic Press, New York.
1989 *Winterville: Late Prehistoric Culture Contact in the Lower Mississippi Valley.* Archaeological Report 23, Mississippi Department of Archives and History, Jackson.

Brain, Jeffery P., and Philip Phillips
1996 *Shell Gorgets: Styles of the Late Prehistoric and Protohistoric Southeast.* Peabody Museum Press, Cambridge, Massachusetts.

Braley, Chad
1998 *Yuchi Town (1RU63) Revisited: Analysis of the 1958–1962 Excavations.* Southeastern Archaeological Services, Athens, Georgia. Report submitted to Environmental Management Division, Directorate of Public Works, U.S. Army Infantry Center, Fort Benning, Georgia.

Brandon, Peter A.
1909 Aboriginal Remains in the Middle Chattahoochee Valley of Alabama and Georgia. *American Anthropologist* 11:186–198.

Braun, David
1985 Ceramic Decorative Diversity and Illinois Woodland Regional Integration. In *Decoding Prehistoric Ceramics,* edited by Ben A. Nelson, pp. 128–153. Southern Illinois University Press, Carbondale.

Brown, James A.
1985 The Mississippian Period. In *Ancient Art of the American Woodland Indians,* by the National Gallery of Art, pp. 92–145. Harry N. Abrams, New York.

Broyles, Bettye
1963 A Lamar Period Site in Southwest Georgia, 9CLA51. In *Survey of Archaeological Sites in Clay and Quitman Counties, Georgia: 9CLA2, 9CLA7, 9CLA28, 9CLA38, 9CLA51, 9QU25.* University of Georgia Laboratory of Archaeology Series Report No. 5. University of Georgia, Athens.

Caldwell, Joseph R.
1953 *The Rembert Mounds, Elbert County, Georgia.* River Basin Survey Papers No. 6. Bulletin 154. Bureau of American Ethnology, Smithsonian Institution, Washington, D.C.
1955 Investigations at Rood's Landing, Stewart County, Georgia. *Early Georgia* 2(1).
1958 *Trend and Tradition in the Prehistory of the Eastern United States.* Memoir 88. American Anthropological Association, Washington, D.C.

Carneiro, Robert L.
1981 The Chiefdom: Precursor to the State. In *The Transition to Statehood in the New World,* edited by Grant D. Jones and Robert R. Kantz, pp. 37–79. Cambridge University Press, New York.

Chagnon, Napoleon A.
1997 *Yanomamö: The Fierce People.* 5th ed. Holt, Rinehart, and Winston, Orlando, Florida.

Chase, David W.
1955 Rood's Landing Mound B. Unpublished field notes on file at the Columbus Museum, Columbus, Georgia.
1959 *The Averett Culture.* Coweta Memorial Association Papers No. 1, Columbus, Georgia.
1963a A Reappraisal of the Averett Complex. *Journal of Alabama Archaeology* 9(2): 42–61.
1963b Background to the Archaeology of the Middle Chattahoochee Valley, 1955–1963. Unpublished manuscript on file, Columbus Museum, Columbus, Georgia.

Clay, R. Berle
1997 The Mississippian Succession on the Lower Ohio. *Southeastern Archaeology* 16:16–32.

Clayton, Lawrence A., Vernon James Knight Jr., and Edward C. Moore (editors)
1993 *The De Soto Chronicles: The Expedition of Hernando de Soto to North America in 1539–1543.* 2 vols. University of Alabama Press, Tuscaloosa.

Cobb, Charles R., and Brian M. Butler
  2002   The Vacant Quarter Revisited: Late Mississippian Abandonment of the Lower Ohio Valley. *American Antiquity* 67(4):625–641.
Cobb, Charles R., and Patrick H. Garrow
  1996   Woodstock Culture and the Question of Mississippian Emergence. *American Antiquity* 61(1):21–37.
Conkey, Margaret W., and Christine A. Hastorf (editors)
  1990   *The Uses of Style in Archaeology.* Cambridge University Press, Cambridge.
DeBoer, Warren R.
  1990   Interaction, Imitation, and Communication as Expressed in Style: The Ucayali Experience. In *The Uses of Style in Archaeology,* edited by Margaret W. Conkey and Christine A. Hastorf, pp. 82–104. Cambridge University Press, Cambridge.
Deetz, James
  1967   *Invitation to Archaeology.* Natural History Press, Garden City, New York.
Delaney-Rivera, Colleen
  2004   From Edge to Frontier: Early Mississippian Occupation of the Lower Illinois River Valley. *Southeastern Archaeology* 23(1):41–56.
DePratter, Chester B.
  1991   *Late Prehistoric and Early Historic Chiefdoms in the Southeastern United States.* Garland Publishing, New York.
Durkheim, Émile
  1933   *The Division of Labor in Society.* Macmillan, New York.
Earle, Timothy
  1997   *How Chiefs Come to Power: The Political Economy in Prehistory.* Stanford University Press, Stanford.
Ember, Carol, Melvin Ember, and Peter N. Peregrine
  2002   *Anthropology.* 10th ed. Prentice Hall, Upper Saddle River, New Jersey.
Emerson, Thomas E.
  1991   Some Perspectives on Cahokia and the Northern Mississippian Expansion. In *Cahokia and the Hinterlands: Middle Mississippian Cultures of the Midwest,* edited by Thomas E. Emerson and R. Barry Lewis, pp. 221–236. University of Illinois Press, Urbana.
  1997   *Cahokia and the Archaeology of Power.* University of Alabama Press, Tuscaloosa.
Faulkner, Charles H.
  1975   The Mississippian-Woodland Transition in the Middle South. *Southeastern Archaeological Conference Bulletin* 15:38–45.
Fisher-Carroll, Rita, and Robert C. Mainfort
  2000   Late Prehistoric Mortuary Behavior at Upper Nodena. *Southeastern Archaeology* 19(2):105–119.
Flannery, Kent V.
  1998   The Ground Plans of Archaic States. In *Archaic States,* edited by Gary M. Feinman and Joyce Marcus, pp. 15–57. School of American Research Press, Santa Fe.
Fortes, Meyer
  1953   The Structure of Unilineal Descent Groups. *American Anthropologist* 55:17–41.

Fowler, Melvin L.
1978   Cahokia and the American Bottom: Settlement Archaeology. In *Mississippian Settlement Patterns,* edited by Bruce D. Smith, pp. 455–478. Academic Press, New York.

Fox, Gregory L.
1998   An Examination of Mississippian-Period Phases in Southeastern Missouri. In *Changing Perspective on the Archaeology of the Central Mississippi Valley,* edited by Michael J. O'Brien and Robert C. Dunnell, pp. 31–58. University of Alabama Press, Tuscaloosa.

Fox, John W.
1987   *Maya Postclassic State Formation: Segmentary Lineage Migration in Advancing Frontiers.* Cambridge University Press, Cambridge.

Fried, Morton H.
1967   *The Evolution of Political Society: An Essay in Political Anthropology.* Random House, New York.

Fritz, Gayle J.
1992   "Newer," "Better," Maize and the Mississippian Emergence: A Critique of Prime Mover Explanations. In *Late Prehistoric Agriculture: Observations from the Midwest,* edited by William I. Woods, pp. 19–43. Studies in Illinois Archaeology 8, Illinois Historic Preservation Agency, Springfield.

Gatschet, Albert S.
1969   *A Migration Legend of the Creek Indians,* Vol. 1. AMS Press, New York.

Gosselain, Olivier P.
1998   Social and Technical Identity in a Clay Crystal Ball. In *The Archaeology of Social Boundaries,* edited by Miriam T. Stark, pp. 78–106. Smithsonian Institution Press, Washington, D.C.

Griffin, James B.
1967   Eastern North American Archaeology: A Summary. *Science* 156:175–191.
1985   Changing Concepts of the Prehistoric Mississippian Cultures of the Eastern United States. In *Alabama and the Borderlands: From Prehistory to Statehood,* edited by R. Reid Badger and Lawrence A. Clayton, pp. 40–63. University of Alabama Press, Tuscaloosa.

Griffin, John W.
1950   Test Excavations at the Lake Jackson Site. *American Antiquity* 16:99–112.

Gronenborn, Detlef, and Carlos Magnavita
2000   Imperial Expansion, Ethnic Change, and Ceramic Traditions in the Southern Chad Basin: A Terminal Nineteenth-Century Pottery Assemblage from Dikwa, Borno State, Nigeria. *International Journal of Historical Archaeology* 4:35–70.

Haas, Jonathan
1982   *The Evolution of the Prehistoric State.* Columbia University Press, New York.

Hair, Joseph F., Jr., and William C. Black
2000   Cluster Analysis. In *Reading and Understanding More Multivariate Statistics,* edited by L. G. Grimm and P. Yarnold, pp. 147–205. American Psychological Association, Washington, D.C.

Hally, David J.
1986   The Identification of Vessel Function: A Case Study from Northwest Georgia. *American Antiquity* 51:267–295.

1993   The Territorial Size of Mississippian Chiefdoms. In *Archaeology of Eastern North America, Papers in Honor of Stephen Williams,* edited by James B. Stoltman, pp. 143–168. Archaeological Report No. 25. Mississippi Department of Archives and History, Jackson.

1994a The Chiefdom of Coosa. In *The Forgotten Centuries: Indians and Europeans in the American South, 1521–1704,* edited by Charles Hudson and Carmen Chaves Tesser, pp. 227–253. University of Georgia Press, Athens.

1994b An Overview of Lamar Culture. In *Ocmulgee Archaeology 1936–1986,* edited by David J. Hally, pp.144–174. University of Georgia Press, Athens.

1996   Platform-Mound Construction and the Instability of Mississippian Chiefdoms. In *Political Structure and Change in the Prehistoric Southeastern United States,* edited by John F. Scarry, pp. 92–127. University Press of Florida, Gainesville.

Hally, David J., and Leila Oertel

1977   *Archaeological Investigations at the Park Mound Site (9TP41), Troup County, Georgia, 1972 Season.* University of Georgia, Athens. Report submitted to the National Park Service. Copy on file, Department of Anthropology, University of Georgia.

Hawkins, Benjamin

1980   *Letters, Journals, and Writings of Benjamin Hawkins,* edited by C. L. Grant. Beehive Press, Savannah, Georgia.

Hegmon, Michelle

1992   Archaeological Research on Style. *Annual Review of Anthropology* 21:517–536.

Hickerson, Harold

1965   The Virginia Deer and Inter-Tribal Buffer Zones in the Upper Mississippi Valley. In *Man, Culture, and Animals,* edited by Anthony Leeds and Andrew P. Vayda, pp. 43–65. American Association for the Advancement of Science, Washington, D.C.

Hilgeman, Sherri Lynn

2000   *Pottery and Chronology at Angel.* University of Alabama Press, Tuscaloosa.

Hodder, Ian

1982   Sequences of Structural Change in the Dutch Neolithic. In *Symbolic and Structural Archaeology,* edited by Ian Hodder, pp. 162–177. Cambridge University Press, Cambridge.

1985   Boundaries as Strategies: An Ethnoarchaeological Study. In *The Archaeology of Frontiers and Boundaries,* edited by Stanton W. Green and Stephen M. Perlman, pp. 141–159. Academic Press, Orlando.

Howard, James H.

1968   *The Southeastern Ceremonial Complex and Its Interpretation.* Memoir No. 6. Missouri Archaeological Society, Columbia.

Hudson, Charles M.

1976   *The Southeastern Indians.* University of Tennessee Press, Knoxville.

1979   *Black Drink: A Native American Tea.* University of Georgia Press, Athens.

Hudson, Charles M., Marvin T. Smith, David J. Hally, Richard Polhemus, and Chester B. DePratter

1985   Coosa: A Chiefdom in the Sixteenth-Century United States. *American Antiquity* 52:840–885.

Hurt, Wesley R.
1975   The Preliminary Archaeological Survey of the Chattahoochee Valley Area
        in Alabama. In *Archaeological Salvage in the Walter F. George Basin of the
        Chattahoochee River in Alabama*, edited by David L. DeJarnette, pp. 5–85.
        University of Alabama Press, Tuscaloosa.

Huscher, Harold A.
1959a   *Appraisal of the Archaeological Resources of the Walter F. George Reservoir
        Area, Chattahoochee River, Alabama and Georgia*. River Basin Surveys,
        Smithsonian Institution, Washington, D.C.
1959b   *Appraisal of the Archaeological Resources of the Columbia Dam and Lock Area,
        Chattahoochee River, Alabama and Georgia*. River Basin Surveys, Smith-
        sonian Institution, Washington, D.C.
1961   Two Mississippian Mound Sites in Quitman County, Georgia. Paper pre-
        sented at the 18th Annual Meeting of the Southeastern Archaeological
        Conference, Macon, Georgia.
1963   The Cool Branch Site, 9QU5, Quitman County, Georgia: A Fortified Mis-
        sissippian Town with Tower Bastions. Paper presented at the Eastern United
        States Archaeological Federation, Philadelphia.
1971   Two Mississippian Mound Sites in Quitman County, Georgia. *Southeastern
        Archaeological Conference Newsletter* 10(2):35–36. [Edited version of the
        1961 paper].

Jackson, H. Edwin, and Susan L. Scott
1995   The Faunal Record of the Southeastern Elite: The Implications of Economy,
        Social Relations, and Ideology. *Southeastern Archaeology* 14(2):103–119.

Jenkins, Ned J.
1978   Prehistoric Chronology of the Lower Chattahoochee Valley: A Preliminary
        Statement. *Journal of Alabama Archaeology* 24(2):73–87.
2003   The Terminal Woodland/Mississippian Transition in West and Central Ala-
        bama. *Journal of Alabama Archaeology* 49(1–2):1–62.

Jennings, Jesse D., and Charles H. Fairbanks
1939   Pottery Type Descriptions. *Southeastern Archaeological Conference Newslet-
        ter* 1(2).

Johnson, Allen W., and Timothy Earle
1987   *The Evolution of Human Societies from Foraging Group to Agrarian State*.
        Stanford University Press, Stanford.

Johnson, Gregory A.
1977   Aspects of Regional Analysis in Archaeology. *Annual Review of Anthropology*
        6:479–506.

Johnson, Jay K.
2000   The Chickasaws. In *Indians of the Greater Southeast, Historical Archaeology
        and Ethnohistory*, edited by Bonnie G. McEwan, pp. 85–121. University
        Press of Florida, Gainesville.

Jones, Charles C.
1999   *Antiquities of the Southern Indians, Particularly of the Georgia Tribes*, edited
        and with an Introduction by Frank T. Schnell Jr. University of Alabama
        Press, Tuscaloosa.

Kellar, James H., Arthur R. Kelly, and Edward V. McMichael
1961   *Final Report on the Mandeville Site, 9Cla1, Clay County, Georgia: Seasons*

1959, 1960, and 1961. University of Georgia. Report submitted to the National Park Service. Report on file, Department of Anthropology, University of Georgia, Athens.

Kelly, John E.

1990 The Emergence of Mississippian Culture in the American Bottom Region. In *The Mississippian Emergence,* edited by Bruce D. Smith, pp. 113–173. Smithsonian Institution Press, Washington and London.

1991 Cahokia and Its Role as a Gateway Center in Interregional Exchange. In *Cahokia and the Hinterlands: Middle Mississippian Cultures of the Midwest,* edited by Thomas E. Emerson and R. Barry Lewis, pp. 61–80. University of Illinois Press, Urbana.

2000 The Nature and Context of Emergent Mississippian Cultural Dynamics in the American Bottom. In *Late Woodland Societies: Tradition and Transformation across the Midcontinent,* edited by Thomas E. Emerson, Dale L. McElrath, and Andrew C. Fortier, pp. 163–178. University of Nebraska Press, Lincoln.

Kidder, Tristram R.

2002 Woodland Period Archaeology in the Lower Mississippi Valley. In *The Woodland Southeast,* edited by David G. Anderson and Robert C. Mainfort Jr., pp. 66–90. University of Alabama Press, Tuscaloosa.

King, Adam

2003 *Etowah: The Political History of a Chiefdom Capital.* University of Alabama Press, Tuscaloosa.

King, Adam, and Maureen S. Meyers

2002 Exploring the Edges of the Mississippian World. *Southeastern Archaeology* 21:113–116.

Kirch, Patrick

1991 Prehistoric Exchange in Western Melanesia. *Annual Review of Anthropology* 20:141–165.

Knapp, A. Bernard, and Wendy Ashmore

1999 Archaeological Landscapes: Constructed, Conceptualized, Ideational. In *Archaeologies of Landscape,* edited by Wendy Ashmore and A. Bernard Knapp, pp. 1–30. Blackwell, Malden, Massachusetts.

Knight, Judith

1978 Evidence of Prehistoric Learning by Imitation. *Journal of Alabama Archaeology* 24(1):69.

Knight, Vernon James, Jr.

1979 Ceramic Stratigraphy at the Singer-Moye Site, 9SW2. *Journal of Alabama Archaeology* 25:138–151.

1981a Mississippian Ritual. Unpublished Ph.D. dissertation, Department of Anthropology, University of Florida, Gainesville.

1981b Appendix 1: Radiocarbon Dates. In *Cemochechobee: Archaeology of a Mississippian Ceremonial Center on the Chattahoochee River,* edited by Frank T. Schnell, Vernon J. Knight Jr., and Gail S. Schnell, pp. 247–251. Ripley P. Bullen Monographs in Anthropology and History 3. University Press of Florida, Gainesville.

1986 The Institutional Organization of Mississippian Religion. *American Antiquity* 51:675–687.

1989   Symbolism of Mississippian Mounds. In *Powhattan's Mantle: Indians of the Colonial Southeast,* edited by Patricia H. Wood, Gregory A. Waselkov, and M. T. Hatley, pp. 279–291. University of Nebraska Press, Lincoln.

1990a Social Organization and the Evolution of Hierarchy in Southeastern Chiefdoms. *Journal of Anthropological Research* 46:1–23.

1990b *Excavation of the Truncated Mound at the Walling Site: Middle Woodland Culture and Copena in the Tennessee Valley.* Alabama State Museum of Natural History, Division of Archaeology, Report of Investigations 56. University of Alabama, Tuscaloosa.

1994a The Formation of the Creeks. In *The Forgotten Centuries: Indians and Europeans in the American South, 1521–1704,* edited by Charles Hudson and Carmen Chaves Tesser, pp. 373–392. University of Georgia Press, Athens.

1994b Ocmulgee Fields Culture and the Historical Development of Creek Ceramics. In *Ocmulgee Archaeology, 1936–1986,* edited by David J. Hally, pp. 181–189. University of Georgia Press, Athens.

1998   Moundville as a Diagrammatic Center. In *Archaeology of the Moundville Chiefdom,* edited by Vernon James Knight Jr. and Vincas P. Steponaitis, pp. 44–62. Smithsonian Institution Press, Washington, D.C.

Knight, Vernon J., Jr., and Tim S. Mistovich

1984   *Walter F. George Lake, Archaeological Survey of Fee Owned Lands, Alabama and Georgia.* Report of Investigations 42, Office of Archaeological Research, University of Alabama, Tuscaloosa.

Knight, Vernon James, Jr., Lyle W. Konigsberg, and Susan R. Frankenburg

1999   A Gibbs Sampler Approach to the Dating of Phases in the Moundville Sequence. Unpublished manuscript on file, Department of Anthropology, University of Alabama, Tuscaloosa.

Knight, Vernon James, Jr., and Vincas P. Steponaitis (editors)

1998   *Archaeology of the Moundville Chiefdom.* Smithsonian Institution Press, Washington, D.C.

Kopytoff, Igor (editor)

1987   *The African Frontier: The Reproduction of Traditional African Societies.* Indiana University Press, Bloomington.

Kowalewski, Stephen, Richard E. Blanton, Gary M. Feiman, and Laura Finsten

1983   Boundaries, Scale, and Internal Organization. *Journal of Anthropological Archaeology* 2:32–56.

Krause, Richard A.

1985   Trends and Trajectories in American Archaeology: Some Questions about the Mississippian Period in Southeastern Prehistory. In *Alabama and the Borderlands: From Prehistory to Statehood,* edited by R. Reid Badger and Lawrence A. Clayton, pp. 17–39. University of Alabama Press, Tuscaloosa.

Kreisa, Paul P.

1998   Pottery, Radiocarbon Dates, and Mississippian-Period Chronology Building in Western Kentucky. In *Changing Perspectives on the Archaeology of the Central Mississippi Valley,* edited by Michael J. O'Brien and Robert C. Dunnell, pp. 59–79. University of Alabama Press, Tuscaloosa.

Kurjack, Edward B.

1975   Archaeological Investigations in the Walter F. George Basin. In *Archaeological Salvage in the Walter F. George Basin of the Chattahoochee River in Ala-*

bama, edited by David L. DeJarnette, pp. 86–198. University of Alabama Press, Tuscaloosa.

Lamb, H. H.
1984 Climate and History in Northern Europe and Elsewhere. In *Climatic Changes on Millennial Basis: Geological, Historical and Instrumental Records,* edited by N. A. Morner and W. Karlen, pp. 225–240. D. Reidel, Dordrecht, Netherlands.

Lafferty, Robert H., III
1973 An Analysis of Prehistoric Southeastern Fortifications. Unpublished Master's thesis, Department of Anthropology, Southern Illinois University, Carbondale.

Lafferty, Robert H., III, and James E. Price
1996 Southeast Missouri. In *Prehistory of the Central Mississippi Valley,* edited by Charles H. McNutt, pp. 1–45. University of Alabama Press, Tuscaloosa.

Ledbetter, R. Jerald
1997a *The Bull Creek Site, 9ME1, Muscogee County, Georgia.* Occasional Papers in Cultural Resource Management 9. Georgia Department of Transportation, Atlanta.
1997b *The Victory Drive Site, 9ME50, Muscogee County, Georgia.* Occasional Papers in Cultural Resource Management 8. Georgia Department of Transportation, Atlanta.

Lewis, Thomas M. N., and Madeline Kneberg
1946 *Hiwassee Island: An Archaeological Account of Four Tennessee Indian Peoples.* University of Tennessee Press, Knoxville.

Lindauer, Owen, and John H. Blitz
1997 Higher Ground: The Archaeology of North American Platform Mounds. *Journal of Archaeological Research* 5:169–207.

Little, Keith J.
1999 The Role of Late Woodland Interactions in the Emergence of Etowah. *Southeastern Archaeology* 18(1):45–56.

Long, Austin, and James E. Mielke
1967 Smithsonian Radiocarbon Measurements IV. *Radiocarbon* 9:368–381.

Long, Austin, and Bruce Rippeteau
1974 Testing Contemporaneity and Averaging Radiocarbon Dates. *American Antiquity* 39:205–215.

Longacre, William A.
1991 Sources of Ceramic Variability among the Kalinga of Northern Luzon. In *Ceramic Ethnoarchaeology,* edited by William A. Longacre, pp. 95–111. University of Arizona Press, Tucson.

Lorenz, Karl G.
1996 Small-Scale Mississippian Community Organization in the Big Black River Valley of Mississippi. *Southeastern Archaeology* 15:145–171.

Lorenz, Karl G., and John H. Blitz
2003 Measuring the Scale of Regional Integration in Mississippian Societies. Paper presented at the Visiting Scholar Conference, *Borne on Litter with Much Prestige: Leadership and Polity in Mississippian Societies.* Center for Archaeological Investigations, Southern Illinois University, Carbondale.

Luer, George M.
1992 Mississippi-Period Popeyed Bird-Head Effigies in West-Central and Southwest Florida. *Florida Anthropologist* 45:52–62.

MacEachern, Scott
1998 Scale, Style, and Cultural Variation: Technological Traditions in the Northern Mandara Mountains. In *The Archaeology of Social Boundaries*, edited by Miriam T. Stark, pp. 107–131. Smithsonian Institution Press, Washington, D.C.

Mainfort, Robert C., Jr.
1999 Late Period Phases in the Central Mississippi Valley: A Multivariate Approach. In *Arkansas Archaeology: Essays in Honor of Dan and Phyllis Morse*, edited by Robert C. Mainfort Jr. and Marvin D. Jeter, pp. 143–167. University of Arkansas Press, Fayetteville.

Marrinan, Rochelle, and Nancy M. White
1998 Smoke and Mirrors in Modeling Fort Walton Culture, Northwest Florida. Paper presented at the 55th Southeastern Archaeological Conference, Greenville, South Carolina.

Mason, Ronald J.
2000 Archaeology and Native American Oral Traditions. *American Antiquity* 65:239–266.

Masson, Marilyn A.
2001 Changing Patterns of Ceramic Stylistic Diversity in the Pre-Hispanic Maya Lowlands. *Acta Archaeologica* 72:159–188.

McMichael, Edward V., and James H. Kellar
1960 *Archaeological Salvage in the Oliver Basin.* Laboratory of Archaeology Series No. 2. University of Georgia, Athens.

Mehrer, Mark W.
1995 *Cahokia's Countryside: Household Archaeology, Settlement Patterns, and Social Power.* Northern Illinois University Press, DeKalb.

Milner, George R., and Sissel Schroeder
1999 Mississippian Sociopolitical Systems. In *Great Towns and Regional Polities in the Prehistoric American Southwest and Southeast*, edited by Jill E. Neitzel, pp. 95–107. University of New Mexico Press, Albuquerque.

Moore, Clarence B.
1907 Mounds of the Lower Chattahoochee and Lower Flint Rivers. *Journal of the Academy of Natural Sciences of Philadelphia* 13:426–456.

Moore, Carmella, and A. Kimball Romney
1994 Material Culture, Geographic Propinquity, and Linguistic Affiliation on the North Coast of New Guinea: A Reanalysis of Welsch, Terrell, and Nadolski (1992). *American Anthropologist* 96:370–396.

Moorehead, Warren K.
1910 *The Stone Age in North America.* Houghton Mifflin, Boston.

Morse, Dan F.
1977 The Penetration of Northeast Arkansas by Mississippian Culture. In *For the Director: Research Essays in Honor of James B. Griffin*, edited by Charles E. Cleland, pp. 186–211. Museum of Anthropology, Anthropological Papers 61, University of Michigan, Ann Arbor.

Muller, Jon

1997   *Mississippian Political Economy.* Plenum Press, New York.

1999   Southeastern Interaction and Integration. In *Great Towns and Regional Polities in the Prehistoric American Southwest and Southeast,* edited by Jill E. Neitzel, pp. 143–158. University of New Mexico Press, Albuquerque.

Nassaney, Michael S., and Charles R. Cobb

1991   Patterns and Processes of Late Woodland Development in the Southeastern United States. In *Stability, Transformation, and Variation: The Late Woodland Southeast,* edited by Michael S. Nassaney and Charles R. Cobb, pp. 285–322. Plenum Press, New York.

Neuman, Robert W.

1959   Two Unrecorded Pottery Vessels from the Purcell Landing Site, Henry County, Alabama. *Florida Anthropologist* 12:101–103.

1961   Domesticated Corn from a Fort Walton Mound Site in Houston County, Alabama. *Florida Anthropologist* 14:75–80.

Noakes, John E., and Betty Lee Brandau

1974   University of Georgia Radiocarbon Dates III. *Radiocarbon* 16:131–141.

Pauketat, Timothy R.

1983   A Long-Stemmed Spud from the American Bottom. *Midcontinental Journal of Archaeology* 8:1–15.

2004   *Cahokia and the Mississippians.* Cambridge University Press, Cambridge.

Pauketat, Timothy R., and Susan M. Alt

2003   Mounds, Memory, and Contested Mississippian History. In *Archaeologies of Memory,* edited by Ruth M. Van Dyke and Susan E. Alcock, pp. 151–179. Blackwell, Malden, Massachusetts.

Pauketat, Timothy R., and Thomas E. Emerson (editors)

1997   *Cahokia: Domination and Ideology in the Mississippian World.* University of Nebraska Press, Lincoln.

Payne, Claudine

1994   *Mississippian Capitals: An Archaeological Investigation of Precolumbian Political Structure.* Ph.D. dissertation, University of Florida, University Microfilms, Ann Arbor.

Peebles, Christopher S.

1971   Moundville and Surrounding Sites: Some Structural Considerations of Mortuary Practices. In *Approaches to the Social Dimensions of Mortuary Practices,* edited by James A. Brown, pp. 68–91. Memoir 15. Society for American Archaeology.

1978   Determinants of Settlement Size and Location in the Moundville Phase. In *Mississippian Settlement Patterns,* edited by Bruce D. Smith, pp. 369–416. Academic Press, New York.

Peebles, Christopher S., and Susan M. Kus

1977   Some Archaeological Correlates of Ranked Societies. *American Antiquity* 42:421–448.

Phillips, Philip

1970   *Archaeological Survey in the Lower Yazoo Basin, Mississippi, 1949–1955.* Papers of the Peabody Museum of Archaeology and Ethnology, Harvard University, Vol. 60. Cambridge, Massachusetts.

Pluckhahn, Thomas J.
  1996   Joseph Caldwell's Summerour Mound (9FO16) and Woodland Platform Mounds in the Southeastern United States. *Southeastern Archaeology* 15(2): 191–211.
  2003   *Kolomoki: Settlement, Ceremony, and Status in the Deep South, A.D. 350 to 750*. University of Alabama Press, Tuscaloosa.
Prent, Mieke
  2003   Glories of the Past in the Past: Ritual Activities at Palatial Ruins in Early Iron Age Crete. In *Archaeologies of Memory*, edited by Ruth M. Van Dyke and Susan E. Alcock, pp. 81–103. Blackwell, Malden, Massachusetts.
Renfrew, Colin, and Eric V. Level
  1979   Exploring Dominance: Predicting Polities from Centers. In *Transformations: Mathematical Approaches to Culture Change*, edited by Colin Renfrew and K. L. Cooke, pp. 145–167. Academic Press, New York.
Roberts, Frank H. H., Jr.
  1962   *Seventy-Eighth Annual Report of the Bureau of American Ethnology, 1960–1961*. Smithsonian Institution, Washington, D.C.
  1963   *Seventy-Ninth Annual Report of the Bureau of American Ethnology, 1961–1962*. Smithsonian Institution, Washington, D.C.
Roberts, John M., Jr., Carmella C. Moore, and A. Kimball Romney
  1995   Predicting Similarity in Material Culture among New Guinea Villages from Propinquity and Language. *Current Anthropology* 36(5):769–788.
Rouse, Irving B.
  1958   The Inference of Migrations from Anthropological Evidence. In *Migrations in New World Culture History*, edited by Raymond H. Thompson, pp. 63–68. University of Arizona Social Science Bulletin 27, Tucson.
Sackett, James R.
  1985   Style and Ethnicity in the Kalahari: A Reply to Wiessner. *American Antiquity* 50:154–159.
  1990   Style and Ethnicity in Archaeology: The Case for Isochrestism. In *The Uses of Style in Archaeology*, edited by Margaret W. Conkey and Christine A. Hastorf, pp. 32–43. Cambridge University Press, Cambridge.
Sahlins, Marshall D.
  1961   The Segmentary Lineage: An Organization of Predatory Expansion. *American Anthropologist* 63:322–345.
Scarry, John F.
  1980   The Chronology of Fort Walton Development in the Upper Apalachicola Valley, Florida. *Southeastern Archaeological Conference Bulletin* 22: 38–45.
  1984   *Fort Walton Development: Mississippian Chiefdoms in the Lower Southeast*. Ph.D. dissertation, Case Western Reserve University, University Microfilms, Ann Arbor.
  1990   Mississippian Emergence in the Fort Walton Area: The Evolution of the Cayson and Lake Jackson Phases. In *The Mississippian Emergence*, edited by Bruce D. Smith, pp. 227–250. Smithsonian University Press, Washington, D.C.
  1996   The Nature of Mississippian Societies. In *Political Structure and Change in*

the Prehistoric Southeastern United States, edited by John F. Scarry, pp. 12–24. University Press of Florida, Gainesville.

1999 How Great Were the Southeastern Polities? In *Great Towns and Regional Polities in the Prehistoric American Southwest and Southeast,* edited by Jill E. Neitzel, pp. 59–74. University of New Mexico Press, Albuquerque.

2000 Ceramic Types from Florida State University and Case Western Reserve University Investigations at the Yon Site in 1960 and 1974: Units 1, 2, 10, and 12. Unpublished manuscript in possession of the author.

Scarry, John F., and Claudine Payne

1986 Mississippian Polities in the Fort Walton Area. A Model Generated from the Renfrew-Level XTENT Algorithm. *Southeastern Archaeology* 5:79–90.

Schnell, Frank T.

1968 Untitled. *Southeastern Archaeological Conference Newsletter* 12(2):7–8.

1970 A Comparative Study of Some Lower Creek Sites. *Southeastern Archaeological Conference Bulletin* 13:133–136.

1981 Late Prehistoric Ceramic Chronologies in the Lower Chattahoochee Valley. *Southeastern Archaeological Conference Bulletin* 24:21–23.

1998a Archaeological Excavations at the Columbus Museum's Singer-Moye Archaeological Site. Unpublished manuscript on file, Columbus Museum, Columbus, Georgia.

1998b Ceramics in the Southern Half of the Chattahoochee Valley. *Journal of Alabama Archaeology* 44(1–2):99–130.

Schnell, Frank T., Vernon J. Knight Jr., and Gail S. Schnell

1979 *Cemochechobee: Archaeological Investigations at the Walter F. George Dam Mound Site, 9ClA62, Clay County, Georgia.* Columbus Museum of Arts and Sciences, Inc. Report submitted to the U.S. Army Corps of Engineers-Mobile District. Report on file, Columbus Museum, Columbus, Georgia.

1981 *Cemochechobee: Archaeology of a Mississippian Ceremonial Center on the Chattahoochee River.* Ripley P. Bullen Monographs in Anthropology and History 3. University Press of Florida, Gainesville.

Schnell, Frank T., and Newell O. Wright Jr.

1993 *Mississippi Period Archaeology of the Georgia Coastal Plain.* Laboratory of Archaeology Series No. 26. University of Georgia, Athens.

Schnell, Gail S.

1981 A Preliminary Political Model for the Rood Phase. *Southeastern Archaeological Conference Bulletin* 24:23–24.

Sears, William H.

1951 *Excavations at Kolomoki, Season I.* University of Georgia Series in Anthropology 2. University of Georgia Press, Athens.

1956 *Excavations at Kolomoki: Final Report.* University of Georgia Series in Anthropology 5. University of Georgia Press, Athens.

1958 *The Wilbanks Site (9CK5), Georgia.* River Basin Survey Papers No. 12. Bulletin 169. Bureau of American Ethnology, Smithsonian Institution, Washington, D.C.

1967 The Tierra Verde Burial Mound. *Florida Anthropologist* 20(1–2):25–73.

Service, Elman R.

1962 *Primitive Social Organization: An Evolutionary Perspective.* Random House, New York.

Shennan, Stephan J. (editor)
1989 *Archaeological Approaches to Cultural Identity.* Unwin Hyman, London.
Shepard, Anna O.
1980 *Ceramics for the Archaeologist.* Publication 609. Carnegie Institution of Washington, Washington, D.C.; Braun Brumfield, Ann Arbor.
Sinopoli, Carla M.
2003 Echoes of Empire: Vijayanagara and Historical Memory, Vijayanagara as Historical Memory. In *Archaeologies of Memory,* edited by Ruth M. Van Dyke and Susan E. Alcock, pp. 17–33. Blackwell, Malden, Massachusetts.
Smith, Betty A.
1979 The Hopewell Connection in Southwest Georgia. In *Hopewell Archaeology: The Chillicothe Conference,* edited by David S. Brose and Naomi Greber, pp. 181–187. Kent State University Press, Kent, Ohio.
Smith, Bruce D. (editor)
1978 *Mississippian Settlement Patterns.* Academic Press, New York.
1984 Mississippian Expansion: Tracing the Historical Development of an Explanatory Model. *Southeastern Archaeology* 3:13–22.
1990 Introduction. In *The Mississippian Emergence,* edited by Bruce D. Smith, pp. 1–8. Smithsonian Institution Press, Washington, D.C.
Smith, Marvin T.
1987 *Archaeology of Aboriginal Culture Change in the Interior Southeast: Depopulation during the Early Historic Period.* Ripley P. Bullen Monographs in Anthropology and History 6. University Press of Florida, Gainesville.
1989 Aboriginal Population Movements in the Early Historic Period Southeast. In *Powhatan's Mantle: Indians in the Colonial Southeast,* edited by P. H. Wood and M. T. Hatley, pp. 21–34. University of Nebraska Press, Lincoln.
Southall, Aidan W.
1956 *Alur Society: A Study in Process and Types of Domination.* Heffer, Cambridge.
Spielmann, Katherine A.
2002 Feasting, Craft Specialization, and the Ritual Mode of Production in Small-Scale Societies. *American Anthropologist* 104:195–207.
Stahle, David W., and Malcolm K. Cleaveland
1994 Tree-Ring Reconstructed Rainfall over the Southeastern U.S.A. during the Medieval Warm Period and the Little Ice Age. *Climatic Change* 26: 199–212.
Steponaitis, Vincas P.
1978 Locational Theory and Complex Chiefdoms: A Mississippian Example. In *Mississippian Settlement Patterns,* edited by Bruce D. Smith, pp. 417–453. Academic Press, New York.
1983 *Ceramics, Chronology, and Community Patterns: An Archaeological Study at Moundville.* Academic Press, New York.
1986 Prehistoric Archaeology in the Southeastern United States, 1970–1985. *Annual Review of Anthropology* 15:363–404.
1991 Contrasting Patterns of Mississippian Development. In *Chiefdoms: Power, Economy, and Ideology,* edited by Timothy Earle, pp. 193–228. Cambridge University Press, New York.
Stoltman, James B.
2000 A Reconsideration of the Cultural Processes Linking Cahokia to Its North-

ern Hinterlands during the Period A.D. 1000–1200. In *Mounds, Modoc, and Mesoamerica: Papers in Honor of Melvin L. Fowler*, edited by Steven R. Ahler, pp. 439–454. Illinois State Museum Papers, Vol. 28, Illinois State Museum, Springfield.

Stuiver, M., P. J. Reimer, E. Bard, J. W. Beck, G. S. Burr, K. A. Hughen, B. Kromer, F. G. McCormac, J. V. D. Plicht, and M. Spurk

1998 INTCAL98 Radiocarbon Age Calibration, 24,000-0 BP. *Radiocarbon* 40: 1041–1083.

Swanton, John R.

1911 *Indian Tribes of the Lower Mississippi Valley and Adjacent Coast of the Gulf of Mexico*. Bulletin No. 43. Bureau of American Ethnology, Smithsonian Institution, Washington, D.C.

1928 Social Organization and Social Usages of the Creek Confederacy. *Forty-Second Annual Report 1924–1925*:25–475. Bureau of American Ethnology, Smithsonian Institution, Washington, D.C.

1931 *Modern Square Grounds of the Creek Indians*. Miscellaneous Collections 85(8). Smithsonian Institution, Washington, D.C.

Thomas, Julian

1987 Relations of Production and Social Change in the Neolithic of Northwestern Europe. *Man* 22(3): 405–430.

Trigger, Bruce

1990 Monumental Architecture: A Thermodynamic Explanation of Symbolic Behaviour. *World Archaeology* 22(2):119–132.

Van Dyke, Ruth M., and Susan E. Alcock

2003 Archaeologies of Memory: An Introduction. In *Archaeologies of Memory*, edited by Ruth M. Van Dyke and Susan E. Alcock, pp. 1–13. Blackwell, Malden, Massachusetts.

Vansina, Jan

1986 *Oral Tradition as History*. University of Wisconsin Press, Madison.

Walthall, John A.

1980 *Prehistoric Indians of the Southeast: Archaeology of Alabama and the Middle South*. University of Alabama Press, Tuscaloosa.

Waring, Antonio J., Jr.

1968 The Southern Cult and Muskhogean Ceremonial. In *The Waring Papers*, edited by Stephen Williams, pp. 30–69. Papers of the Peabody Museum of Archaeology and Ethnology 58, Harvard University, Cambridge.

Wauchope, Robert W.

1966 *Archaeological Survey of Northern Georgia with a Test of Some Cultural Hypotheses*. Memoirs No. 21. Society for American Archaeology, Salt Lake City.

Welch, Paul D.

1991 *Moundville's Economy*. University of Alabama Press, Tuscaloosa.

Welch, Paul D., and Margaret Scarry

1995 Status-Related Variation in Foodways in the Moundville Chiefdom. *American Antiquity* 60:397–419.

Wesler, Kit L.

2001 *Excavations at Wickliffe Mounds*. University of Alabama Press, Tuscaloosa.

Wheeler-Voegelin, Erminie, and Remedios W. Moore

1959 The Emergence Myth in Native North America. In *Studies in Folklore*, edited by W. Edison Richmond, pp. 66–91. Indiana University Press, Bloomington.

White, Nancy M.

1982 *The Curlee Site (8JA7) and Fort Walton Development in the Upper Apalachicola–Lower Chattahoochee Valley.* Ph.D. dissertation, Case Western Reserve University, University Microfilms, Ann Arbor.

1996 *Test Excavations at the Yon Mound and Village Site (8LI2), Middle Apalachicola Valley, Northwest Florida.* Report Submitted to the Division of Historical Resources, Florida Department of State, Tallahassee.

1998 Northwest Florida Archaeology: Artifact Typology and Sorting Criteria. Unpublished manuscript on file, University of South Florida Archaeology Lab, Tampa.

Wiessner, Polly

1983 Style and Social Information in Kalahari San Projectile Points. *American Antiquity* 49(2):253–276.

Wilkinson, Leland, Mary Ann Hill, and Erin Vang

1992 *SYSTAT: Statistics, Version 5.2 Edition.* SYSTAT, Inc., Evanston, Illinois.

Willey, Gordon R.

1949 *Archaeology of the Florida Gulf Coast.* Smithsonian Miscellaneous Collections 113. Smithsonian Institution, Washington, D.C.

Willey, Gordon R., and Philip Phillips

1958 *Method and Theory in American Archaeology.* University of Chicago Press, Chicago.

Williams, Mark

1994 The Origin of the Macon Plateau Site. In *Ocmulgee Archaeology, 1936–1986,* edited by David J. Hally, pp. 130–137. University of Georgia Press, Athens.

Williams, Mark, and Gary Shapiro

1990 Paired Towns. In *Lamar Archaeology: Mississippian Chiefdoms in the Deep South,* edited by Mark Williams and Gary Shapiro, pp. 163–174. University of Alabama Press, Tuscaloosa.

1996 Mississippian Political Dynamics in the Oconee Valley, Georgia. In *Political Structure and Change in the Prehistoric Southeastern United States,* edited by John F. Scarry, pp. 128–149. University Press of Florida, Gainesville.

Williams, Stephen, and Jeffery P. Brain

1983 *Excavations at the Lake George Site, Yazoo County, Mississippi, 1958–1960.* Papers of the Peabody Museum of Archaeology and Ethnology 74, Harvard University, Cambridge, Massachusetts.

Willis, W. S., Jr.

1980 Fusion and Separation: Archaeology and Ethnohistory in Southeastern North America. In *Theory and Practice: Essays Presented to Gene Weltfish,* edited by Stanley Diamond, pp. 97–123. Moulton, The Hague.

Wobst, H. Martin

1977 Stylistic Behavior and Information Exchange. In *Papers for the Director: Research Essays in Honor of James B. Griffin,* edited by Charles Cleland, pp. 317–342. Anthropological Paper 61. University of Michigan Museum of Anthropology, Ann Arbor.

Worth, John E.

2000 The Lower Creeks: Origins and Early History. In *Indians of the Greater*

Southeast: Historical Archaeology and Ethnohistory, edited by Bonnie G. McEwan, pp. 265–298. University Press of Florida, Gainesville.

Wright, Henry T.
 1984 Prestate Political Formations. In *On the Evolution of Complex Societies: Essays in Honor of Harry Hoijer, 1982,* edited by Timothy K. Earle, pp. 41–78. Undena Press, Malibu, California.

Index